Is That True Or Did You Hear it On The BBC?

Is That True Or Did You Hear it On The BBC?

Disinformation and the BBC
Vol. I

DAVID SEDGWICK

Sandgrounder

First Printing, 2022
ISBN-978-1-9993591-7-1

Sandgrounder Publishing

Contents

Preface

I had originally intended calling this book *Inverting Reality: The BBC and Disinformation*. As titles go, it ticked all the requisite boxes: clear, simple and concise. But I had another title in mind, one which seemed less sober and perhaps more memorable: *Is That True Or Did You Hear It On The BBC?* Between the two, I was not sure which title would be the most suitable and so flitted back and forth. It wasn't until the final week of editing that the title issue was finally settled and it's worth recalling the event which tipped the balance.

I'd always known that there existed such a thing as an archetypal BBC consumer, the type of person who sits in front of the TV every evening and who soaks up BBC content without any kind of critical engagement whatsoever. Meeting one face to face, when it happened, was still a shock though. My wife and I had accepted an offer of coffee from a fellow dog-walker and so one morning sat down in a lounge dominated by a large, wall-mounted plasma television set. To non-TV watchers like us, it seemed like a version of hell: how did my neighbour tolerate the blaring noise and the inane shrillness of those voices? How did he manage to *even think* amid that constant din? Perhaps he didn't. Thankfully, our host turned the noise off upon returning to the lounge.

Not more than ten minutes had elapsed when our host suddenly brought up Putin – specifically the topic of the Russian president's evilness. Seemingly he wanted to discuss the Ukraine conflict. My wife and I weren't biting; we tend to steer clear of politics – dogs are much safer ground. However, it became apparent that by declining to join in with this anti-Putin/Russia mantra, we had not reacted as expected, and the more we resisted, the more our host began to make ever more pointed statements about Putin and

Russia. Did we not agree, he asked us almost plaintively, that 'bombing innocent children was evil?' For his part, our host could not understand why anybody would wish to do such a terrible thing; the only reason must be wickedness. He shook his head. Putin had, he went on, specifically targeted children taking shelter in a (Mariupol) theatre. *Children! How could he?*

I sipped my coffee. Our host looked expectantly towards us. Evidently the time had come to add our own condemnation. I took a deep breath. Before joining mein host I sought clarification on a number of issues:

How did Putin know there were children in the theatre? And would he have still bombed the theatre had there been no children present? Why does the Russian president hate children so much? Is it an individual quirk or is perhaps a Russian thing? Having planted these seeds, I took a long sip of coffee.

Our host looked perplexed. Was he, mused I, on the point of a serious malfunction? He pointed towards the plasma TV set and mumbled something about watching the BBC news. It transpired that a certain Clive Myrie had reported the incident of the theatre bombing from Ukraine. Our host had seen this report 'with his own eyes.' Ergo, Putin had deliberately bombed children. It took several minutes for my neighbour to accept that what he had in fact witnessed with his own eyes was a member of the BBC, albeit one clad in camouflage, reading from a prepared script. 'So what,' retorted my acquaintance: 'why would the BBC not present the truth: 'It's their job…'

Besides, he declared, 'everybody knows' that Russia is a threat to the world and that the Russian president, as well as evil, is corrupt. Had he not managed to infiltrate the White House itself?

Is that so? I tried to sound as innocent as possible. Just how had he managed to do this?

Once upon a time Putin had acquired 'dirt' ('something to do with sex and prostitutes') on a certain US businessman called Donald Trump. My neighbour knew this sordid affair to be true because he had heard it on BBC news, not just once 'but several times…' It transpired that Putin has a 'dossier' on Trump and that when the businessman became US president one day – which he assuredly would – the Russians would blackmail him for reasons my host could not quite explicate.

At this point I wondered whether the name Christopher Steele rang any bells? Negative. Fusion GPS? Negative. Robert Mueller? Negative. I decided against asking if he had ever heard of Chomsky, let alone read *Manufacturing Consent*…Shaken but not especially stirred and becoming vaguer by the minute, my host went on to insist that though it had been Trump sitting in the White House between 2016-2020, 'it might as well have been Putin.'

I had to smile. Here we were, a couple of years on since the whole Russiagate hoax had been thoroughly debunked (though not by the BBC) and yet my friend *still* believed. When I asked him if he truly believed Trump had been on the Kremlin payroll, trapped in a cunning piece of Soviet-style kompromat, he pointed automatically to the faithful plasma television screen.

I understood him perfectly: he'd heard all about it on the BBC, and, what is more, believed every single word of it.

The trust that our audience has in all our content underpins everything that we do. We are independent, impartial and honest. We are committed to achieving the highest standards of accuracy and impartiality and strive to avoid knowingly or materially misleading our audiences.

— Learn how the BBC is working to strengthen trust and transparency in online news

If you tell a lie big enough and keep repeating it, people will eventually come to believe it. The lie can be maintained only for such time as the State can shield the people from the political, economic and/or military consequences of the lie. It thus becomes vitally important for the State to use all of its powers to repress dissent, for the truth is the mortal enemy of the lie, and thus by extension, the truth is the greatest enemy of the State.

— Joseph Goebbels (attributed to)

Introduction:
BBC disinformation: Cui bono?

This is a book ostensibly about disinformation. It is a book which specifically focuses on disinformation produced by the 'British' Broadcasting Corporation, arguably the world's most prolific exponents of this nefarious art. Disinformation though is merely a means to an end. What may become apparent as the chapters unfold is that the book's actual topic is power; specifically, the crucial role played by the BBC in legitimising a structure of power that would otherwise be much less sure of itself, more open to challenge, vulnerable even. As gate-keepers come, they don't get any more dedicated to the task than the BBC.

For some readers this bold assertion might come as a surprise. Isn't the BBC a disinterested observer, operating without fear or favour? Not quite. As Christopher Lasch, the celebrated cultural critic observes in *The Culture of Narcissism*:

> The master propagandist, like the advertising expert, avoids obvious emotional appeals and strives for a tone that is consistent with the prosaic quality of modern life – a dry, bland matter-of-factness. Nor does the propagandist circulate "intentionally biased" information. He knows that partial truths serve as more effective instruments of deception rather than lies.

Nothing works better than sobriety. The skilled propagandist knows a thing or two about gaining public trust, of looking and sounding the part. He or she also knows the importance of not under-estimating the audience. Better to mix lies with truth – what is known nowadays as 'truthiness.' Lasch goes on to note that: 'In Propaganda, as in advertising, the important consideration is not whether information accurately describes an objective situation but whether it sounds true.'[1] We'll meet plenty of truthiness within the pages of this book – particularly in terms of climate change, Ivermectin and Russia, the Big Bad Wolf of western imaginings.

Exposing BBC disinformation is thus a relatively simple task; it is often a case of simply locating source information that has been minimised, misrepresented or omitted entirely from its reports and which, once obtained, will invariably provide important contextual information.[2] What usually emerges is a much more nuanced picture. More often than not the BBC version of a news story is eventually proven to be partly or wholly incorrect – the key word is eventually. It happens rather a lot.

For example, when a BBC 'health and disinformation reporter' asserts that: 'Myocarditis is actually more common after catching Covid than after the vaccine,'[3] reference to the published research tells an entirely different story. Researchers who studied post-Covid symptoms in almost 200,000 adults conclude that: 'We did not observe an increased incidence of neither pericarditis nor myocarditis in adult patients recovering from COVID-19 infection.'[4] French researchers meanwhile found 'increased risks of myocarditis and pericarditis during the first week following vaccination.'[5] Less truth, more lies, the broadcaster is treading precariously here.

Take another example, this one with a much higher degree of truthiness. In November 2021 an inflatable dinghy carrying 30 migrants capsized in the English Channel killing 27. 'In that terrible tragedy where so many people were killed off the coast of the UK,' commented yet another member of the broadcaster's 'disinformation' team on a BBC Radio 4 broadcast, 'a large number of them were from Afghanistan. And we've all seen what's happened there over the past 6 months, especially, and the Taliban takeover…'[6] The dinghy had in fact capsized in French territorial waters, not 'off the coast of the UK.' Of the 27 victims only 4 had been from Afghanistan. Easy enough to debunk, yet the facts would only have been available to those *actively seeking them*. It's important to bear this in mind.

Another BBC headline from June 2022 declared that a (black) male 'tasered by police falls into Thames.'[7] The man in question had been wielding a screwdriver on Chelsea Bridge. As multitudes of social media users pointed out after being tasered by police, he had picked himself up, run over to the side of the bridge, vaulted over safety barriers and then *jumped* into the river – a sequence confirmed by video footage. The verb 'falls' had been used in order to mislead the BBC audience – presumably to give it the false impression of police culpability.[8] With its insinuation of a racial motive it's just the kind of story that *might have sounded true* to consumers of BBC content.

Misleading stories like these account for a significant proportion of BBC content; and, just as Lasch advises are based upon seeds of truth, enough at any rate to convince the average BBC consumer that he or she is bearing witness to truthful reporting. Certainly, the broadcaster is far too cunning to present blatant falsehoods. Some do filter through, but can be breezily dismissed as 'honest mistakes' and forgotten about.

So, what's going on here? Clearly, BBC audiences are being primed, conditioned to react in predictable ways to stimuli which appeals not to intellect, but rather to emotion. This is where truthiness comes into its own. When a story 'feels right,' when it accords with prejudice or ideological belief, the actual truth can and often does fall short of expectations. For the propagandist lack of critical engagement is a green light.

And so, it continues. Readers will no doubt be familiar with the plethora of BBC stories which strongly implied that Donald Trump was a Russian spy working on behalf of Vladimir Putin, or that Brexit would lead to starvation due to empty supermarket shelves etc. Both these BBC narratives were completely untrue. But here's the rub: as ludicrous as these narratives appear to the critical thinker, fed a diet rich in Trump-Russia and Brexit scare stories to the average BBC audience member these stories would not have necessarily sounded like disinformation. On the contrary, it would have all sounded highly plausible.

For the consumer of BBC content that the broadcaster weaves truth and untruth together behind a façade of professionalism presents an insoluble problem: to verify each and every BBC claim would clearly be an impossible task. And so, like lorries at the port of Dover, the vast majority of the broadcaster's claims are waved through, left unchecked. Disinformation thereby sneaks in to the public forum every day.

At the heart of this operation to shape and form the opinions and behaviour of the masses is that word 'narrative.' Central to the broadcaster's playbook, it is a concept worthy of analysis.

Narrative can be understood as a vehicle that introduces and consolidates certain ideas into the arena of public consciousness. Like advertising, the aim of a narrative is to persuade. But while adverts sell products, media narratives sell ideas which shape our view of reality, modify and change how we perceive the world itself. Whether selling ideas or product, the objective is the same: to make some more prominent than others. In the case of the BBC, it goes further; not only does the broadcaster promote certain ideas over others, it also presents them as being the *only possible* ways of engaging with the world - the thought processes of all reasonable, 'educated' people. The danger of such an approach is all too obvious for narrative, like advertising, is of course not synonymous with truth. It is merely a version of reality a producer *wants* or *is obliged* to tell. Just as the advertising agency will do whatever is required to increase sales – exaggerate, cherry-pick, suppress, lie etc. – so the unethical media operator will also do whatever it takes to sell certain ideas. Media narratives, we might say, are ideological adverts. Hence, its false claims regarding myocarditis, drowned Afghans, Trump's links with the Kremlin and post-Brexit supermarket shelves bereft of sandwiches can be thus understood as components of BBC narratives all of which seek to mislead on key issues. This leads to a further consideration:

If supplanting truth with untruth is a conscious decision – which we assume it is – then there must be a rationale. An act of deception is rarely, if ever, an end in itself. The question becomes not *if* the BBC misleads its audience, rather *on whose behalf* it does so: cui bono?

In a heterogenous world there might be expected to exist any number of opinions and viewpoints. That certain narratives become dominant over others is a reflection of society-at-large where resources can purchase not only material goods, but intangible elements like influence, access, compliance. It is hardly a surprise to learn that the preferred narratives of the rich and powerful are those which prevail, for in a mercantile world the 'truth' – *that which is accepted as truth* – like every other commodity has a price. As we shall see later in this book when discussing the various activities of a certain Microsoft founder, provided the price is right, even air-time on BBC broadcasts can be acquired.

With its intimate connection to mass media and all that implies in terms of public perception, it is easy to see why the powerful both want and need to control the narrative. Being able to decide which messages are seen on the television news every evening (and what is *not seen*) – messaging repeated not only all over the BBC's vast platform, but also recycled by the broadcaster's colleagues at ITV, Channel 4 etc. – affords tremendous power.

Imagine if just one business monopolised available advertising space. That business could ensure rivals ceased to exist. Apart from the shareholders of the dominant company, for the majority such a situation could have serious consequences, not least in terms of price-fixing etc.

While it is expected that commercial enterprises seek to increase profit, it's not quite as clear-cut for those seeking to sell ideas and worldviews – those wishing to increase their power and influence. Adverts are explicit, narratives invariably implicit. After all, buying say a croissant or a muffin is a rather different proposition than buying into ideas or entire worldviews. And so, as Robert Greene explains in *The 48 Laws of Power*, when it comes to power, those seeking to expand the realm of influence are advised to mask their true intentions:

> No one wants less power; everyone wants more. In the world today, however, it is dangerous to seem too power hungry, to be overt with your power moves. We have to seem fair and decent. So we need to be subtle-congenial yet cunning.[9]

Thus, naked ambition tends to repel rather than attract. So tread carefully; present a benign public face, speak the language of utopia, or so Greene appears to be advising. Such practices may strike the reader as obvious – the way of the world – but in its role as establishment gatekeeper the BBC is quick to label such realities as 'conspiracy.' Conspiracy is arguably the corporation's favourite concept of all time. In fact, just about any critique of establishment power is automatically deemed as conspiracy by the broadcaster. The alacrity with which the BBC moves to shut down criticism of (establishment-approved) power is nothing if not impressive.

'Conspiracy' though is a somewhat stratified term, at least as far as the broadcaster is concerned. It works in just one direction.

16

In BBC-land collusion, corruption, buying of influence etc. does not occur amongst the Bidens, Faucis, Gates or any other member of the global establishment, but only between wrong-thinkers - *those who stand outside of it*: between Donald Trump's lawyers and Petro Poroshenko; between Boris Johnson and pro-Brexit supporter Sir James Dyson etc.[10]

As the various chapters in this book will illustrate, mainstream media narratives share certain common features which are used to manipulate the end user - the trusting individual who, tired after a long day at work and therefore more than happy to be spoon-fed information, sits down in front of the television each evening to watch the news. Corporate-legacy media narratives are invariably:

- Simplistic - rely heavily on polarisation e.g. good v evil
- Hyperbolic - replete with threats, warnings, disasters etc.
- Emotive - e.g. seek to inflame: 'Putin bombs children'
- Partial – lack inconvenient information; one-sided

Take that inaccurate story about large numbers of drowned Afghans. This was part of a BBC narrative that promotes mass immigration into the UK (and western Europe). It is a narrative the aim of which is to exponentially increase the proportion of non-native inhabitants in the country, part of a wider objective which seeks to undermine national sovereignty of western nations transferring ever more power away from the demos to unelected technocrats.[11] In order for this story to harmonise with these broader objectives, the broadcaster exaggerated (hyperbole) the number of Afghan victims; by doing so it assumed that focus would be restricted to 'desperate' refugees (emotion[12]) forced to make the crossing rather than the reality i.e. a decision freely taken by economic migrants many of whom had paid thousands of dollars to professional smuggling networks (partiality). Meanwhile, the location shift from French to British waters enabled the broadcaster to imply responsibility had lain with Britain. Guilt was of course the aim; if the BBC could succeed in stoking guilt where none ought to exist, the path towards ever more prolific levels of immigration would have just gotten a step closer - much to the approval of corporate and ideological power.

Nor is creating truthiness especially difficult. Even the most mundane journalist can impose a narrative upon events however unpromising the facts first appear – 'framing' as it is often called. Indeed, BBC activists are trained to do exactly this – frame stories. If a story cannot be re-purposed to fit a set narrative in this way, it can simply be omitted from the news feed altogether.

The point has been made before, but is worth restating: BBC employees are journalists only in the loosest definition of the word, in that they produce work for an organisation classified as media. That's where any similarity begins and ends. Journalism is so much more than simply writing or broadcasting a news story. The fourth estate must be prepared to expose wrong-doing and corruption wherever it occurs, be that in public or private spheres irrespective of narrative. Above all else it must never act on behalf of exterior influence. Once a broadcaster, editor or journalist suppresses, modifies or enhances the facts to the advantage of an ally or benefactor – this is the moment he or she crosses the line from journalist to that of propagandist. While a real journalist says: *I don't know how the story will end*, a fake journalist by contrast says: *This is how the story ends*. Put simply journalism is guided by a single sacred principle: the quest for truth.[13] Real journalists are fearless; fake journalists – those whose role is to protect the wealthy and powerful from scrutiny – are, at their core, cowards. That is not say these impersonators/stenographers don't have teeth. It means that in common with the schoolyard bully, they select their prey with the utmost care i.e. targets approved by the establishment, those that are perceived to threaten its pre-eminence. Fake journalists invariably 'expose' the weak and powerless, ordinary people. Safest of safe grounds.

In this book we shall see a recurring example of this practice when discussing the BBC approach to two very disparate groups: QAnon and WEF. Now one of these groups chooses to base itself in the million-billionaire enclave of Davos to where the ultra-rich and powerful make annual pilgrimages. This unelected Swiss quango boasts an alumni consisting of some of the world's most powerful and influential individuals e.g. Trudeau, Merkel, Ardern, Johnson, Macron, Mark Carney, Prince Charles and other royalty. Amongst what it calls former and current 'Young Global Leaders' (YGL) are to be found the likes of Chelsea Clinton, Bill Gates, Jeff Bezos, Tony Blair, Sergey Brin (Google), Mark Zuckerberg etc. The other group meanwhile has neither wealth or political influence. It consists largely of the working poor. Rather than palaces and luxury yachts, followers of the group known as QAnon are more likely to inhabit much less salubrious locations – trailer parks, social housing etc.

So then, which of these two groups continually finds itself in the broadcaster's crosshairs, the subject of forensic examination by BBC 'disinformation' activists intent on exposing it? The ultra-powerful WEF or the totally powerless QAnon?

Looking back into the history of the corporation it soon becomes apparent that the broadcaster has always advocated on behalf of certain powerful interests, that such behaviour is hardwired into its DNA. Take the episode known as The General Strike.

The 'British' Broadcasting Company was still in its infancy when, in 1926, workers called for a nationwide strike in an attempt to secure improved conditions and rights – a manifesto fiercely opposed by the country's industrialist millionaire class and its government acolytes. In order to swing public opinion towards the masters and away from the workforce BBC wireless broadcasts ensured that the former group had its voice amplified wherever possible. By contrast, it endeavoured to suppress the voice of the workers. 'Everywhere' remarks renowned historian Asa Briggs, 'the complaints were bitter that a national service subscribed to by every class should have given only one side during the dispute.'[14] As anticipated, constantly exposed to just one side of the debate – that of the industrialist capitalist class – the BBC was able to shift public support from the powerless (workers) to the powerful (capitalists).

'The failure of the BBC to assume anything resembling an impartial position during the General Strike,' observes Mills (2016) 'has been readily acknowledged in the many histories of the BBC and British broadcasting, although the extent of these failures and the level of collusion between the BBC and the government has been hugely underplayed.'[15] Some idea of the extent of that collusion is hinted at in the private diaries of Lord Reith, the first BBC Director General, who, in an entry dated 10 May 1926 confides that: 'The government know they can trust us not to be really impartial.'[16]

From Suez to US-directed regime change in Iraq, Libya and Ukraine through Brexit and Covid that trust government has in the BBC to support its objectives remains well-founded. Thanks in no small part to the BBC, The General Strike collapsed on 12 May after just nine days. In many cases workers returned to even worse conditions than before. The establishment had crushed the strike, but it could not have done so without assistance. A reality not often appreciated by those analysing the strike and the BBC role is that the corporation performed splendidly – at least in the eyes of a tiny minority. The BBC achieved what it had been set up to do: protect the powerful, crush its enemies.

Fast forward to 1984. Despite its aversion to Mrs Thatcher, the broadcaster yet again played a significant role in crushing revolt from below this time the miners who, like their 1926 counterparts, were lobbying for better conditions and job security – the right to live a decent life. Déjà vu, BBC activities ensured the establishment triumphed once more. 'Britain's national broadcasting organisation has served as the propaganda arm of the British government,' observes Professor Nicholas Cull and his colleagues in their definitive reference guide to propaganda.[17]

Almost a century has elapsed since that ignominious episode of 1926, but little has changed in the interim. While the clique that sets the limits of public discourse might have gradually shifted its base from London to Washington DC during the twentieth century, as for the 'British' Broadcasting Corporation its mission remains unchanged: to facilitate the interests of society's most powerful entities, to normalise[18] their agendas, attack opponents – to continue, in effect, to do what it did to working people so effortlessly in 1926 and again in 1984: punch down.[19]

The question of who benefits from BBC disinformation answers itself therefore: the most powerful actors in society, those with sufficient resources to enable them to control the messages seen on TV, radio, online and elsewhere.[20] In this book the term US-(UK) corporate-political power and variations of it is used to refer to an exclusive clique whose interests the 'British' Broadcasting Corporation so dutifully promotes and which incorporates gigantic largely US-based entities such as the military industrial complex, Wall Street, the pharmaceutical industry, Silicon Valley etc. It also includes the US political system as manifest in the Democrat and Republican uniparty.[21] Hence, the BBC occupies a pivotal position within a structure of power that stretches from the City of London, all the way to the east coast of the United States and its urban power centres – what Chomsky terms as 'the Washington consensus' and what in *The News Class War*, Michael Lind calls 'the transatlantic elite.'

It was this same London-Washington-New York cabal whose noses were so badly put out of joint in 2016. For the election of

Donald Trump in the US and the success of Brexit in the UK undeniably triggered some of the mightiest political and economic powerhouses in town. It was a year unlike any previous election cycle. Arguably, it was the first time in living memory that the hegemony of what Arnold Toynbee calls the dominant minority had been not only challenged, but formally defeated in a way that would never be allowed to happen under the traditional Labour-Tory/Democrat-Republican uniparty system, which ensures the triumph of neo-liberalism each and every election.[22] Ranging from disbelief to horror and often descending into contempt, the reaction of the BBC to both events, though baffling and perplexing to the uninformed (isn't it supposed to be impartial?) was in fact wholly commensurate with its role as one of the most important proxies for ultra-powerful interests which reside either side of the Atlantic and whose feathers had been so badly ruffled by the outcomes of both votes.

However, it's not only events of 2016. Readers are invited to cite a single example wherein the 'British' state broadcaster has dissented from the neo-liberal global narrative or genuinely questioned the actual wealth and power consensus.[23]

Attacking those who supported Trump in the US or Brexit in the UK was a task the BBC undertook but it wasn't alone. For, along with its fellow travellers in the mainstream media such as ITV, *The Times* and *The Guardian*, the BBC-Ofcom is one of a number of UK-domiciled wealth and power proxies whose role is to 'sell' the agendas of the transatlantic power nexus to the British masses.

The task of promoting narrative over truth is, however, fraught with danger. Institutions like the BBC must try to convince people not to trust their own senses or instincts, but trust instead the opinions of BBC correspondents and hand-picked 'experts.' This entails, for example, convincing people there really is a 'climate emergency' even as those who preach this alarming message fly around the world in private jets between multiple homes.[24] It means persuading that mankind truly is in the grip of a deadly pandemic even when reality proves stubbornly resistant. It means informing audiences that there really are 100 genders, that it's not women who get pregnant, but 'people.' As the BBC is obliged to invert reality in multiple ways on a daily basis, reputational damage thus becomes a real possibility. But that's ok. As a result of its truth-bending behaviour brand BBC might continue to plummet but *not* among those who matter. Within circles of power and influence the broadcaster's stock remains as high as ever, higher.[25] Quid pro quo.

Surely though it can only be a matter of time until the public realises the world presented on the TV or radio bears hardly any resemblance to the world as they experience it? Not necessarily. Wealth and power proxies overcome this jeopardy by adopting a collegiate approach, sticking together. They simply drown out opposition. Not by accident are BBC headlines interchangeable with those of *The Guardian*, *The Huffington Post*, *The New York Times*, CNN etc. Besides, the pay-offs are by no means insignificant. In fulfilling what is a vital PR-gatekeeping role, the BBC and its employees remain within a golden circle of influence – rewarded for their compliance with hugely inflated salaries, more than generous perks and gilded future career paths.[26]

Telling the truth does not require inducement or reward. To tell lies on the other hand…

One hundred years after its formation, the BBC shows no signs of changing course. And why would it? Enabling the establishment to control the narrative is why the broadcaster came about in the first place. As long as it continues to promote the narratives of US-(UK) imperialist hegemonic power, the BBC's well-being is guaranteed. Nor will the UK's Labour-Tory uniparty – itself a (political) proxy of wealth and power - ever curb the broadcaster's subversive activities, not as long as it promotes the narratives of the transatlantic 'elite.'[27]

That the BBC is currently promoting the narrative of rule by technocrats should therefore come as no surprise, nor should its support for unelected quangos such as the UN, EU, WHO, WEF, IPCC etc. As the rich and powerful decide that the time has arrived for unprecedented top-down control, that democracy has had its day and technocratic autocracy is the way forward, who but the BBC should be busily assisting an authoritarian agenda many find so sinister? Under the guise of various 'emergencies' zealously promoted by the broadcaster, since 2020 (but in reality, well before) hugely powerful entities have begun to set in motion an agenda of authoritarian control which aims to disenfranchise the ordinary citizen while increasing the power of a tiny number of individuals and institutions – what politicians from Obama to Bush have referred to as a 'new world order.' Once again, without the assistance of a 'trusted' proxy such an agenda would struggle to get off the ground. And it is precisely this public relations role which explains the broadcaster's seeming invincibility as well as its longevity: for the 'British' Broadcasting Corporation is a vital asset of global power – arguably its most precious resource of all.

Where then does this all leave us? It leaves us at the mercy of an especially unethical actor, one happy to exploit its privileged position on behalf of hugely powerful concerns – the majority of whom are unknown to the public and have minimal affinity with it. And what that in turn means is that despite the scandals, gaffs and mockery that comes its way, the BBC is here to stay.[28] For the very sobering fact of the matter is that dishonesty pays and always has. 'Serial deceit,' as the journalist Glenn Greenwald observes:

> is not a liability for a thriving career in corporate journalism but rather a vital asset provided that the lies are in service of ruling class policies.[29]

Which explains quite a lot; it explains, for instance, why the BBC can campaign to unseat a democratically-elected (wrong-thinking) Prime Minister and escape any kind of censure whatsoever; it explains why the same broadcaster can undermine the (wrong) result of public referenda without even a suggestion of sanction against it; and it also explains how the broadcaster can insult the (wrong-thinking) President of the United States without so much as the mildest of rebukes. Meanwhile, at the time of writing the broadcaster is still ignoring the numerous scandals swirling around the (right-thinking) Biden family – especially Hunter Biden.

Sad to say, but it's impossible to envisage the broadcaster acting any other way. It's a shame, because had it not been a proxy of wealth and power the BBC could perform actual journalism. Instead of protecting power, it could hold it to account. Instead of punching down as it did in 1926, 1984 and on innumerable occasions before and since, it could punch upwards. Don't hold your breath. [30]

SUMMARY

The BBC was formed by the British establishment in order to control the narrative. Media Narratives facilitate the social and economic objectives of society's wealthiest and most powerful entities. The BBC does not report news. It reports narrative. As such it is a hugely valuable asset of global power.

A note on the text

The reader will observe the use of 'quotation marks' throughout the book. All headings and sub-headings are quotations directly made by BBC activists or by third-parties on the broadcaster's platform. They are just a tiny fraction of a much bigger disinformation cache. The reader will also observe extensive notes. While referring to notes can be a tiresome business, the reader is advised to make the effort; the notes in this book are not just citations, but comments which expand the text.

'This is a paradise faced with extinction'

'Maldives Paradise soon to be lost:'
bbc.co.uk, 28 July 2004

When it comes to reporting of climate the BBC has a well-established modus operandi: any opportunity it gets to highlight a freak weather event it grabs with both hands, for the broadcaster likes nothing more than to tell stories of record levels of sunshine, snow and rain; 'the sunniest day on record, the rainiest winter on record, the driest April on record,' etc.[1] The use of that phrase 'on record' is key. If records are being broken, surely it is proof that Anthropogenic Global Warming (AGW) is a real and present danger?[2]

Dig beneath the alarmist headlines and inevitably a much more nuanced picture emerges: 'Record Easter temperatures in three nations of the UK' duly went a BBC headline of April 2019. The highest temperature of the week-end in question had been recorded on the Hampshire coast at Gosport – 77.9F on Easter Saturday. However, on Easter Saturday 1949 the temperature had hit a roasting 85F in Camden; on the same day in 1893 it had reached 84F in Cambridge.[3] Prior to these dates it is impossible to know just how hot the Easter holiday period had been. That's because covering a period of little more than 150 years, climate records can only have limited relevance. Given the age of the earth and a future of unknown length records for the period 1870-2020 are such a tiny drop in a vast ocean to be virtually meaningless in this much wider context.[4]

As well as alarmist in tone – devised to ratchet up the level of

27

fear - BBC climate change reports have yet another ubiquitous feature: they are invariably hypothetical - projections that always insist on a worst-case scenario. For example, in 2021 BBC Sport presented various Doomsday scenarios which had been 'creatively imagined' and which showed how climate change *could* affect major sporting events.[5] According to the broadcaster, by the year 2050 there *could* be 'football fixture chaos' due to torrential rain; test match cricket *could* be abandoned because of scorched pitches; the Australian open tennis tournament *could* be moved indoors due to the number of 'unplayable days' and there *could* be 'no more skiing in Chamonix' due to a lack of snow at the French ski resort.

It becomes apparent that the broadcaster is peddling a specific narrative which states that AGW is a real and present danger, that in order to avoid its deleterious effects urgent action must be taken.[6] Given our own hypothesis that the broadcaster acts as a wealth and power proxy, its behaviour with regard to climate fits that hypothesis perfectly. According to some commentators the AGW agenda is a trojan horse that will allow governments to exercise unprecedented power over the citizenry, the like of which would never be acceptable outside of 'emergencies' such as climate change and Covid-19 'pandemics.' Like Covid, tentacles of the AGW agenda ultimately extend into everyday life in the form of limitations and restrictions e.g. travel, diet etc. The endgame for the AGW lobby, which itself is a merger of powerful global financial interests, was hinted at by Commonwealth Secretary General Sir Shridath Ramphal when decreeing back in the 1980s that: 'Governments must yield national sovereignty to multilateral authorities able to enforce laws across environ-mentally invisible frontiers if the green-house effect, which threatens the future of whole nations, is to be overcome.'[7]

Yield national sovereignty to multilateral authorities able to enforce laws...In other words transfer power from the demos to a tiny coterie of unelected and unaccountable actors who can override the democratic laws of sovereign nations. When viewed in relation to the long-term objectives of a small, but immensely powerful coterie of actors, unbridled BBC enthusiasm for climate propaganda becomes entirely explicable.

A full discussion of the AGW climate agenda is beyond the scope of this book, but it ought to be noted that until the last decade or so, the world had been experiencing warmer temperatures, part of a larger cyclical phenomenon of warming and cooling periods which have occurred since time began. Far from denying that climate does indeed change, sceptics agree whole heartedly that climate is *always changing* – mainly in accordance with solar activity. The bone of contention is the extent, if any, that *human activity* contributes to these patterns. Although the BBC would never admit as much there is in fact a spectrum of opinion ranging from scientists who believe human activity is wholly, partly or minimally responsible for the warmer temperatures experienced in the 20th century.

Despite the robustness of a debate that is still evolving and with so many unknowns, as far as climate change is concerned the BBC continues to insist that the 'science is settled.' The inherent absurdity with this statement is obvious enough: real science is consistently involved in a process of testing conflicting and emerging hypotheses – it thus advances, refines and modifies; the type of 'science' that refuses to open itself up to enquiry is the type that may just have something to hide for real science does not hide away from, but rather welcomes scrutiny. Notwithstanding, the broadcaster clings tenaciously to its claim. Nothing strange about that – it's precisely the line taken by a galaxy of wealth and power proxies from fellow travellers in the corporate MSM to NGOs and various celebrities.

However, when it talks of settled science it ought to be borne in mind that the broadcaster is deliberately conflating entirely separate phenomenon – politics with science. While the political consensus does indeed appear to be 'settled' the scientific debate rages on. In order to trick its audience into believing the opposite – that the debate is indeed closed – the BBC reverts to a favoured trick: amplify voices that agree with its absolutist narrative, marginalise (and demonise) those that disagree. It is this very method by which unscrupulous actors can create consensus where none exists. In doing so, the broadcaster facilitates the financial and ideological objectives of international corporate-political power, manifestations of which includes the (permanent) British state and its net-zero emissions policy.

While the ideological goal of creating a worldwide meta-government via an 'emergency' is nothing new, it is worthwhile briefly assessing the staggering financial inducements which also underpin the climate debate. That the so-called science cannot be challenged, modified or even rejected as per the scientific method is partly due to the enormous financial interests at stake; there is also the question of reputational damage to consider.[8] For the science has long since been corrupted by economic and ideological interests. Climate change has morphed into a massive industry, one which according to Inc.com now represents a '$26 trillion growth opportunity.'[9] In the US alone federal funding for climate change research went from $2.4 billion in 1993 to $11.6 billion in 2014 with an extra $26.1 billion available for climate change programs and activities.[10] 'Any academic whose research dares question the 'settled science' of the climate change complex,' ruefully notes Heritage.org. 'is instantly accused of being a shill for the oil and gas industry or the Koch brothers.'[11]

Certainly, the financial (and career) rewards for those towing the establishment climate change narrative can be substantial. And so, like all self-fulfilling prophecies, the debate takes on a life of its own whereby a vast system of financial reward helps to create and sustain a whole community of vested interests whose aim is to keep their business profitable.[12] Incentivise sightings of fairies with grants, acclaim and career advancement and overnight sightings of fairies will increase exponentially to the point where their existence is no longer in question, rather it becomes a case of how can fairies be preserved/saved from extinction from fairy-deniers. Thus, is born the fairy industry with its very own set of powerful advocates. Put it another way: while there is almost unlimited funding available for researchers pushing the agenda of immensely wealthy and powerful governmental institutes and NGOs, there is not a *single dime* nor shred of acclaim available to scientists who would seek to take issue with the man-made theory. On the contrary, career ruination awaits. In stark contrast, the most vociferous climate lobbyists can and do become very, very rich.[13]

This reality of personal enrichment might help answer a question posed by Professor Richard Lindzen, former Alfred P. Sloan Professor of Meteorology at the Massachusetts Institute of Technology, who, when ruminating about the theory of man-made global warming asked: 'how do otherwise intelligent people come to believe such arrant nonsense despite its implausibility, internal contradictions, contradictory data, evident corruption and ludicrous policy implications?'[14] Follow the money.

'Come here fast before it disappears'
The headline which greeted visitors to the BBC news website one day in July 2004 was typically cataclysmic: 'Maldives: Paradise soon to be lost.' Paradise lost? It sounded almost biblical. How could a paradise possibly be lost? The answer of course was climate change. With the polar caps melting and the oceans of the world rising, this collection of low-lying coral islands and atolls would sink into the sea, lost to mankind forever. Disaster!

'To visit the Maldives,' begins the BBC article, 'is to witness the slow death of a nation.'[15] It doesn't get any more calamitous than that: a nation dying and what is more dying slowly! Visitors to the BBC website would no doubt have read those words with growing anxiety. According to the BBC, an entire nation was about to become extinct because of climate change. Indeed, a little further on the article suggests that should the current inaction re climate continue, the islands' 360,000 citizens would be forced to evacuate.

Having told of the dire situation apparently facing the Maldives, the article ends with a call to action: 'So come here fast, before it disappears. This is a paradise faced with extinction.' Lost paradise...evacuation...extinction...BBC choice of language could not have been more nerve-wracking.

The (near) future seemed bleak in the extreme, but were the report's extraordinary claims true? With the majority of its 1,190 coral islands situated less than 1 metre above sea level, the Maldives has long since been characterised as a nation under threat, susceptible to wave-driven flooding and prone to freshwater shortage, a prime climate change casualty. In the late 1980s authorities warned that rising sea levels would 'completely cover' the islands within 30 years. 'But the end of The Maldives could come sooner,' observed *The Canberra Times*, 'if drinking water supplies dry up by 1992, as predicted.'[16] Water supplies of course did not dry up.

As for the tourism industry, the data contradicts the BBC's grim forecasts:

Maldives' Visitor Arrivals	
2004	616 000
2008	683 000
2012	958 000
2016	1 286 000
2020	555 000
2021	1 321 000

Source: Ministry of Tourism

The broadcaster might have told its audience that time was running out fast, that it should urgently visit the Maldives before the atolls became extinct but arrivals data reveals a gulf between the broadcaster's rhetoric and reality. While the BBC article speaks of the island nation's imminent 'slow death,' nobody appears to have told its residents; in 2004, at the time when the broadcaster was making its dire predictions, the population of the Maldives stood at 311,264, a figure which had increased to 540,985 by 2022.[17]

Far from dying, the country is in fact thriving. Investment is pouring into the Maldives. For example, Maafaru international airport opened in December 2021 - a project funded by the Abu Dhabi Fund for Development to the tune of $60 million, part of a luxury tourism zone established on Noonu atoll.[18] The development includes a 2.2 kilometre runway designed to accommodate international flights and private jets.

Meanwhile, Velena International Airport on Hulhulé Island is undergoing a major expansion to meet the increasing passenger demand which is projected to reach 7.3 million by 2030. The project is expected to cost $800m.[19] The Maldives continues to prosper.

Indeed, the picture presented by the BBC seems ever more fallacious as time goes by, part of a narrative presumably constructed to stoke irrational fears. Reality is very much at odds with the broadcaster's apocalyptic messaging. For example, a 2019 study investigated 709 islands in Pacific and Indian ocean atolls. Researchers found that no atoll lost land area and that almost 90% of the islands were either stable or had *increased in area*. 'Over the past decades,' concluded the study, 'atoll islands exhibited no widespread sign of physical destabilization in the face of sea-level rise.'[20] As reported by Australia's abc news, these findings were corroborated by a team of researchers from the University of Auckland. In their analysis of atolls, which included

The Marshall Islands and The Maldives archipelago, the scientists noted an 8% increase in land mass having occurred over a period of six decades.[21] Not quite the scenario subscribed to by the BBC – one whereby endless numbers of atolls in the Pacific and Indian oceans are submerged under rising sea levels caused by AGW. In fact, as remarked by abc in its report, the opposite is true: 'hundreds of Pacific Islands are getting bigger.'

As it stands, the Maldives is preparing to welcome record numbers of tourists. Tourism Minister Dr Abdullah Mausoom has in fact estimated 2 million tourists will visit the islands in 2022.[22] Despite BBC proclamations, there has never been a better time to visit the islands. Nor is there any hurry. The Maldives is not sinking nor have they ever been. All the evidence suggests this island paradise will continue to attract increasing number of visitors for some time to come.

SUMMARY

In 2004 the BBC urged its audience to visit the Maldives before the islands disappeared because of climate change. In 2022 record numbers of visitors are expected to visit the islands and investment continues to develop the islands' infrastructure.

'The death toll is rising around the world'

Panorama: Britain's Wild Weather,
BBC One: 3 November 2021

It starts with storms, floods and the sound of screaming voices. The music is ominous, nerve-jangling. A voiceover of BBC climate editor Justin Rowlatt[1] grimly insists that 'climate change IS going to effect all of our lives' - one of many such predictions which introduces *Britain's Wild Weather*, a documentary produced by BBC Panorama. Naturally, for an organisation that believes as far as climate is concerned the science is settled, the BBC documentary duly paints an apocalyptic picture of Britain's future.[2] As with the broadcaster's similarly catastrophic post-Brexit scenario, virtually all of the film's dire predictions are predicated on just one word: *could*:

'We'll show you how extreme it [weather] **could** get... This is what we think **could** happen... how much wetter **could** our winters get... by around 2070 winter rainfall **could** rise... it **could** be as much as a third more rain in winter... the arctic **could** get from 18-14 degrees hotter... summers in the UK **could** get between 1 and 6 degrees hotter...'[3]

And so on and so forth. These BBC proclamations are 'credible scenarios' of what 'could happen' in the future. Before going any further it is worth noting how the broadcaster routinely breaks not only its obligations under the royal charter, but how it even flouts its own proclamations with impunity: 'The BBC,' reads a document produced by the BBC Trust, 'has many public purposes of both ambition and merit – but joining campaigns to save the planet is not one of them...'[4]

Nonetheless, the programme is replete with a plethora of context-free claims which have a distinct feel of campaigning about them. At one point, Rowlatt asserts that a Siberian heatwave 'recorded 38 degrees in a town inside the arctic circle.' Arctic circle – isn't it usually very, very cold up there? Scared? You ought to be. Without context it is easy to see how such assertions can instil fear. Rowlatt is in fact referring to a place called Verkhoyansk which, on 20 June 2020, recorded a temperature of 100.4°F. What BBC Panorama failed to disclose is that Fort Yukon, Alaska, recorded the first-ever 100°F day north of the Arctic Circle as long ago as 1915; Verkhoyansk also hit 99.1°F in 1988. High temperatures are in fact not unusual in the Arctic circle. In an interview conducted with *National Geographic* Walt Meier, a climate scientist at the US National Snow and Ice Data Center, observed that: 'At this time of the year, around the summer solstice, you get 24 hours of sunlight,' adding: 'that's a lot of solar energy coming in. So, in these high-latitude areas—80 degrees, 90 degrees, that's not unheard of.'[5]

Not for nothing does the broadcaster pump out a never-ending diet of hypothetical scenarios and context-free assertions, all of which point to Armageddon for humanity. The objective is of course to foment fear and panic. It has long since been known that when people are placed under sustained stress cognitive function can be impaired. Indeed, prolonged exposure to stress leads to loss of neurons.[6] Individuals suffering from anxiety can become ever more susceptible to manipulation and as a result may be more likely to seek and meekly accept any solution offered. Hence, should an 'impartial' and 'trusted' broadcaster suggest net zero is the answer to these horrific occurrences, however outlandish and bogus, it stands a fighting chance of being accepted by those whose cognitive faculty has been negatively impacted.

And what could be any more alarming than mass deaths caused by climate change? *Britain's Wild Weather* makes some pretty wild claims during its 58-minute running time, none wilder than when asserting that the death toll due to climate change: 'is rising around the world and the forecast is that worse is to come.'

However, according to the World Meteorological Organisation (WMO) the *opposite* is true: the death toll associated with climate change is *falling* – and falling steeply. In the 1970s and 1980s an average of 170 deaths per day related to climate were recorded; in the 1990s the figure almost halved to 90 related deaths per day; by the 2010s that figure had more than halved to 40 related deaths per day.[7] The facts make the BBC's further claim that 'worse is to come' rather difficult if not impossible to justify.[8] Disinformation at its finest.

'Statistics can be slippery'

WMO data is corroborated by research conducted by the Office of National Statistics for the period 2001-2020 which notes a 'net decrease in deaths' related to climate in the UK. The report also observes that: 'Over a 20-year period the estimated change in deaths associated with warm or cold temperature was a net decrease of 555,094, an average of 27,755 deaths per year.'[9]

Contradicting its narrative of spiralling climate-induced death so comprehensively, the ONS research was not exactly welcomed by the BBC, nor for that matter Justin Rowlatt who seemed to imply something nefarious afoot when observing that, 'Statistics can be slippery, as these new climate-death figures show.'[10] Having informed Panorama viewers of a rising death-toll, denial of facts is an understandable reaction. Thus, it was a report that gained little traction and rather than splashed all over the broadcaster's vast platform, ended up buried away on the Science and Environment page of its website; nor were there any references on news and current affairs programmes. It's almost as if the report had never happened. For, provided official statistics back up its climate alarmism, the corporation will accept and promote that data without question, and with something akin to glee. Official data which does not support the BBC's Armageddon narrative becomes suspect – 'experimental' in the words of the broadcaster or just plain 'slippery' in the words of its climate editor. All of which goes to illustrate the immutability of a BBC narrative. Facts inconvenient to the narrative are simply dismissed as irrelevant, or, as on this occasion, suspect.

But death-tolls are not the only misleading item on show. The programme is dripping in claims which have been cherry-picked and presented without context. Justin Rowlatt and his Panorama team also visit Yorkshire. Footage follows of the storms of 2020 which flooded areas of the Calder Valley, an area through which the river Calder runs and which incorporates towns including Hebden Bridge and Mytholmroyd. On the same evening – 7 December 2020 – that *Britain's Wild Weather* was broadcast on BBC 1 prime-time, BBC Look North Yorkshire transmitted its own alarmist segment drawing on and supplementing some of the material from Rowlatt's documentary.

'Next tonight' begins the presenter, 'a warning that flooding in the Calder Valley *could* become even more frequent *if* [*our italics*] climate change continues…' A flood warden then tells a BBC reporter that: 'People do get worried and they get anxious and they just feel that anxiety every time it rains even if it's a small amount of rain, it's that worry: what if?'[11]

Anxiety every time it rains…

Back with Panorama, *Britain's Wild Weather* also journeys around the Calder Valley.[12] Mytholmroyd has suffered three floods since 2012 viewers are informed. Referring to the town, a Met Office spokesperson predicts 'heavy rainfall that will see a big increase, 20-30%.' However, all is not lost because: 'If we cut our emissions then these changes won't be as severe.' Consuming this BBC programme, the viewer might well be left with the impression that severe flooding is a consequence of climate change, that Britain's reliance on fossil fuels has led to catastrophic disruption to its ecosystem and that places like the Calder Valley face a horrific future.

As often happens with the BBC it is not necessarily what the audience is told, but rather *what it is not told* that matters. By presenting information stripped of context propagandists are able to mislead with impunity. A quick assessment of the area's topography helps to shed light on the extreme weather events experienced in towns such as Mytholmroyd and Hebden Bridge, known administratively as Calderdale. Topographically, the area is characterised by steep valleys, hillsides and its riverside communities. The River Calder rises to 1,300 ft above sea level on the eastern slopes of the Pennines; periods of heavy rainfall thus make the area susceptible to flooding.[13]

'The River Calder burst its banks'

For an (incomplete) record the following is a summary of just a few *major* floods recorded in the Calder area.[14] Hebden Bridge suffered flooding in 1837 – 'the highest flood recorded' – and again in 1849 and 1866. The 1891 flood turned the town's Market Street into a 'canal.' Its main thoroughfare was again under water in a flood which occurred in November 1901. Neighbouring Mytholmroyd was hit by flooding in February 1920. Both it and Hebden suffered badly in a particularly severe flood of 1946.[15] The River Calder reportedly rose over 6 foot in just a couple of hours precipitating a flood in 1954, the water level reaching 10 foot above its normal level in some parts of the town by the end of the day. Meanwhile, the 1967 flood...' Flooding has always been a fact of life in Calderdale.

Naturally, the BBC would never place the floods occurring since 2012 in a historical context when to do so would severely damage its objective to instil fear. As devastating as the recent floods have been,' observes *The Yorkshire Examiner* 'they're nothing new in Yorkshire.'[16] The paper chronicles previous floods which occurred in the county; one such flood in 1852 resulted in 81 fatalities in the Holmfirth, a town located 13 miles south of Mytholmroyd.

Floods are indeed part of life for certain areas of the UK and the wider world. If they *seem* to occur more frequently then this perception is likely due to several factors:

1 Consistent record-keeping since the start of the 20th century aided by improvements in technology which replaced non-existent or partial records.

2 Politicisation of climate whereby alarmists benefit from massive public and private funding in order to promote the AGW hypothesis.

3 The activities of climate lobbyists which includes the de-contextualised, partisan output of organisations such as the BBC who consider 'the science settled' and who thereby invest considerable resources in creating vehicles such as *Britain's Wild Weather* replete with its many falsehoods and inaccuracies.

At one point in *Britain's Wildest Weather* an ever-breathless Rowlatt announces with RADA-like incredulity that 'The River Calder burst its banks.'

Concluding this foray into flooding, suffice to say the whole of the British Isles has been subject to extreme weather events throughout its history. For example, in the year 1099 the east coast of Britain was hit by a flood which, according to *The Anglo-Saxon Chronicle*, 'sprung up to such a height and did so much harm as no man remembered before.'[17] Similarly, 'Huge and mighty hills of water' moving 'faster than a greyhound can run' was how eye witnesses described the Bristol Channel flood of 1607.[18] Water levels reached heights of almost eight metres and spread over five kilometres as far as Pembroke and Glamorgan. In May 1920, 1,200 million gallons of rain fell on the Wolds near Louth; the River Lud rose over sixteen feet in just 15 minutes and the Lincolnshire town was hit by a raging torrent that would leave 23 people dead. The list goes on and on and on.[19] Extreme weather events have always occurred throughout the British Isles and always will. They have nothing whatsoever to do with fossil fuels, the thesis of 'Britain's Wild Weather' – the same programme that falsely claims 'The death toll [from climate change] is rising around the world…'

Had Justin Rowlatt and BBC Panorama been around in Louth in 1920, imagine how they might have reacted to and reported an epic flood such as this – a flood caused by natural phenomenon – aka weather…

SUMMARY

BBC Panorama claimed deaths resulting from climate change are increasing. Since the 1990s, climate-related deaths have in fact been significantly decreasing. It also implied that adverse weather events are increasing. The records that do endure demonstrate that the British Isles has always experienced adverse – often severe - weather events, especially flooding.

'In steep decline because of climate change'

Russia with Simon Reeve:
BBC Two: Sunday 28 September 2017

A t the start of *The Grand Chessboard*, a geopolitical analysis of the world from a US perspective written by Zbigniew Brzezinski, scholar of international relations, director of the Trilateral Commission and adviser to US President Jimmy Carter, the book sets out an important US credo: 'For America,' asserts its author, the chief geopolitical prize is Eurasia.' Brzezinski goes on to state that: 'America's global primacy is directly dependent on how long and how effectively its preponderance on the Eurasian continent is sustained.'[1] Short as it is, this brief introduction provides a remarkably candid insight into US foreign policy thinking which has changed little in the 25 years since Brzezinski was writing. As far as the United States is concerned, there is room for only one global superpower in Eurasia: The United States.

As alluded to in the introduction to this book, proxies of US corporate and political power such as the US-UK mainstream media have long since been co-opted into what is essentially a long-term propaganda campaign aimed at undermining the Russian state at every opportunity. It has been observed for example (Tsygankov, 2017) how western media frequently portrays Russia as a sinister 'neo-Soviet autocracy.' Tsygankov also notes how the media 'plays important social functions validating, developing, or challenging various collectively held myths, prejudices and stereotypes.'[2]

What then to expect when a BBC activist is given free rein to travel around a country long since targeted by US-UK hegemonic power as a serious rival to its geo-political and economic dominance? While an ethical operator would treat the subject matter fairly and equitably, an actor whose loyalties lie very much with US (and UK) interests as articulated by Brzezinski might be tempted to exploit the opportunity, to consolidate the dominant narratives of their partners and allies.

'Feeling the effects of our warming world'

The BBC blurb for its three-part serial *Russia with Simon Reeve* in which the eponymous host travels around the world's largest country, gives a hint of things to come in the series:

> Throughout his stay Simon is followed and harassed by the authorities, finally being forced to leave the area. It is a powerful reminder of Russia's authoritarian and corrupt system...[3]

As far as 'authoritarian' systems go, the BBC could of course choose to investigate virtually any country in the world – the US or UK for example where holding 'wrong' opinions of the sort not approved by the establishment (i.e. being politically incorrect, or conducting real journalism as in the case of Julian Assange) can have serious consequences in terms of reputation and career prospects and, in the case of Assange, personal liberty.[4] When it comes to corruption it would have a field day with trans-national organisations such as the EU, the UN, the WHO etc. Alas, targets of BBC investigations are invariably selected with the utmost care.[5]

Nor is this the only political axe that will be ground in the series. 'Simon ends his journey on the rim of a giant crater,' continues the BBC blurb, 'that has emerged in the Siberian landscape - chilling evidence of the impact of global climate change.' Two of the most favoured and enduring narratives of US-UK hegemonic power for the price of one: Russian villainy and man-made climate change. Full speed ahead.

It doesn't take long for the series to arrive at the first of these pet subjects. In episode one Reeve spends some time with a family of reindeer herders in Kamchatka, a remote area of eastern Russia. 'It's a fragile existence,' Reeves says, 'And in recent years, the consequences of our changing climate have been disturbing.' According to the narrator the unpredictable weather is impacting the lives of said herders: because of the frozen ground reindeer cannot access its staple diet of lichen. Without reindeer there is no livelihood for the area's nomadic people. As a sad fiddle strikes up Reeve then remarks that:

> Across northern Russia many reindeer populations are **in steep decline because of climate change**. Tens of thousands of reindeer have died. People and wildlife who survive at the edge of existence are already feeling the effects of our warming world.

Are reindeer populations really 'in steep decline?' Or is the picture a little more nuanced that the broadcaster would have its audience believe? It was Lord Lawson who took up the cudgels in what would turn out to be a fairly standard example of BBC climate-related chicanery. The former Chancellor of the Exchequer submitted a complaint to the corporation protesting its assertion that many reindeer populations were 'in steep decline.' Lawson called the claim 'a distortion of known facts and constitutes a serious factual error.'[6] In sharp contrast to the broadcaster who once again had put narrative ahead of facts, Mr Lawson had done his homework.[7] What he discovered bore no relationship at all to what the BBC programme had asserted.

The producers of *Russia with Simon Reeve* indeed appeared oblivious to the work of researchers such as Konstantin Klokov from the Faculty of Geography at Saint Petersburg State University. The academic has an extensive track record related to reindeer ecology. For example, in a 2012 paper he concluded that herd numbers are most closely connected to changes in Russia's political context.[8] His paper also notes that following stabilisation of the Russian economy and starting around the turn of the century, reindeer numbers had 'crept up gradually.' Having assessed the evidence Klokov gives his verdict on the fluctuating fortunes of the country's reindeer numbers: 'In Russia, the huge changes in reindeer numbers provoked by the instability of political, social, and economic life make it nearly impossible to find any link to long-term climatic changes.'

Similarly, research by Uboni *et al* (2016) mirrored Klokov's assessment. This project studied data pertaining to nineteen reindeer populations in the region over a 70-year period. Between 1941-2012 the authors found that reindeer populations in the region had undergone 'significant socio-economic changes.' When it came to climate however the researchers found minimal impact on long-term trends in population numbers. 'Proxies of climate variability,' they conclude 'mostly failed to explain population growth rates and synchrony. For both wild and semi-domesticated populations, local weather, biotic pressures, loss of habitat and human disturbances appear to have been more important drivers of reindeer population dynamics than climate.'

The evidence is extensive and unequivocal: multifarious factors determine the fecundity of northern Russia's reindeer population. Had the BBC cared to peruse the literature it could not possibly have made such misleading claims as aired in *Russia with Simon Reeve*. The socio-economic context is apparent throughout the published research as noted by Rees *et al* (2008) who, in their investigation into Eurasian reindeer husbandry remark that:

Models of vulnerability to climate change should be tempered by paying greater attention to changes in socio-economic factors. When compared with the potential effect of changing these socioeconomic factors, the vulnerability of reindeer husbandry to projected climate change appears to be comparatively small.

Faced with overwhelming evidence to the contrary, the BBC had no option but to accept the facts. Several months after the programme had aired the broadcaster added a brief paragraph to the Corrections part of its website whereby it clung to its original falsehood: 'This programme suggested that many reindeer populations are in steep decline because of climate change. It would have been more accurate to say that many reindeer populations are threatened by it.' When is a correction not a correction? What made this BBC statement even more egregious was the fact that the recent (2016) paper authored by Uboni *et al* had clearly stated that of the nineteen reindeer populations studied, nine had increased in overall number while seven had decreased in population size. It would not therefore have been 'more accurate' to maintain a narrative that was clearly contradicted by study after study all of which asserted the minimal role played by climate change. In fact, this correction could not have been any more inaccurate.

Meanwhile, Reeve had some dubbing to do. Episode one of *Russia with Simon Reeve* has subsequently undergone some cosmetic touch-ups:

Across northern Russia many reindeer populations are **under threat.** Tens of thousands of reindeer have died **in events linked to climate change**. People and wildlife who survive at the edge of existence are already feeling the effects of our warming world.

As can be seen from this new (unacknowledged) commentary, the broadcaster's narrative is peculiarly impervious to truth. 'Under threat' has replaced 'steep decline' and in an effort to salvage its falsehood a baseless claim has been added regarding the reason why so many reindeer have died: 'in events linked to climate change.' However, no such claim can be inferred from the published research. Once again, the point is made by Uboni *et al* who conclude that: 'Most of the synchrony in reindeer population dynamics we detected does not seem to be explained by the climate indices we considered.' The researchers note that the stability of just two of the populations *might* have been effected by climate. 'Our study has shown,' they also note, 'that generalizations about the future abundance of this species should be avoided.'

So much for the catastrophic destruction of reindeer herds due to climate. What about that other BBC pet narrative? Perhaps the broadcaster could at least further its campaign against Russia's president Putin.

'It threatens to cook our world'
With its history of aggressive anti-Russian propaganda, perhaps it's not that surprising to find the BBC production team under close scrutiny by the authorities. Reeve certainly takes pains to paint a grim picture of the country around which he is travelling: the people are not free and the media is controlled.

'Russia under Vladimir Putin,' asserts Reeve, 'often behaves like a police state.' Maybe so, but it's worthwhile recalling that it was UK police who descended on the home of Harry Miller, a 53-year-old in 2019 in order to 'check his thinking' after he had retweeted an allegedly offensive poem. It was the UK where a cartoonist lost her job after being reported for a 'transphobic' cartoon recorded by Avon and Somerset police recorded as a 'non-crime hate incident.'[9] It is in fact the UK, not Russia, where a citizen can be arrested for looking at somebody in a way 'perceived' by 'the victim' to be 'hateful.' Are some police states more equal than others in BBC-land?

Creepy music underscoring his every word, Reeve informs us that he and his crew are indeed under surveillance. BBC reputation apart, it's not clear what if anything the production crew has done to warrant this attention; whatever, it makes for great TV while also managing to consolidate the broadcaster's narrative that portrays Russia as a sinister, criminal backwater.

Reeve ends this first instalment at the edge of a Siberian crater. The villain is of course climate change, the phenomenon of craters presumably unknown before fossil fuel use. 'If, as scientists fear,' says a subdued Reeve, 'the permafrost melts it releases incredible quantities of methane into the atmosphere, it threatens to cook our world. Methane could accelerate unstoppable global warming.' *Could* + *if* + lashings of hyperbole… the usual suspects of BBC climate reports.

'I'm going to puke'

Episode two of the series starts with a voiceover in which Reeve promises to discover what happens to people who 'speak out in Russia.' The programme's titles next show the host in a boxing ring. It appears he's been undergoing some training and looks a little fragile. The voiceover continues: 'I'll meet the tough blokes fighting for what they say are traditional Russian values.' 'I'm going to puke,' next says an exhausted Reeve addressing the camera in an typically innocent piece of BBC juxtaposition. The broadcaster it appears doesn't much care for traditional Russian values.

What follows is a series of speculative and evidence-free statements of which the following are fairly typical examples: Russia took over Crimea 'then organised a questionable refer-endum;'[10] Putin 'encouraged, perhaps orchestrated an armed uprising in the east of Ukraine' etc. And that's not all. A programme like this would not be complete without liberal doses of innuendo. Reeve's ruminations about President Putin more than fill the gap: 'What's astonishing to me is just how incredibly talented so many of his [i.e. Putin's] judo buddies must have been because so many of them now seem to be running this country or owning it...'[11]

Reeve next arrives in Moscow. Now, there is art and culture to spare in this beautiful city; the Russian capital is arguably home to some of the world's finest museums, theatres and galleries. It is a city of bridges and home to architectural wonders which include Red Square and St Basil's Cathedral with its brightly coloured 'onion' domes. Indeed, there is an inexhaustible supply of cultural artefacts on offer. Notwithstanding, the BBC heads for an area of the city home to an area of housing known as Khrushchyovka. Here it interviews a female resident threatened with eviction and who clearly does not wish to relocate. Reeve follows her all the way to court. Upon demolition of her home, the poor woman will be cast out onto the street by the wicked Russian government of Vlad Putin. Well, that's the BBC narrative. The truth is of course somewhat more nuanced.

Named after Russian president Nikita Khrushchev, Khrushchyovka apartments were built in the 1950/1960s to meet the housing needs of an expanding city. As a consequence of being built so rapidly and so cheaply these cramped, pre-fabricated homes were of such poor structural quality they had not been expected to endure into the 21st century. 'They were only meant to last for 25 years,' reported *The Moscow Times,* 'but many have stood for twice as long, turning into dilapidated eyesores.'[12] Apartments had low ceilings, terrible sound insulation, no elevators etc. Bathrooms were tiny – on average 2 square metres. One-bedroomed flats were 16 square meters in size, two-bedroomed 22 square metres. In an article about Ukraine's own Khrushchyovkas, *Al Jazeera* called the apartments 'grim.'[13] The five-storey blocks became known as Khrushchobi - a blend of Khrushchev's name and *trushobi*, Russian for slum.

Although new apartments had been earmarked for residents, as might be expected not everybody wanted to uproot their lives. The majority of residents though had agreed to move and seemed happy to do so. City officials promised replacement accommodation would be larger, better quality and more comfortable than Khrushchyovka stock. Car parking spaces would increase and urban planning would be improved; residents with disabilities would also be catered for. The modernisation project would be developed along with Moscow's transport network.[14]

However, viewers of *Russia with Simon Reeve* would have been left with the distinct impression that the rotten Russian government was forcing people to leave their homes purely for the hell of it, to inconvenience them. It's a little more complicated than the BBC's simplistic narrative though. Naturally Reeve does not bother speaking to any residents glad to be leaving or any Moscow housing officials; BBC cameras don't bother filming in the new, spacious stock and talk to satisfied residents. No, it's all about one woman's desire to remain in her flat, a fight against tyranny.

There are three instalments of this stuff, and Reeve takes any opportunity afforded to have a dig at Russia - especially its president. It's all rather unedifying, but we'll end with one such dig: 'There's long been some sort of unspoken agreement here between President Putin and the Russian people,' asserts a BBC travel activist now in full rhetorical flow, 'and it goes something like: 'I will give you jobs, a bit of money, you'll have a chance to buy stuff and occasionally take a foreign holiday but don't question my power...'[15]

Russia with Simon Reeve is not all climate alarmism and anti-Russian disinformation. There are a few shots of the unique landscape. But the programme's crowning glory surely comes when, with what appears to be absolute sincerity, the host makes the assertion that 'Russia's not alone in having broadcasters who pump propaganda...'

SUMMARY

The BBC claimed that reindeer populations in Russia had declined because of climate change. With a few exceptions the herds in question have actually stabilised or increased in number over the past seventy years. According to the published research, reindeer population size is dependent upon a range of factors most importantly those related to socio-economic policy.

'The Brexit Murder?'

BBC Radio 4 The Corrections: 28 Nov 2019

The death of Arkadiusz Jozwik in August 2016 was allotted virtual round-the-clock coverage by the BBC. The 40-year-old factory worker had been involved in a late-night altercation with a gang of youths who were hanging around The Stow shopping precinct in the town of Harlow, Essex. There had been a scuffle. A punch had been thrown. Mr Jozwik fell to the ground, his head striking the concrete. Two days later, he died in Addenbrookes hospital.

On the face of it the incident was yet another tragedy in a long list of comparable incidents wherein anti-social behaviour – often fuelled by alcohol and/or drugs – can and does lead to violent encounters. The cases of Garry Newlove (Warrington, 2007) and Duncan Browne (Liverpool, 2020) are two incidents described as 'unprovoked' and which also resulted in fatalities. While the vast majority of such incidents rarely make an impact on the BBC radar, Harlow was a different matter. No sooner had the victim been taken to hospital than swathes of BBC reporters arrived in town, among them Daniel Sandford, Home Affairs correspondent and John Sweeney of BBC Newsnight.

The story of a late-night punch up in a nondescript Essex town duly led not only the broadcaster's main 6 o'clock news bulletin, but occupied a similarly prominent slot later that evening on Newsnight. Clearly, the broadcaster's interest had been piqued. Yes, somebody had died in terrible circumstances, but compared to other cases its coverage seemed out of all proportion. What could explain this particular case's attraction to the BBC?

In a word: Brexit.

As Mr Jozwik happened to be a Polish national and had died just months after the UK had voted to leave the European Union, sensing an opportunity to promote its anti-Brexit narrative the broadcaster had seized upon this tragic event with relish. *Foreign national killed in post-Brexit Britain!* For an organisation that had spent the run-up to the 2016 European Union Referendum pumping out pro-EU propaganda as per its allegiance to international corporate-political power, bruised and increasingly bitter in the aftermath of defeat, Mr Jozwik's was a tragedy ripe for exploitation. BBC activists were soon crawling all over the Essex town.

As distasteful as it was, corporation anticipation should have come as no surprise. Its post-Brexit wounds were, after all, still raw. The 'British' Broadcasting Corporation was seeking redress – a way to conclusively prove its utterly nonsensical thesis which posited that leaving the EU had uncorked what it termed 'a hate crime epidemic.' Had not the UK voted to leave the EU; months later had not a foreign national died on British soil? The link between democratic vote and random attack might have been tenuous in the extreme, to say nothing of a brazen attempt to exploit a human tragedy for political gain, but the UK's state broadcaster seemed not to care on either count. Indeed, even before Sandford, Sweeney & co descended upon Essex, the BBC had its narrative already written: *the Harlow killing had happened because the UK had voted to leave the EU.*

'The fear is,' Daniel Sandford duly told BBC news viewers, 'that this was a frenzied racist attack triggered by the Brexit referendum.' Introducing the story on that evening's edition of Newsnight host Evan Davis began by stating there were obvious worries within Harlow's Polish community 'at what looks like a hate crime.' In his report direct from the town, Davis' colleague John Sweeney continued the Brexit hate crime theme by cueing up an associate of the dead man to infamously assert that in light of the tragedy Brexit figurehead Nigel Farage 'had blood on his hands.' Meanwhile, BBC Radio 4's *Today* programme interviewed Polish Prime Minister Mateusz Morawiecki. 'We had a Polish man attacked and killed in Harlow in Essex on Saturday,' began the host, Dominic O'Connell, going on to ask a typically leading BBC question: 'do you fear that some Poles might be motivated to return simply because they fear the Brexit vote has stirred some racist feeling against them?'[1]

Fast forward to 2019. By now the facts of the case had long since been established. And they bore no resemblance to the narrative peddled by the BBC. As had been clear from the start, Mr Jozwik's death had nothing whatsoever to do with a Brexit-inspired 'hate crime.' Having consumed a quantity of alcohol, it had been Mr Jozwik together with a friend who had first approached the gang of youths - at least one of whom had been of mixed-race descent and against whom a racial slur is said to have been directed. From there the situation had escalated.

The BBC thus had a problem. Having led the 'Brexit hate crime' charge as per its predilections with round-the-clock coverage, memories of its inflammatory and wholly erroneous reporting lingered on. *The Corrections* is a programme produced by BBC Sounds which purports to: 'revisit news stories that left the public with the wrong idea about what really happened and investigates how and why the narrative went awry.' In October 2019 the series aired an investigation into the reporting of Mr Jozwik's death. BBC Sounds chose to call this edition, *The Brexit Murder?*

Brexit and *murder* – an interesting even inflammatory combo. Could the sneaky broadcaster be attempting to forge a link between those two words, to plant a seed - the same broadcaster that had always insisted Mr Jozwik's death had been a Brexit-related hate-crime? Curiously, the suggestion that the Polish national had been murdered was never made at the time – certainly not by the police and with good reason: the investigation into the death had not yet begun.[2] Thus, it would have been highly imprudent for any reputable organisation to have made such a dubious as well as sensational and unsubstantiated claim. Early indications pointed in just one direction as regards cause: anti-social behaviour of the worst possible kind. Indeed, the sixteen-year-old who had delivered the punch which knocked the victim to the floor would be eventually found guilty of manslaughter.

'In reviewing the evidence,' observed the Chief Crown Prosecutor for the East of England, 'we were satisfied there was no intent by the youth to kill Mr Jozwik or that he thought that his actions would result in the death of a man.'

Given that Mr Jozwik's death had not been murder nor had it been related to Brexit, BBC Sounds had chosen an especially misleading title for its production. Although far from perfect, *The Brexit Manslaughter?* would have been slightly more accurate than the title chosen. Admittedly 'Brexit' and 'manslaughter' do not carry the same lurid associations as 'Brexit' and 'murder,' but on the plus side the false connection between an *unlawful* death and Brexit could still have been made.

It's worth considering a few more aspects of that carefully chosen BBC Sounds title, specifically the use of punctuation. Notice the use of the interrogative (?) While some might wonder whether this is a cynical tactic used to create doubt, others will claim the question mark is merely indicative of the confusion surrounding the case as summer turned to autumn back in 2016; the media had mistakenly assumed a murder had been committed. To re-iterate: at the time of Mr Jozwik's death in August of that year up to and including the conviction of the perpetrator in July 2017, murder had never been an item on the news agenda, which makes that use of a question mark (*The Brexit Murder?*) rather difficult if not impossible to justify.

What then was the broadcaster playing at? When it wishes to

highlight an opinion with which it does not agree the BBC, along with other media, typically uses quotations marks. Thus, '*The Brexit Murder*' would indicate the supposition has little or no validity – at least from the BBC perspective. But no. For reasons best known to itself, the broadcaster opted for *The Brexit Murder?* The only logical explanation appears to be that the broadcaster is indeed trying to cement a link between its detested 'Brexit' and 'murder' in the minds of its audience, irrespective of the reality, inviting it to wrongly believe that the question is far from over. BBC audiences can thus continue to discuss Brexit in the same breath as murder; the concept is introduced and recycled, running the risk of becoming a reality – at least in the minds of BBC listeners.

Brexit *and* murder...if listeners were expecting some form of BBC mea culpa, they might well have been bemused by what would follow. Despite the broadcaster's leading role in the promotion of the Brexit hate crime narrative, presenter Jo Fidgin takes some pains throughout the programme's 28 minutes to focus on what she calls 'the news machine' and *its* reaction to the story.[3] The broadcaster is therefore able to float the idea of collective guilt; the BBC was merely part of what the host terms a 'media circus.'

'Has it something to do with racism or Brexit?'

In the second half of the programme Daniel Sandford himself makes an appearance. Despite the prominent role he played in attempting to link Mr Jozwik's death with Brexit, the activist remains unrepentant. 'I'm quite proud of being a straight-talking reporter,' he says at one point. 'To not have the Brexit word in the report would have been frankly dishonest.'

It is sometimes the case that with its back against the wall, the BBC will offer up a sacrificial lamb, the 'rogue reporter' defence in which the broadcaster will seek to distance itself from an individual deemed to have acted inappropriately, on their own initiative. However, as noted, the fallacious 'Harlow = Brexit hate crime' narrative was promoted throughout the BBC's huge media platform, from the 6 o'clock news through BBC London, Newsnight and the corporation's vast news website. In fact, the entire BBC network was using Mr Jozwik's death as a means to stigmatise Brexit voters. That the BBC is offering Sandford up as a sacrificial lamb, albeit half-heartedly, becomes apparent when a segment of audio recorded at the Stow precinct is played.

On location in Harlow, BBC Sounds had interviewed the pizzeria worker who served Mr Jozwik and his friend on that fateful night. Sandford, it transpires, had petitioned this same witness. 'Daniel (Sandford) asked me has it something to do with racism or Brexit,' confirms the witness 'and I said no. I didn't think it was a hate crime.' BBC activists such as Sandford and Sweeney had indeed arrived in the town simply looking for any evidence that would clinch their employer's Brexit hate crime narrative. As it stood however, the pizzeria worker's testimony was no good to the BBC. Not only had he told the broadcaster that the gang of youths taunted and annoyed just about anyone who had the misfortune to cross its path, he made other observations antithetical to the BBC thesis: gang members were of mixed race and on the night in question Mr Jozwik and his friend had been 'a bit drunk.' He might have been an eye witness, but Daniel Sandford promptly dismissed the pizzeria worker. After all, the BBC reporter had a mission: to link the death to Brexit. And nothing – facts, truth nor fidelity - was going to prevent him from doing just that.

And there was another problem for the BBC's pre-written narrative: for reasons known only to Mr Sandford himself, omitting the Brexit word from his reports would have apparently been 'dishonest;' yet wherever he turned nobody mentioned Brexit or even alluded to it, not the pizzeria worker nor any other witness. What the townsfolk *did* talk about was Harlow's anti-social problem, especially within the Stow precinct. So, when Mr Sandford breathlessly announced to viewers of BBC news the 'fear' that the killing was related to Brexit, it was not the fear of local residents rather the affected fear of his employer, a vengeful 'British' Broadcasting Corporation desperate to attack Brexit any which way it could. Mr Jozwik – his death – had simply been the means to an especially ignoble end.

As for Nigel Farage, he accused of having 'blood on his hands,' *The Brexit Murder?* fails to mention this infamous smear engineered by its BBC Newsnight colleagues. For a programme promising to investigate how the public 'got the wrong idea' about a given news story, it's a glaring as well as mysterious oversight. Following the BBC broadcast, Mr Farage and his family suffered considerable abuse.[4] That is not to say the politician is overlooked by the programme; Mr Farage *does get mentioned* only not in relation to the infamous and incorrect slur. The programme criticises the former MEP for stating that the Polish men had directed a racial slur towards one of the teenagers thus sparking the incident.

From blaming the 'media circus,' the police and even the town's member of parliament to omitting key aspects such as the BBC's own inflammatory slurs attempting to link a key Brexit figure to the murder, BBC Sounds had managed to whitewash the leading role played by the BBC. Lessons learnt? Apparently not. Because six years after Brexit, the broadcaster is still attempting to link the vote to racism and any number of phantoms.

We'll end this section with what seems like a rare instance of BBC mea culpa. At one point during BBC Sounds' production of *The Brexit Murder?* the narrator remarks that: 'For many of those who wanted to remain in the European Union, the killing of a Polish immigrant looked like proof that the referendum had unleashed violent racism. The true story was rather different.' And that is as close as the broadcaster will ever come to owning up. One pronoun away from truth: 'for many of *those*' ought of course to have read 'for many of *us*.'

SUMMARY

In 2016 the entire BBC news platform implied that the death of a Polish national had been caused because of Brexit. While amplifying this narrative, the broadcaster suppressed both eye witness evidence and testimony of local residents which contradicted the implication. The death had in fact been the result of anti-social behaviour.

'Shot and killed two men during racial justice protests'

BBC 10 o'clock news: 19 November 2021

The headlines chosen by the BBC on 19 November 2021 appeared to tell a shocking story: 'Cleared of murder,' went the introduction to the broadcaster's 10 o'clock news bulletin that evening, 'American teenager Kyle Rittenhouse - who shot dead two people last year during protests against racial injustice.' Similarly, BBC Breaking News declared to its 50 million Twitter followers that:

> US teenager Kyle Rittenhouse, who shot and killed two men during racial justice protests, cleared of homicide after claiming self-defence.

However, it wouldn't be the BBC if some key facts didn't get muddled. Although it had never been in doubt that both victims had been white (the actual killing had occurred *15 months before the trial*) BBC Pidgin informed its users that: 'Di teenager bin shoot and kill two black pipo for protest but di judge find am not guilty of murder.' Which translates as: *The teenager that shot and killed two black people because they were protesting has been found not guilty of murder*. How badly the broadcaster had wanted the victims to be black; that way it would have had a story to stir the pot of racial tension interminably. Alas not.

What the corporation made of the Rittenhouse saga could, as ever, be discerned from the opinions it sought and the language it used to frame the story. Before its deletion, a BBC online article chose for its sub-heading the phrase 'Disgusting verdict' – the opinion of former Mayor of New York and BBC favourite Bill de Blasio.[1] By contrast, Republicans 'approved' of the verdict. The broadcaster was seething despite reminders like this one from its Editorial Policy and Standards Director: 'Our audiences should not be able to tell from BBC output the personal opinions of our journalists or current affairs presenters on matters of public policy, political, or industrial controversy.'[2]

It had all begun in August 2020 when police responded to an emergency call regarding a domestic incident. Upon arrival at a suburb in the midwestern town of Kenosha officers encountered Jacob Blake, a 26-year-old black male who had turned up at the property of his estranged girlfriend brandishing a knife. At the time there had been an active warrant out for his arrest. Officers attempted to execute that warrant only for Blake to resist. Footage picked up law enforcement officers following the fugitive as he headed for his car. Believing Blake was about to retrieve a firearm, an officer fired a volley of shots into his back. Whether those actions were justified or not depends on several factors, but it is worth pointing out a fact the BBC and co did not: between 2001-10 a total of 541 police officers were murdered in the line of duty in the United States.[3] Working on the front line against US criminals can be a deadly occupation.

To Black Lives Matter, who had been co-ordinating protests through summer 2020, the shooting of Blake was just the latest example of America's 'systemic racism.' Without waiting for the facts to emerge high profile Democrat politicians immediately condemned the police and were equally presumptuous in suggesting that race had indeed been a factor. To make matters worse, politicians including Joe Biden refused to call for peaceful protest thereby implicitly endorsing violence. 'It was as if they were sending a signal that it was okay to tear up the town,' remarked *The Washington Times*.[4]

Rioters duly flocked to the town. And so, starting on Sunday

23rd August, as Democrat party officials remained silent and Kenosha police department stood by, downtown Kenosha burned. The unrest went on for several days. On Monday 24th a protest march through Kenosha passed off without incident. However, as night fell the situation started to become tense. Ordered to disperse in abeyance with an 8pm curfew, crowds only increased. ABC 7 Chicago reported the presence of riot police who found themselves confronted by 'a very volatile situation.' Indeed, rioters proceeded to attack police with fireworks and bottles. Vehicles were set on fire. City buildings also came under attack. When CBS Chicago reported the presence of 'a number of out of state [automobile] plates,' it seemed that agitators had indeed arrived with the aim of stoking tensions. Protest marches had long since ended. The situation escalated to such an extent the National Guard was deployed to Kenosha.

That same evening, unrest showing no sign of abating and with Kenosha PD spectating, Kyle Rittenhouse, a teenager from nearby Antioch, grabbed a rifle and headed over to the town. The police standing by while the city burned, Rittenhouse had decided to defend the local businesses which were being ransacked and destroyed - likely by out-of-state actors. The teen had stationed himself outside a car dealership. At some point the Antioch native was chased by a trio of (white) men all of whom had criminal records and who had been participating in the violence. In the melee that ensued the court would later learn that one of these pursuers had been first to draw a weapon as the 17-year-old vigilante had been floundering on the ground, having stumbled. Rittenhouse had fired back, according to the prosecution, 'to save his own skin.' Two of the pursuers died from gunshot injuries and a third man was injured. A freelance journalist who had witnessed the incident testified that Rittenhouse had been attempting to 'de-escalate' a confrontation between rioters and armed guards – not quite how the BBC had been framing the incident.

Though his presence at the scene of the riots and decision to arm himself had been undeniably foolhardy, the teen's claim of self-defence seemed commensurate with the known facts. True, but the facts as they stood did not advance the BBC's preferred narrative. So, when the media falsely asserted, as it was always going to, that the teenager was a 'white supremacist,' along with its fellow travellers in the corporate-legacy media the 'British' state broadcaster had struck gold, or so it thought. Calls went up for Rittenhouse's head. It was no longer about facts but feelings, just the way the broadcaster would have wanted it.

The murder trial thus began in a wave of publicity. For here was a narrative beloved of the mainstream media: an armed 'white supremacist' had decided to kill 'peaceful protesters' who had assembled to protest racial brutality by US police. This was how the likes of CNN and the BBC habitually reported the matter. However, as the trial would establish it was a narrative not based on facts, but rather on the preferred reality of a handful of powerful, politically-motivated media organisations who had already written their stories in order to progress certain objectives.

When trial judge Schroeder gave permission for the individuals Rittenhouse had killed to be referred to as looters and rioters *not* victims - a key moment in the evolution of the affair had arrived: it blew apart a vital component of the media's narrative that the dead men had been peacefully protesting. The teenager had in fact killed the men during a curfew which neither he nor they had any business breaking. In other words, the protests of BBC reporting had long since finished at the time of the shootings. However, in order to inflame public opinion, the broadcaster claimed the killings had taken place 'during' *not after* 'racial justice protests.' Listening to BBC reports one could have been forgiven for thinking that the teenager had burst in on a moment of solace, as protesters held hands and were in the process of lighting candles. 'Teen shoots men in self-defence during riots and looting,' the problem with the truth was that it would not have served BBC purposes. Not that the verdict unduly ruffled the broadcaster. It was a minor inconvenience. In its follow up reports the BBC ploughed on, granting oceans of coverage to anybody voicing the right opinion:

> Derrick Johnson, the president of the civil rights organisation NAACP, tweeted that the verdict "is a reminder of the treacherous role that white supremacy and privilege play within our justice system."[5]

Meanwhile, according to the broadcaster it was 'conservatives' alone arguing that Rittenhouse had acted in self-defence. Donald Trump and 'right-wing Fox News host Tucker Carlson' were amongst those offering their support.[6] So, did the BBC approve or disapprove of the verdict? Attempting to discern the impartial broadcaster's opinion was, as always, nigh on impossible to discern...

Had Auntie told the truth – that Rittenhouse had been part of a group (however ill-advisedly) protecting property during a curfew broken by violent agitators and that the situation had arisen through cynical politicking by its favoured Democrats - BBC viewers might not have been quite as outraged by a verdict the broadcaster appeared to find so 'disgusting.'

'Disenchanted with the army'

While the BBC could hardly hide the anger it felt towards Kyle Rittenhouse, far from earning the broadcaster's wrath mass murderers will in fact sometimes attract its *sympathy* and even a hint of sneaky admiration. It all depends on *who* is doing the killing and the skin colour of the victims.

The 2016 murder of five white Dallas police officers by ex-US army officer and black nationalist Micah Johnson met with rather different BBC treatment than had been meted out to Rittenhouse. A report broadcast by BBC news on 12 July 2016 whilst ignoring the victims, told viewers that a tour of Afghanistan had left Johnson 'disenchanted with the army.' Rather than interview relatives of the five victims – their wives and loved ones, the BBC chose instead to platform *the mother of the murderer*. 'The ideal that he thought what the military represented,' Johnson's mother told a respectful BBC activist, 'it just didn't live up to his expectations.' So, it was Johnson who was the real victim here which helped explain BBC reverence towards the murderer and his family while also helping to explain the snub towards the dead officers and their families.

Now in full-on apologist mode the BBC reporter explains that: 'Johnson's murderous rampage was fuelled by recent examples of the victimisation of black suspects by white police officers.'[7]

The report next platforms a black medic, comments from whose press conference the broadcaster co-opts into its bizarre report. BBC activist David Willis ends his piece by informing that President Obama will be flying back from Europe immediately motivated by 'the desire not to see other potentially divisive forces filling the void left by his absence…'

As demonstrated by the Rittenhouse and Johnson cases, the BBC applies quite different criteria to certain stories; while Rittenhouse's case was plastered all over its media platform, the Micah Johnson case barely troubled the same broadcaster; Rittenhouse aired on all major BBC news bulletins while Johnson garnered a few brief mentions *but only* on the broadcaster's US/Canada website portal.[8] As eager as it was to promote the false narrative of a 'white supremacist' killing peaceful BLM protesters the broadcaster was just as eager to ensure its audience had minimal opportunity to hear about Johnson's appalling crimes – unless it was through the carefully curated prism of a BBC narrative which told of the killer's disappointment with army life.[9]

Omission is by far the broadcaster's most favoured tactic when it comes to reporting (or not) racial incidents. Ignoring anti-white racism seems to be a way of life down at Broadcasting House, which is what occurred in May of 2022 when the hiring manager of Dropbox publicly stated that what she needed in her life were 'feminism, comedy, truth and less white people.' Dropbox is a popular file hosting service used by millions of people every day. Yet this shocking admission of anti-white discrimination failed to obtain even a cursory mention on any BBC platform.[10]

Readers will have their own theories to account for these glaring double standards. Suffice to say it is behaviour that is by no means accidental. What is witnessed with the Rittenhouse, Micah Johnson cases and Dropbox incident is (unofficial) BBC editorial policy that seeks to amplify certain incidents, suppress others. The broadcaster's approach can be summarised the following way:

Victim	Offender	BBC coverage[11]
Non-white	White	●●●●●●●●●●●●●●●
White	White	●●●●●●●●●
Non-white	Non-white	●●●
White	Non white	●

The police officers killed by Johnson, a black male, had all been white. Their murders had been racially-motivated – a reality that presented all sorts of difficulties to organisations like the BBC wedded to an especially dishonest narrative that insists white people pose a (violent) threat to non-whites while non-whites present little or no threat back.

'Is there a way to live without whiteness?'
The question is not *if* the BBC applies quite different approaches to journalism based on ethnicity (as well as many other criteria

e.g. religion, class, gender and political affiliation etc.) but rather *why* it should act in this way. The answer, as ever, is found in its role as proxy of international wealth and power. If the public can be convinced that white people are inherently violent and non-white inherently peaceful, there can be no objection to mass migration into the continent from Africa and sub-Saharan Asia - at least that appears to be the current thinking of US-UK corporate-political power. History teaches that a nation divided into myriad ethnic groups will almost certainly fragment and thereafter may become destabilised; a broken nation state may be unable to resist ceding sovereignty to trans-national umbrella organisations such as the UN, EU and WHO. After all, if nations no longer exist in terms of distinct cultures, peoples, traditions etc. then what harm in 'progressing' to a form of government beyond nationalism e.g. technocratic globalism. World government run for and on behalf of the rich and powerful would become not only feasible but even irresistible.

Moreover, mass immigration provides a cheap and plentiful pool of labour to be exploited by international corporate power. Clearly, a labour force that is transitory and disparate is likely to be one which may lack the ability to come together, to unionise in order to fight for better conditions. Those who are suspicious of one another are hardly likely to join forces to fight oppression. By promoting false stories of gun-toting 'white supremacists' in the mould of Rittenhouse while suppressing the crimes of non-white demographics the 'British' Broadcasting Corporation assumes it can manufacture consent for mass immigration into the west as per the long-term objectives of the ultra-rich neo-liberal powerbrokers of US (and UK) the economic (and social) interests of whom it so diligently promotes.

When this context is understood, BBC behaviour which may at first glance seem inexplicable, madcap even, becomes entirely understandable. It explains, for instance, why the same publicly-funded broadcaster that demands the UK flings open its borders to unlimited migration also bombards those same immigrants with incessant anti-white messaging; for the BBC endgame has a name: entropy – the breakdown of one system (nation state democracy) and the heralding in of a new, global system (technocratic communism). Indeed, it explains all manner of BBC output.

Take for example a BBC Radio 4 production titled *White Mischief* in which: 'Ekow Eshun traces where whiteness came from and how its power has remained elusive.' On this odyssey into 'whiteness' the presenter asks many questions, amongst them: 'Is there a way to live without whiteness?'[12] Towards the end of episode three the presenter asks a writer, Nikesh Shukla:

Eshun: What is the vison of the world that…doesn't necessarily centre whiteness as the superior position?

Shukla: Everyone's beige (*Laughter*)

While we leave the broadcaster to ponder the mystery of why what it refers to as 'whiteness' should be so pervasive in Europe and Britain and ponder if there is some way of living without it, the next section demonstrates the lengths the broadcaster will actually go to in order to promote one its most favoured narratives.

'Killed at the hands of four white police officers'
It is highly likely consumers of BBC content have never heard the names Tony Timpa or Ariel Roman; almost certainly they *have heard* the name 'George Floyd.' Indeed, searching the BBC news website (bbc.co.uk/news) for either of the first two names draws a blank. But not in the case of George Floyd for whom a search of the same database returns hundreds of BBC articles, programmes and features.

Ariel Romano was a 33-year-old (white) Idaho male who, in February 2020, was shot inside Chicago's Grand subway station by a police officer after resisting arrest. Officers had been alerted to a male hopping between rail carriages. Two officers were filmed restraining Romano. One of the officers – a black female – shot the unarmed Romano twice – once in the stomach and, as he fled up the escalator, again in the lower back. As far as the corporate-legacy media and BBC was concerned there was nothing to see here. It was merely an incident whereby police used due force to prevent a suspect from fleeing, nothing remotely racial to it. Certainly, the question of why the officer used a firearm and whether it had been a proportionate response to a case of possible fare-dodging did not seem to concern the media. Such was the unconcern, this shocking case slipped right by BBC antennae usually so finely-tuned into what is after all one of its most cherished narratives i.e. police brutality and race.

Like Romano, Tony Timpa apparently also did not fit with the broadcaster's idea of a worthy victim: he also just so happened to be white. In August 2016 Timpa, suffering perhaps from a schizophrenic episode, made an SOS call to Dallas police. Officers handcuffed the 32-year-old and pinned his arms behind his back for almost 14 minutes while one officer knelt on his back. 'You're gonna kill me!' Bodycam footage captured Timpa pleading more than thirty times with the officers, one of whom was black. Mr Timpa died at the scene.

With regards to George Floyd, BBC consumers will be all too familiar with this case. In a situation that eerily echoed that of Timpa, Floyd was also restrained by officers using controversial methods. However, while the former had requested assistance, the latter, high on drugs, had been *resisting* arrest. In stark contrast to those of Mr Romano and Mr Timpa, Floyd's case was afforded massive coverage by the broadcaster.[13]

Previously, we have drawn attention to the BBC propensity to subvert truth to any of its preferred narratives. As with Kyle Rittenhouse the broadcaster wished to impose a certain narrative over the facts: George Floyd had died as a result of the actions of racially-motivated police. However, there was a rather large fly in this disingenuous ointment: two of the four officers involved in the incident had been non-white. Still, such trivialities were not going to prevent the broadcaster from promoting the story it wanted to tell. The BBC 10 o'clock news broadcast on 4 June 2020 duly made Mr Floyd's funeral service its top story, the presenter introducing the bulletin thus: 'Tonight at Ten: An emotional memorial service in Minneapolis for George Floyd, the black man killed at the hands of four white police officers.'

Footage of the incident had gone viral and had clearly shown that two of the four officers in attendance had been non-white. Further, the footage had been in circulation for *ten days* prior to the BBC bulletin. As demonstrated by the following statements which appeared on the Corrections part of the broadcaster's website, while all those millions who saw the footage could be left in no doubt regarding the ethnicity of the officers, the BBC appeared to be having all sorts of difficulty identifying the racial composition of the same quartet of officers:

Clarification #1: 7 June 2020
We referred to George Floyd's death as occurring during an encounter with white police officers. The officer who knelt on his neck is white, but two of the other three involved are not.

Upon receipt of complaints the BBC has a protocol which ensures such 'errors' cannot reoccur: 'We circulate your complaint over-night to producers and managers.'[14] It is reassuring to know the BBC responds so swiftly to complaints. And what could be more important than correcting misleading information published at a time of heightened racial tension? Unscrupulous actors – those working to an agenda – could so easily imply that Mr Floyd had been murdered by a gang of racist cops - an assumption that could only increase tensions.

The next clarification popped up a few weeks after the previous one. It is worth recalling that Mr Floyd had died on 25 May – a whole month before the latest raft of BBC broadcasts were aired:

> **Clarification #2: 24 June 2020**
> We reported that George Floyd died 'at the hands of white police officers.' George Floyd died after a police officer who is white knelt on his neck for more than seven minutes. Two of the other three police officers also in attendance are not white.

It can only be assumed that a communication breakdown had occurred. Presumably, the complaints had not reached senior BBC staff. Perhaps the broadcaster's night staff had been taking their regular naps as revealed by an investigation carried out by *The Sun* a few years previously, and had thereby missed the overnight messages circulated to producers and managers. The same 'error' happened again, a month after the previous clarification:

> **Clarification #3: 23 July 2020**
> We referred to George Floyd's death as occurring during an encounter with white police officers. The officer who knelt on his neck is white, but two of the other three involved are not.

Thus, the BBC had to consistently clarify and correct its reporting of what appeared to be a very basic component of the story. Eager to highlight the (white) ethnicity of the officer who knelt on Mr Floyd's neck and to thereby imply the arrest had been racially-motivated, it had to similarly underplay/ignore the role of (non-white) colleagues who had stood by and watched Mr Floyd's discomfort and who could have intervened at any moment.

Reports of 'four white officers' was little more than wishful thinking, the broadcaster's preferred scenario. The presence of the two non-white police officers certainly appeared to have thwarted an otherwise perfect BBC narrative. As for the likes of Tony Timpa and Ariel Romano – victims too of police brutality, the 'British' Broadcasting Corporation has had nothing whatsoever to say about the deaths of these two white males at the hands of police.

SUMMARY

When reporting crime, the BBC amplifies or suppresses stories depending on racial characteristics. As illustrated by its handling of the Kyle Rittenhouse and George Floyd cases, its main objective is to portray non-whites as the perpetual victims of racially-motivated crimes by whites.

'The [Pfizer] vaccine is 100% safe for children'

BBC Newsround: 8 June 2021

A iring since 1972 BBC Newsround is a news programme aimed primarily at children. An edition broadcast in June 2021 featured Professor Devi Sridhar, chair of global public health at the University of Edinburgh. Though neither a qualified virologist nor epidemiologist, Sridhar was answering questions in a segment titled, 'Pfizer vaccine for 12–15-year-olds: Your questions answered.'[1]

Unsurprisingly, the habitual BBC contributor could not express sufficient enthusiasm for the vaccines. According to Sridhar not a single child who received the Pfizer vaccine contracted Covid during the manufacturer's own trial. She did not however mention the negligible risk posed by Covid to children.[2] Nor did she mention that the same small trial alluded to had resulted in *seven* serious adverse reactions among its cohort of 12–15-year-olds.[3,4]

Asked about potential side-effects, Sridhar confidently said children might experience similar reactions to adults: fatigue, headache and feeling generally unwell. The claim was also made that being vaccinated would mean: 'you're likely to not infect your parents, the people you live with and your teachers,' a claim not even made by Pfizer.[5] In an accompanying article, Newsround also makes the claim that, 'The Pfizer vaccine offers up to 95% protection against Covid-19…' It also states that, 'It's not unusual for vaccines to make people feel a bit unwell for a few hours after being jabbed.'

But it's what Sridhar went on to claim in the video segment that caused uproar: 'So far,' said a smiling BBC 'expert' 'trials

73

have shown the vaccine is 100% safe for children.'[6] Neither the video segment nor article contained any challenge to this or any other of her sweeping statements. Newsround viewers and readers had been assured by the BBC that Covid vaccines were 100% safe for children and teens. However, it was an assertion that did not tally with increasing reports of a range of vaccine-related side effects experienced by teenagers – some of them serious. Had they been exposed only to BBC Newsround disinformation, it's a reality about which many parents would have remained unaware.

After receiving complaints the broadcaster swiftly removed the '100% safe' claim from the segment though none of the other spurious claims. Usually when caught out spreading disinformation the BBC instinct is to fight tooth and nail, to swear night is day, that black is blue. On this occasion the claim was removed with such speed it strongly suggested its inclusion had been no accident. And it wasn't just the aforementioned trial data which flatly contradicted Sridhar's '100% safe' assertion. Prior to the BBC Newsround broadcast the CDC had published data pertaining to post-vaccination cases of myocarditis and pericarditis, rates of which seemed to be considerably higher than anticipated – especially in adolescent males.[7]

Rather than taking down the misleading piece in its entirety the broadcaster chose to simply edit out the 100% safe claim. One moment it was there, the next it had vanished. Too little too late – who knows how many parents had been misled by this egregious falsehood? 'Editing a feature after it has already been circulated and viewed by huge numbers of the public and children,' wrote the UK Medical Freedom Alliance in an open letter 'without a publicized explanation or apology, is highly irregular.'[8]

The letter labelled 'a gross misinterpretation' another of Sridhar's claims, that the main downside to the vaccine would be just 'another injection into your arm.' Clearly, the broadcaster was going all out to sell the Covid vaccine to parents. Given the evidence of adverse events following vaccination, this was an especially misleading claim, one echoed by Jeremy Vine on his BBC Radio 2 phone-in who characterised vaccine adverse reactions as little more than a 'pain in the arm.' Leaving to one side serious post-vaccination reactions, it appears neither BBC Newsround nor BBC Radio was keeping up with FDA updates. In May 2021,[9] just weeks prior to Sridhar's broadcast, the US regulatory body had remarked that: 'Syncope (fainting) may occur in association with administration of injectable vaccines, in particular in adolescents. Procedures should be in place to avoid injury from fainting.'[10,11] The FDA also ominously notes that: 'Additional adverse reactions, some of which may be serious, may become apparent with more widespread use of the Pfizer-BioNTech COVID-19 Vaccine.' According to the BBC though these same vaccines had been 'fully tested.'

Indeed, concern with regards to vaccine adverse reactions in children-teens had been growing for some time. With regards to heart inflammation the FDA noted 'increased risks of myocarditis and pericarditis, particularly within 7 days following the second dose.'[12] A Hong Kong study conducted in summer 2021 which investigated the incidence of acute cases of heart inflammation agreed when concluding that: 'There is a significant increase in the risk of acute myocarditis/pericarditis following Comirnaty vaccination among Chinese male adolescents, especially after the second dose.'[13]

Of even more worry an FDA Fact Sheet goes on to admit that regarding the long-term prognosis of vaccine-induced heart conditions in teens: 'Information is not yet available about potential long-term sequelae.'[14,15] A study which looked at cardiac imaging in children who had suffered myocarditis after Covid vaccination similarly concluded that the 'long term risks remain unknown.'[16] During its ten week duration the study assessed 15 cases at a single paediatric referral facility. Symptoms started 1 to

6 days after vaccination and included chest pain, myalgia and headache.

Case studies submitted to VAERS such as the following which pertains to a 16-year-old male in California became more and more common:[17]

> Since receiving his second dose of COVID-19 vaccine (Pfizer) on Sunday 2/21 he has had fever (tmax 103.0 F), headache, and stomach ache. His fever started on 2/21 and had persisted through 2/24. He woke up from a nap on 2/24 in the afternoon at 1600 had onset of severe chest pain. Then reoccurring multiple times throughout the evening. He was taken to a local hospital and the transferred to another hospital for higher level of care. Paediatric cardiology was consulted and treatment was started for suspected atypical pericarditis.

This patient managed to recover, though as noted the long-term effects of such trauma remain unknown.[18] Others have not been so lucky. Three days after receiving the Pfizer shot in summer 2021, a 13-year-old Michigan boy died in his sleep.[19] A few months later a 12-year-old died in the German town of Cuxhaven two days after also taking the Pfizer vaccine.[20] On 27 October 2021 a question was raised in the European Parliament with regards to safety following the deaths of three Italian adolescents following vaccination.[21] Just 20 minutes after her vaccination a teenage Vietnamese girl:

> Experienced tightness in her chest, dizziness, difficulty breathing, and seizures. She received emergency treatment on the spot before being transferred to the Ha Hoa District medical center. She began to vomit blood upon arrival. She then fell into a coma and her heart stopped.[22]

An Ohio 12-year-old meanwhile ended up in a wheelchair after receiving her second dose of Pfizer during the company's vaccine trial. The girl complained of severe abdominal and chest pain. 'It feels like my heart is being ripped out through my neck,' the young girl told her mother.[23]

Evidence of harmful side effects impossible to ignore – despite the best attempts of certain actors - in its advice to vaccinators, the FDA cautioned that: 'In order to mitigate the risks of using this unapproved product [i.e. Covid vaccine] under EUA,' recipients should be informed about potential serious adverse events listed as:[24]

- Death
- A life-threatening adverse event
- Inpatient hospitalization or prolongation of existing hospitalization
- A persistent or significant incapacity or substantial disruption of the ability to conduct normal life functions

By Autumn 2021 Iceland, Sweden and Finland had suspended the Moderna vaccination for the under 30s. Denmark and Norway formally advised against the Covid vaccination for those under 18.

Meanwhile the BBC confidently told children (and concerned parents) that they might expect to experience, at the very worst, a sore arm post vaccination...it most certainly did not tell them about any of the 'risks' involved with what the FDA described as an 'unapproved product.'[25]

'People die from all sorts of causes every day'

As for the BBC it was sticking to its guns. In an article written by a pair of 'disinformation' activists in December 2021 unironically titled: 'Covid: Misleading vaccine claims target children and parents,' the broadcaster declared that: 'someone dying after a jab does not mean the vaccine is responsible. People die from all sorts of causes every day.'[26] Yet the same broadcaster had been asserting that a significant number of deaths (especially in the over 70s) which had occurred throughout 2020-21 had been as a direct result of Covid infection. Incredible as it may appear, the BBC approach to this subject really could be summarised thus: Octogenarians – often having multiple co-morbidities – had definitely died of Covid and thus proof positive of a virulent, 'global pandemic;' meanwhile, healthy teenagers dying within hours or days of a Covid vaccination were nothing to worry about because 'people die from all sorts of causes every day…'

Though it had been forced to withdraw a serious falsehood which had been aimed at children (and their parents), it was business as usual at Broadcasting House; nothing to see here. 'Covid: 'Getting vaccinated is best for my child' – was an article which appeared on the BBC website in February 2022, one of a multitude attempting to still sell Covid vaccines for children despite the increasing evidence of severe side-effects.

'It may sound incredible,' observed a BBC production purporting to investigate false claims circulating around Covid-19, 'but deliberate disinformation around vaccines is being sown by international political actors playing on our deepest fear.'[27] A Rhodes scholar, Chatham House associate, WEF and Oxford university graduate (and Professor) Devi Sridhar fits the bill of an 'international political actor' better than most.[28] Indeed, in such high regard does Sridhar appear to be held within the corridors of the 'British' Broadcasting Corporation, in spite of or perhaps *because of* her infamous declarations, via its Radio 4 programme *Book of the Week* the broadcaster next happily promoted a book written by the academic about the pandemic. *Preventable: How a Pandemic Changed the World & How to Stop the Next One* according to BBC blurb is 'A gripping insider's view of the pandemic.'

IS THAT TRUE OR DID YOU HEAR IT ON THE BBC?

'We now have a whole ward full of [Covid] children here'
This was not the first time the broadcaster had pushed medical misinformation aimed at persuading parents to get their children vaccinated. Months earlier, in January 2021, BBC Radio 5 had conducted an interview with a member of staff from a London hospital.

Notwithstanding the fact that Covid poses virtually no danger to children, and after previously having firmly excluded the possibility, by the beginning of 2021 the British state had seemingly performed a complete U-turn. The Boris Johnson government seemed determined to 'jab' children who the scientific literature strongly suggested required no such medical intervention. Had the government always intended to inject children? It started to look that way. However, rather than challenging what appeared to be a cynical volte face and holding power to account as per its avowals, the 'British' state broadcaster had begun doing the precise opposite: facilitating a policy which many medical professions warned would not only be counter-productive, but dangerous too.

Thus, on the 1st January Radio 5 Live's *Chiles on Friday* show interviewed a matron at King's College Hospital who told the BBC that 'It [Covid] was minimally affecting children in the first wave.' She then went on to assert that, 'We now have a whole ward of children here and I know that some of my colleagues where they have whole wards full of children with Covid.' On the 2 January, BBC Radio 5 Live tweeted its guest's ominous words to its 650,000+ followers.

Parents listening to the broadcast or reading the tweet would have been suitably shaken: according to information broadcast by the 'trusted' BBC, children were now at grave risk from Covid. Hospital wards were 'full' of children who had caught the virus. Clearly, there was only one thing to do and that was to get kids vaccinated without further delay.

Following the broadcast, a complaint was submitted to the

BBC. The complainer contended that *Chiles on Friday* had not contested any of the extraordinary claims made by its contributor thereby spreading misinformation with regards to incidence and severity of Covid infections among the young. 'There was no reason to think a matron with 18 years' experience would not convey what she saw and what she had heard,' replied the BBC in response to complaints. 'She did not say the children were seriously ill, nor did we.'

Given that admission to a dedicated Covid hospital ward indicates the illness has reached a certain level of severity, this particular BBC response was nothing if not baffling. Moreover, the broadcaster had taken the trouble to locate and then interview a matron whose message strongly implied that children were exactly that i.e. seriously ill. But the objective here was neither truth nor logic, but rather to scare parents into taking a step into the unknown with their children's health. Indeed, submitting children at miniscule risk of serious illness to Covid vaccination was considered little short of reckless by many experienced health professionals – professionals whom the BBC was routinely attempting to smear as 'conspiracy theorists' and worse.[29]

'I've been an on-call consultant in a London children's hospital all week,' tweeted Dr Ronny Cheung in response to the BBC interview adding, 'It's simply not true.' The paediatrician also observed that the claims made on *Chiles on Friday,* aimed at panicking parents, had been 'irresponsible in the extreme.'[30] Meanwhile, on the same day The Royal College of Paediatrics and Child Health confirmed Dr Cheung's observations: 'As of now we are not seeing pressure from Covid-19 in paediatrics across the UK.'[31] Similarly, The Evelina, a specialist children and families hospital located in Lambeth, South London, remarked later that week that, 'We currently have very few children with COVID-19 at our hospital.'[32]

Following a freedom of Information request submitted by

Citizen Journalists, the actual facts emerged. On 2 January 2021 in its 12-bed paediatric ward which had been converted into a Covid-19 only ward, King's College Hospital had two children i.e. 16% capacity.[33]

With evidence so clear and unequivocal BBC promotion of such contrary information might have seemed puzzling – at least to the casual consumer. But in its role as the PR arm to the wealthy and powerful its course of action was entirely predictable. In order for the pharmaceutical industry to maximise profit children were always going to be targeted sooner or later. It was just a question of time. Alarming parents with lurid tales of 'wards full of [Covid] children' - untruths broadcast by the BBC - were thus a crucial element in overriding resistance to vaccine uptake. Announcing that the same vaccine was '100% safe for children' was the next stage of the broadcaster's calculated disinformation campaign.

SUMMARY

Throughout the coronavirus 'pandemic' the BBC sought to persuade parents to expose their children to a vaccine research strongly suggested was unnecessary, and also possibly dangerous to them. In order to achieve this aim, it platformed selected 'experts' while ensuring that information regarding side effects – some serious – was unavailable. BBC donor Bill Gates expects to make a 20-1 profit on vaccines – provided the whole world i.e. adults and children get 'jabbed.'

'Some racial slurs about Muslims can also be heard'

BBC News London: 2 December 2021

A news organisation whose activities are governed by narratives at the expense of objective journalism will, sooner or later, invariably find itself in hot water. Disseminating propaganda on behalf of the rich and powerful however compels the 'British' Broadcasting Corporation to do just this: impose a pre-conceived version of events onto reality with the aim of subverting truth. It's an approach to journalism fraught with danger.

Thus, nobody should have been *that* surprised by the manner in which the broadcaster reported a horrific antisemitic incident which occurred in London's Oxford Street one winter evening.

Before going any further it should be noted that in some situations the BBC is prone to misconstruing certain utterances. For example, when Donald Trump addressed the UN General Assembly in 2018, the broadcaster reported that the US President had actually threatened war with Iran during his speech! According to the BBC, when discussing Iranian sanctions, the president had declared that 'war will follow' – a threat which the broadcaster recycled throughout its huge media platform. The president had in fact said 'more [sanctions] will follow.'

The antisemitic incident in question occurred towards the end of November 2021. A group of orthodox Jewish children had travelled by coach to Oxford Street in order to celebrate Chanukah, an eight-day celebration which commemorates the recovery of Jerusalem. As early evening shoppers went about their business the group danced on the pavement and distributed sweets to passers-by. Video footage then captured the approach of three males of Asian appearance behaving in an intimidating fashion, spitting and swearing. One of their number appeared to make a Nazi salute. F*** Israel was one of several insults to be heard. Fleeing back to their bus, the children were clearly upset by the incident. As the bus pulled away from the scene the three males pursued, banging and kicking against the side of the vehicle.

While the incident provoked outrage within and without of the Jewish community, it presented somewhat of a headache for the narrative-lead BBC. In the world of the broadcaster the state of Israel is indisputably bad while its Arabic foes are indisputably good. Events in Oxford Street thus presented the organisation with a conundrum: unable to ignore such a horrifying incident, how could it possibly mitigate this naked example of antisemitism? The broadcaster found a way.

'An alleged antisemitic attack'

On 2 December a story appeared on the BBC news website. In what the broadcaster described as an 'alleged antisemitic attack' its report about events in Oxford Street also stated that, 'some racial slurs about Muslims can also be heard from inside the bus.' On that evening's report from BBC News London a reporter, Guy Lynn, reported that: 'We at BBC London did watch this footage and you can hear some racial slurs about Muslim people which does come from the bus.'

Twenty-four hours after first appearing, the BBC amended its online report from 'racial slurs' in the plural to: 'a slur.'[1] Given the poor quality of the clip's audio it was not immediately clear how the broadcaster had been able to establish its claim about slurs, specifically that somebody on the bus had said 'dirty Muslims.' The BBC had not, as far as could be ascertained, subjected the audio to any advanced form of analysis, expert or otherwise. Moreover, the children and adults accompanying them categorically denied such words had been said. Nonetheless, the broadcaster pressed ahead in publishing what were unsubstantiated as well as contested claims.

The question that unsettled many was, why? Why hone in on an undecipherable segment of audio and insist on an interpretation based on what seemed to be gut instinct at best, political bias at worst? After all, had the children been abused by a trio of British National Party members, BBC editors would hardly have taken so many pains to scrutinise the audio for comments that could mitigate any actions. Indeed, cries of 'far right racists' would have echoed throughout the BBC platform for days, weeks. But not on this occasion. The conviction that BBC reporting was linked to its biased presentation of the Israel-Palestine conflict was getting harder to shake.

BBC News London claimed to have heard the anti-Muslim comment about three seconds into the video. However, those wishing to confirm this claim would have been confounded had they relied on the videoclip presented alongside BBC news stories, for the broadcaster had purposely bleeped out the soundtrack at the precise moment they were claiming the slur(s) occurred – at the 2-3 second mark.[2] No matter because the clip was widely available on social media.

In order to make its claim, the broadcaster had made not just one but two suppositions: 1 – the language being spoken was English, not Hebrew and 2 – that the phrase 'dirty Muslims' had been 'clearly' uttered. And yet when the audio reveals a cacophony of noise, drawing conclusions firm or otherwise seems wildly presumptuous. To go on to then publish this guesswork on a national media platform seems not only unjustified, but intentional. Talk about jumping the gun.

Early technical analysis did not bode well for Auntie. At the point in the clip identified by the BBC it was suggested by multiple sources that one of the terrified children might have said in Hebrew, 'call someone, it's urgent.' Like the BBC conclusion, such interpretations were nothing more than speculation; the audio would clearly require expert analysis. 'Even an audio forensic specialist would struggle to get something useful,' concluded a sound and audio professional who assessed the clip, confirming just how poor was the quality of sound.[3] It had been nigh on impossible to decipher the audio yet the BBC had seemingly managed to do just that.

Unease with how the broadcaster was attempting to portray what had been an especially unedifying episode of antisemitism soon spread over the Internet. The American Jewish Committee was aghast. Its tweet of 5 December summed up public disbelief:

Jewish children get abused by a bunch of antisemitic racists. The BBC's response? Falsely claim the kids used anti-Muslim slurs. We won't drop this until the BBC owns its lies.[4]

The BBC's behaviour triggered an avalanche of criticism. In a statement posted to Facebook on 6 December, The Board of Deputies of British Jews said it was 'dismayed' at the broad-caster's refusal to correct its reporting. 'I have always defended the BBC,' observed Lord Austin writing in *The Telegraph* on the same day, 'but can't imagine an incident involving any other group being reported in this way.'[5] In its own letter of protest sent to the BBC, The British Board of Jews referenced what it termed the broadcaster's 'Deeply irresponsible journalism.'[6] In response to the hive mentality encountered as BBC editors and journalists predictably sought to evade and stone-wall enquiry, the letter also criticised what it called BBC 'wagon circling.'

What had dismayed many commentators was not just the alacrity with which the broadcaster promoted its baseless slur claim, but how it was trying to imply some kind of equivalence between that very claim and the horrific abuse experienced by the Jewish children. For starters, the three men had approached the children; the level of abuse aimed at them had been so extreme they had been forced to seek sanctuary inside the bus; even then the assault had continued from outside. If one of the teenagers had indeed responded to the intimidation in the way described by the BBC i.e. a single, muffled comment – *and it was a big if* – it would have been a retort to an unprovoked and sustained racist attack of the worst kind imaginable. Further, the 'slur' had occurred *onboard the bus*, when the assault had almost finished. Though almost certainly spurious, the broadcaster was thus comparing 'a slur' uttered from the interior of the bus and thus only audible to fellow passengers, with abusive and threatening behaviour initiated by the thugs and which had continued until the bus had been obliged to depart Oxford Street. Chalk and cheese.

The BBC implication of proportionality, that this was a tit-for-tat scenario, was then nothing if not bizarre. And it was precisely the way in which the broadcaster was attempting to introduce this subtext into its narrative which many found so disconcerting. It had not escaped wider attention that while the broadcaster was referring to an 'alleged' antisemitic incident, one nonetheless that had been witnessed by the hundreds of thousands who saw the clip, the supposed 'racial slurs' it reported as de facto truth…

But what really appalled onlookers was the BBC's quid pro quo insinuation that the Jewish children had somehow *deserved* what had occurred: all's fair in love and war.

When the Metropolitan police announced it had found no evidence of an 'anti-Muslim' slur on the clip, expectations rose that the broadcaster would finally do the right thing. 'The revelation will place the BBC under intense pressure,' remarked *The Jewish Chronicle*, 'as it continues to refuse to retract the allegations and apologise.'[7] The Campaign Against Antisemitism rallied outside Broadcasting House on 13 Dec imploring the broadcaster 'to tell the truth' and 'stop blaming Jews.' Alas, in the weeks leading up to Christmas those expecting contrition would be disappointed. On the contrary, the broadcaster's wagon circling only intensified.

Not for the first time BBC executives found themselves in a sticky spot. Admitting that its reports had deliberately sought to mislead would naturally lead to another question: why? And that answer would inevitably lead into areas the broadcaster very much wished to avoid at all costs: its own alleged antisemitism largely manifest, but by no means limited to, its reporting of the Israel-Palestine conflict.[8] In fact, this latest example of perceived BBC bias chimed with long-held concerns in the Jewish community.

In its annual *Global Anti-Semitism Top Ten Report of 2021*, The Simon Wiesenthal Centre had placed the 'British' Broadcasting Corporation at the number 3 spot in its list of most antisemitic organisations, behind Iran (1) and Hamas (2). In its brief mention of the Oxford Street assault, the report succinctly summarises the rationale behind the broadcaster's seemingly bizarre actions: 'BBC falsely reported that anti-Muslim slurs could be heard from within the bus deftly turning the victim into the victimizer.'[9] When asked how they rated television representation of matters of Jewish interest in a 2020 survey, two-thirds of respondents said BBC coverage was 'unfavourable' towards the Jewish community.[10]

As 2021 drew to a close the broadcaster was doing what it always does when caught red-handed: digging itself an even bigger hole. Disbelief was palpable. 'What takes this from an egregious failure to something far more sinister,' opined Marie van der Zyl, 'is the BBC's behaviour when confronted with its mistake. Instead of admitting it was wrong, it has doubled and tripled down.'[11] The stakes really were *that high*: admission would, corporation hierarchy knew, open a great, big can of worms. Solution: double, triple, quadruple down. Do whatever it took to avoid telling the truth.

But the Jewish community in particular was not prepared to let

Auntie off the hook. D3 Audio, a company specialising in sound engineering, were commissioned to analyse the videoclip. The results confirmed the plethora of anecdotal reports concerning what had or had not been said 2-3 seconds into the clip:

> Our analysis of the entire audio track by a native Hebrew speaker confirms that the sound is a mix of Hebrew and English. We can categorically confirm that the spoken phrase is Hebrew: 'Tikrah lemishu, ze dachuf' meaning: 'Call someone, it is urgent.'[12]

'D3 Forensics unequivocally confirms that the audio does not contain any racial slur,' summarised Camera-UK.[13] It was a conclusion confirmed in a detailed report of analysis undertaken by Professor Ghil'ad Zuckermann, Chair of Linguistics and Endangered Languages at the University of Adelaide who remarked that he had been, 'unable to detect any anti-Muslim slur at any point in the footage: neither in Israeli nor in English.'[14] The professor hypothesised that BBC editors/reporters may have been subconsciously primed to 'mishear' the audio content, thereby imposing their own frame of reference upon it. In order to support its own case, it might have been expected that the broadcaster would commission its own analysis of the audio. Alas, it never happened.

'We take complaints very seriously'

The saga dragged on into the new year. Rabbi YY Rubinstein, a BBC contributor for 30 years, resigned from the corporation in protest over its 'inexcusable' handling not only of the Oxford Street incident, but antisemitism in general.[15] Observers were further infuriated when, a few days later, an article appeared on the broadcaster's website stating it was seeking to resolve the matter 'as swiftly as possible.' Despite unequivocal evidence to the contrary, in its article claiming that 'we take complaints very seriously'[16] the broadcaster was still referring to what it called 'an alleged antisemitic incident.' When it comes to antisemitism, the burden of proof appears to be that much higher down at Broadcasting House in comparison to certain other faiths, indecipherable 'slurs' against whom are invariably not reported as 'alleged.'

What is also noticeable about the article is the complete lack of reference to the aforementioned analysis of the audiotape, that the Metropolitan Police as well as independent experts concurred that there was no evidence of 'anti-Muslim slurs' as per the BBC assertion – an assertion, so the article goes on to say, the Board of Deputies of British Jews 'disputed.'[17] Indicative of two sides in a debate both of equal validity, not for nothing has the verb 'dispute' been chosen. Reading this article without prior knowledge the casual observer might well assume that there is nothing to see here. He or she might also assume that a partisan organisation is merely picking an argument with a 'trusted' broadcaster, that the evidence must be far from conclusive.

Eventually, on the 26 January, the BBC's Executive Complaints Unit released its report into the BBC's actions. Predictably, the ECU all but exonerated its colleagues.[18] Amid the inevitable twisting and turning, some potentially new information however did emerge. According to the ECU the audio tape had been, 'assessed by at least seven members of BBC London news staff and a senior editor in network news, all of whom agreed that the phrase 'Dirty Muslims' could be heard...'[19]

Then it becomes *really* interesting. Having been assessed by seven BBC members of staff who all agreed with one another, the broadcaster apparently then approached an organisation called The Community Security Trust, a charity which provides help and guidance to the UK's Jewish community. Whatever the CST had said or not said, the ECU decided it had been 'entirely reasonable' for its BBC colleagues to assume the organisation had verified the presence of its anti-Muslim slur on the audio.[20] The CST replied to the BBC claim in a Twitter thread which is worth reading in full:

> CST completely rejects the claim in today's BBC report that CST confirmed to the BBC on 2nd December that an anti-Muslim phrase had been spoken on the Chabad bus that was attacked on Oxford Street.
>
> CST was not asked for any such confirmation by the BBC and was in no position to provide any confirmation: we had no prior knowledge of the allegation and had not sought to confirm it with any of the witnesses or victims at that point.
>
> Instead, a BBC journalist who had already been in contact with CST over the incident phoned to tell us that (a) an anti-Muslim slur was audible and (b) the BBC was going to include it in their report. He was definite on both points.
>
> CST replied in a WhatsApp to argue that the alleged slur, even if true, was irrelevant to the dynamic of how the incident occurred and should not be reported. We were in no position to confirm (or not) whether the now much-disputed phrase in question had been spoken.

Not surprisingly the ECU's judgment caused outrage and disbelief. 'It took the BBC two months and four pages,' commented The Campaign Against Anti-Semitism, 'to deliver a whitewash non-apology that stands by its spurious reporting of an anti-Muslim slur and dismisses the monumental offence generated by its coverage.'[21]

Late in January 2022 Ofcom announced it would be launching its own investigation into the matter. However, the watchdog's record of virtual blanket support for the broadcaster may not augur well for those seeking truth. 'Only when the BBC confronts its anti-Israel bias,' observed *The Telegraph*, 'will it find that it makes fewer slips in its handling of Jews.'[22]

SUMMARY

In December 2021 and in order to mitigate a vicious and sustained anti-Semitic attack on a group of Jewish children, the BBC claimed an anti-Muslim slur had been heard from the interior of the bus to which the children had fled. However, audio analysis appears to contradict this assertion. The attack on the children by a trio of males featured various anti-Semitic tropes and had left them shaken. The BBC reported the assault as an 'alleged' anti-Semitic incident.

'The material [on Trump] was of a sexual nature'

'Trump 'compromising' claims:
How and why did we get here?'
bbc.co.uk: 12 Jan. 2017

Throughout his term as US president, the British state broadcaster concocted and disseminated a daily cocktail of misinformation revolving around Donald Trump. The aim was to destabilise the presidency enough in order to facilitate the 2020 election of a Democrat-led administration and along with it, the consolidation and spread of US corporate-political hegemony via proxy wars and aggression all over the world e.g. Syria, Ukraine.

The maverick businessman and reality TV star was considered a wild-card by the US establishment. Could he be relied upon to further its economic and political interests? Not necessarily. The forty-fifth United States' president would therefore have to go. And so, the corporate media, its British allies at the BBC leading the way, set out to do whatever it took to destabilise the Trump White House, mainly via means of propaganda: smears, innuendo, rumour, slander, falsehoods, gossip and speculation – much of which originated from anonymous sources.

BBC misinformation indeed came thick and fast: *Trump's lawyer had accepted a substantial bribe from the president of Ukraine; Mr Trump had mocked a disabled reporter; he had advised US citizens to drink bleach to treat Covid infection; he had threatened war with Iran; he had detained migrant children inside inhumane 'cages' at the US southern border...etc. etc.*

On top of all this BBC activists freely slandered the US president on a daily basis. In one article it was subsequently forced to retract, the impartial broadcaster declared that Mr Trump had what it termed a 'narcissistic hunger for adoration.'[1]

Along with its allies within the US corporate power base, much of the broadcaster's slander revolved around Trump's supposed ties with Russia.[2] In the US the tactic paid off handsomely. Half way through the Trump presidency according to a Gallup poll, a massive 75% of Americans thought Russia had 'interfered' with the 2016 election.[3]

'Could the way he [Trump] does business make him vulnerable to blackmail?' asked one of many BBC productions amplifying claims made in a document which came to be known as the Steele Dossier.[4] This 30 page document, the work of a British spy and based entirely upon anonymous sources, had been commissioned by Trump's political rivals, a consideration which did little to moderate BBC behaviour. In fact, despite its dubious provenance the Steele Dossier became a cornerstone of BBC insinuation and innuendo. One BBC article even claimed it had 'verified' what it called one of the dossier's 'key claims.' In another article it went further. The broadcaster claimed it had contacts within the CIA itself and that the agency had confirmed the existence of tapes featuring Trump and that there was 'more than one tape' on 'more than one date' 'in more than one place' and that the material was 'of a sexual nature.' The CIA belief that the president was thus compromised were 'credible.'[5]

Worryingly, this baseless story began to gain momentum. A poll conducted by Morning Consult in 2018 found 51% of voters believed Russia did have kompromat on Trump.[6] There was method in this apparent madness, because the more organisations like the BBC amplified the dossier and its baseless claims, the more people began to believe the broadcaster's Trump-Russia conspiracy theory.

When it came to Russia-gate misinformation such as that contained within the subsequently discredited Steele Dossier, the

BBC's approach was a familiar one: publish liberal amounts of lurid speculation thereby amplifying the baseless smears and rumours and then, in the interests of 'balance,' publish a single-sentence denial by Trump or a spokesman acting on his behalf and tuck it away towards the end of the hit piece where it might not be seen by the majority of readers. Nor did corporation activists care to investigate too closely the British spy who concocted the BBC's favourite fairy-story, his motivations or paymasters. Steele was, after all, on the same side as the UK state broadcaster. The BBC became incurious.

As to the suggestion of kompromat, the theory hawked around by BBC activists for virtually the entire duration of the Trump presidency, if Putin did indeed possess compromising material, puzzlingly he appears never to have used it as leverage. As noted by Forbes, Trump's first few months in office told an entirely different story to that propagated by the BBC. 'His appointments to key foreign policy positions,' observed the magazine 'are of strong anti-Putin advocates.'[7]

According to Brookings, the Trump administration imposed a grand total of fifty-two policy actions on Russia during its time in office including a raft of harsh economic restrictions and sanctions.[8] Amongst a whole raft of other measures the administration also bombed Russia's close allies Syria and helped arm Ukraine and Poland while extending NATO operations. 'When you actually look at the substance of what this administration has done, not the rhetoric but the substance,' observed Daniel Vajdich, a senior fellow at the Atlantic Council, 'this [Trump] administration has been much tougher on Russia than any in the post-Cold War era.'[9]

All of which might have come as something of a revelation to those who obtain their news and views from the 'trusted' BBC and who could have sworn Putin had caught the US president in a honey trap of a 'sexual nature' claims about which the broadcaster had 'verified' and that Moscow was just waiting to implement this dastardly blackmail plot to the detriment of the US and wider world.[10]

'Her allegations might bring down the president'
Not that trivial considerations such as fidelity to the facts were ever going to prevent the British state broadcaster from proving to its devotees that Mr Trump was indeed a sexual deviant. It was just a matter of finding the requisite proof to back up its dubious hypothesis. No sooner would its latest anti-Trump ruse crash and burn than the broadcaster would set off on its latest one like an excited puppy.

Though the corporation had its 'grab 'em by the pussy' quote, which it hawked around for the entirety of the Trump presidency to little effect, the broadcaster was hungry for something more, something that could clinch the deal, a sexual scandal that could bring the president down. Could a certain self-publicist by the name of Stormy Daniels be the key to bring Trump down? The emergence of this porn actress into the news cycle put BBC activists on high alert. Its hopes had been raised after allegations Trump's lawyer had made 'hush payments' to the porn actress which may, if shown to be true, have violated finance laws pertaining to election campaigning. Daniels alleged she and the businessman had had a consensual sexual encounter in 2006. Trump denied anything had occurred. In May 2021 an official enquiry dropped the case against Mr Trump.

Throughout 2018 the impartial broadcaster couldn't get enough of Stormy Daniels. She was all over the BBC. Story after salacious story came pouring out of Broadcasting House, the aim of course being to humiliate the president. The explanation for the broadcaster's obsession with this non-story was to be found in a BBC Sounds production which devoted a *whole programme* to a profile of the porn actress and which declared that some commentators were 'even suggesting her allegations might bring down the president.' The BBC Sounds production lavished attention on the veteran porn actress, portraying her as an old-fashioned country girl, sweet and innocent who loved horses and the heavy metal band Motley Crew.

The broadcaster even allocated Daniels a platform on its flagship Newsnight programme – whatever it took to humiliate the US president. Quid pro quo: Daniels humiliated the president and the BBC and co allocated her the kind of promotion about which she could only ever have dreamed. Sure enough the programme arrived at the sort of destination beloved by the tackiest of tabloids - the president's genitalia: 'Unless he's had a penis transplant,' said Daniels in reply to the BBC activist's probing, 'then I'm pretty sure that's a checkmate.' Egged on by the programme's host, the porn actress was implying that, should the opportunity ever arise, she would be able to 'identify' the president by his genitals.[11]

'They knew he [Trump] was a sexual pervert''

When it suits, the broadcaster can become credulous to the point of shockingly naïve. It depends. That Daniels had waited a whole decade before revealing the sordid details certainly did not appear to trouble the BBC. Daniels was not the only woman to emerge from the woodwork eager to relate tales of Trump's sexual misdemeanours. And whenever they appeared, the BBC was never far behind. It came as no surprise then when in 2017 the broadcaster took the trouble of interviewing a certain Jessica Leeds whose tale went back even further than Daniels – *three decades* and more.[12]

The 74-year-old Hilary Clinton supporter claimed that once upon a time she and the businessman had sat next to each other on a first-class flight. Trump had then gone on to launch a sexual assault against her. According to Leeds, Trump had virtually raped her. She had also said there had been a witness present – who must presumably have sat back and watched this serious sexual assault take place. Leeds was right: there had been a witness present. But according to the witness – a British businessman - the assault never happened. In this account it was Leeds who was flirting with the billionaire celebrity businessman – 'trying too hard' to win his attentions according to the witness.[13] When Trump visited the toilet, Leeds turned excitedly to the Brit and allegedly said: 'He's one of the richest men in the world!' Bizarrely, Ms Leeds did not report the alleged assault to aeroplane staff; nor did she report it to the airline or even to police. Stranger still, not a single person on the flight had heard the woman's screams for assistance; nor had anyone seen the distressed woman escaping her attacker. Naturally, these were crucial details the BBC did not divulge to its audience. Instead, it allowed Leeds to slander the president with impunity.

'I think the Trump voters knew he was a con artist,' says Leeds as a BBC activist gravely nods her head in agreement. 'They knew he was a sexual pervert and they voted for him anyway.'

That the BBC is platforming baseless slurs from an individual so sorely lacking credibility hardly comes as a surprise; as one of the most important propaganda arms of international corporate-political power it was merely fulfilling its obligations to an oligarchy whose vested interests Trump's policies were deemed to threaten.

Inverting reality – making people believe the opposite to truth – is a vital facet of BBC activity. As of 2022 every single one of the Trump accusers promoted by the BBC - all of whom coincidentally turned up around the time of his ascension to office - have either disappeared from view or had their cases dropped. Odder still, since the election of Joe Biden new allegations have been rather thin on the ground. Perhaps one day, the broadcaster will wonder why, but don't bank on it.

Meanwhile on the BBC news website, the lurid accusations of actors in the mould of Daniels and Leeds are still available, ready to mislead those who have the misfortune to stumble upon them.

SUMMARY

For virtually the entire term of the Trump presidency the BBC parroted the salacious and wholly fallacious claims in the Steele dossier – a scheme devised and paid for by Hilary Clinton and the Democrats. Indeed, in the hope of destabilising the presidency the broadcaster readily amplified its lurid accusations. Meanwhile, the same organisation refuses to report on claims made against the Biden presidency which mainly revolve around Ukraine dealings on the grounds they are 'baseless.'

'Mr Trump suggested injecting patients with disinfectants might help treat coronavirus'

Various BBC outlets: 24-25 April 2020

While the BBC's four-year misinformation campaign against President Trump consisted of myriad propaganda techniques, one method in particular proved especially useful: misrepresentation – defined by Merriam Webster's online dictionary as: 'An intentionally or sometimes negligently false representation made…often for the purpose of deceiving, defrauding…'

From multitude instances of misrepresentation available, two in particularly stand out. The broadcaster circulated the following pair of memes throughout its vast platform at the start of the Covid 'pandemic.' This pair of BBC headlines were contrived to arrest attention:

Trump told people to inject themselves with bleach! Trump told people to drink bleach!

Following an April 2020 White House press conference memes such as these lit up social media. According to the establishment media, in order to treat coronavirus the US president had indeed encouraged citizens to take matters into their own hands, to actually use household bleach as a medicine. Consumers of outlets such as CNN, Yahoo News, *The Guardian* etc. duly expressed their outrage: how could Trump possibly suggest such patently ridiculous as well as dangerous courses of action? For its part, BBC audiences were bombarded with stories in which doctors and scientists 'condemned' the president's outrageous advice.

But had Mr Trump even made such claims? A strawman argument often entails embellishing what a person might have originally said or intimated with spurious additional information; it can also entail stripping context from a speaker's words – whatever it takes to give a misleading impression. Strawman created, the propagandist can then go on to refute something the original speaker never actually said or intended to say.

'Most disinfectants contain bleach'

Thanks in no small part to the 'British' Broadcasting Corporation, the story of Trump's gross irresponsibility gained massive traction in the UK. The following claim made by BBC 'Reality Check' – the broadcaster's 'fact-check' faculty - was repeated to the point of saturation in all manner of BBC broadcasts and articles: 'Mr Trump suggested injecting patients with disinfectants might help treat coronavirus.'[1]

While disinfectant sounds harmful enough, following the lead of its US allies what the BBC really wanted its audiences to believe was that the president had in fact suggested using *bleach* to treat coronavirus – presumably because bleach is a product found in most kitchens and thus makes the suggestion sound that little bit more irresponsible.[2] 'Most disinfectants contain bleach,' announced the Newsround section of the BBC website, 'which would make you very seriously ill and could kill you if it gets inside your body.'[3] In its next sentence the article drops disinfectant altogether: 'Mr Trump's own public health agencies also warn against bleach as a medicine.'

Notice also the logical implication inherent in that last sentence, one which would have been read (and believed) by potentially millions of children and as well as their parents:

Public health is issuing warnings about using bleach as a medicine.
ergo:
Trump must have advised using bleach as a medicine.

However, the broadcaster wasn't finished there. Associating whenever possible household bleach to Mr Trump's comments was merely the first part of its strawman strategy. The second part involved implying that the US president had encouraged people to not only inject the substance but also to *ingest* – i.e. drink it. Had Mr Trump really suggested that? The transcript of what the president actually said will assist in arriving at a judgement; for now, let's stay with what the BBC *implied he had said.*

This is the start of a BBC website article titled, 'Coronavirus: Disinfectant firm warns after Trump comments' – one of dozens of similar reports the broadcaster produced on 24th April 2020, the day of the press call. According to the article 'a leading disinfectant producer' had issued 'a strong warning' not to use its products on the human body 'after Donald Trump suggested they could potentially be used to treat coronavirus.' It continues:

Reckitt Benckiser said 'under no circumstance' should its products be **injected** or **ingested**. Disinfectants are hazardous substances and can be **poisonous if ingested**.

Notice once again the implications inherent in this paragraph:

Disinfectant producer warns against injecting its products
ergo:
Mr Trump must have suggested injecting/ingesting disinfectant

Thus, the article marches boldly on: 'These products have corrosive properties that melt or destroy the lining of our innards,' warns a McGill University thoracic surgeon who also tells the broadcaster that '**ingestion of a household cleaning product** was 'extremely dangerous.' To cap a characteristically impartial BBC report its central claims are once again recycled, this time by a member of its 'disinformation' team who remarks that, '**Not only does consuming or injecting disinfectant risk poisoning and death,** it's not even likely to be effective.'[4]

Nor was the broadcaster quite finished. Continuing the theme of drinking and/or injecting harmful substances, BBC 'Reality Check' weighed in once again by quoting yet another medical professional, this time a professor of toxicology who told the ever credulous broadcaster that: '**Injecting bleach or disinfectant** ...would likely result in significant, irreversible harm and probably a **very unpleasant death.**'[5]

Citing a pulmonologist, another BBC article amplified the broadcaster's carefully constructed narrative yet further: '**This notion of injecting or ingesting any type of cleansing product into the body** is irresponsible and it's dangerous.'[6] After the broadcaster had sought and then published the thoughts of innumerable doctors and scientists all expressing their horror at Trump's supposed comments, its strawman was building nicely: so many medical professionals rebuking the president could only help convince consumers of BBC output that the American president really had said something truly reckless. What else could have disturbed doctors to such a degree?

Consuming, injecting or ingesting bleach (disinfectant) in order to treat coronavirus...why, these were the ramblings of an individual unfit to hold public office, right? Well, that was the broadcaster's story and it was sticking with it.

'Highly dangerous to use disinfectants inside the human body'
So now let's turn to the actual press conference in question. By analysing the context as well as the president's actual words, it will become possible to assess the veracity of the BBC narrative which circulated all through its vast media platform and which remains there to this day. At the conference William Bryan, the

undersecretary for science and technology at the Department of Homeland Security, presented a study that found cleaning agents and exposure to sun can both kill coronavirus on surfaces. Prior to handing over to Mr Trump, the undersecretary concludes by observing: 'I can tell you that bleach will kill the virus in five minutes.'

Turning round to address Mr Bryan, the president starts by outlining that which propagandists prefer to avoid: context. A discussion had already taken place between Mr Trump and his official. 'So I asked Bill [i.e. Mr Bryan] a question some of you are thinking of if you're into that world...' Trump had apparently asked several hypothetical questions regarding the use of ultraviolet or 'very powerful light' to nullify the virus.[7] Still addressing himself primarily to Mr Bryan, the president next raises the topic of disinfectant:

And I then I see the disinfectant, where it knocks it out in one minute, and is there a way you can do something like that by injection inside, or almost a cleaning? Because you see it gets in the lungs, and it does a tremendous number on the lungs. So, it'd be interesting to check that. So, you're going to have to use medical doctors, but it sounds interesting to me, so we'll see. But the whole concept of the light, the way it goes in one minute, that's pretty powerful.

Having presumably witnessed for himself (or been briefed about) the powerful effects of disinfectant on the virus, the president then *asks a question*: is there a way *the effect* can be replicated via injection or a cleaning? Although it is not exactly clear what is meant by a 'cleaning' the salient point is that the president is clearly *asking a question* i.e. Is there a way...?[8] Clearly, this is not an order, edict or even suggestion. It is a query. And like all queries expresses a certain amount of uncertainty.

Next, a reporter from ABC News asks Mr Bryan the following question: 'The president mentioned the idea of a cleaner, bleach and isopropyl alcohol emerging. There's no scenario where that could be injected into a person, is there?'

'It wouldn't be through injections,' Trump confirms. 'You're talking about almost a cleaning and sterilization of an area. Maybe it works, maybe it doesn't work, but it certainly has a big effect if it's on a stationary object.' Unsurprisingly, this part of the press call is not 'fact-checked' by the broadcaster. In fact, it does not receive even the briefest of mentions...

Even anti-Trump 'fact-checkers' could not twist their way out of this one. 'The former President did not instruct people to drink bleach,' correctly observed Logically, 'but he did suggest that the use of disinfectants as a treatment should be researched.'[9] Indeed, that is precisely what the president had done: suggested further research into the efficacy of disinfectants to treat coronavirus. In an article it carried titled, 'No, Trump didn't tell Americans infected with the coronavirus to drink bleach,' Politifact was forced to begrudgingly admit that: 'Trump did not specifically recommend ingesting disinfectants, but he did express interest in exploring whether disinfectants could be applied to the site of a coronavirus infection inside the body, such as the lungs.'[10] Again, that is what the president had suggested: taking the promising results with disinfectant further i.e. via more research.

All of which might have confused consumers of BBC output to whom it had been strongly intimated that Mr Trump had, in the broadcaster's own words, 'suggested injecting and even ingesting bleach in order to treat coronavirus.' As various hostile fact-checkers verified and as the transcript clearly demonstrates, the president suggested no such thing. As to why BBC articles invariably omitted virtually the entire context of what had both preceded and followed the president's comments – including the question from the ABC correspondent - it's back to Politifact:

The briefing transcript shows that Trump did not say people should inject themselves with bleach or alcohol to treat the coronavirus. He was asking officials on the White House coronavirus task force whether they could be used in potential cures.

Presentation of the transcript would have sunk the BBC narrative before it had chance to set sail.[11] However, by the time all this had been clarified BBC audiences had been consistently exposed to an especially iniquitous strawman argument - the majority of whom no doubt firmly believed that president Trump really had advised injecting and/or drinking bleach into their systems in order to treat coronavirus.

In its 'reality check' of what it termed Mr Trump's claims the broadcaster delivered its impartial verdict: 'It is highly dangerous to use disinfectants inside the human body,' asserted the reality checkers. It was time to let that revelation sink in. Swallowing disinfectant really isn't a good idea. And so, the strawman had done its job: the broadcaster had debunked not any assertion made by Mr Trump, but rather its own disinformation. Mission to mislead accomplished.[12]

SUMMARY

The BBC claimed President Trump had advised people to inject and ingest bleach to treat Covid. He had in fact enquired whether further research would be conducted on the use of disinfectants to treat the virus.

'James Dyson is a prominent Conservative supporter'

Various outlets: Wednesday 21 April 2021

March 2020 and UK hospitals were on high alert. According to a mainstream media led as ever by a hyper-ventilating BBC, the national health service was about to be swamped by victims of the coronavirus 'pandemic.' The broadcaster, in its own inimitable way, was helping stoke fears (that would prove completely unfounded) that the entire health system would collapse under such unmitigated pressure. With limited capacity in ICU how could the system cope with thousands of Covid-19 afflicted patients? Panic spread not only through the health service, but government too.

At this early stage of the 'pandemic' the corporate-legacy media was daily berating the government for what it declared was its inadequate response to coronavirus - from lack of personal protective equipment to shortage of ventilators. Boris Johnson and his government were feeling the heat – most of which was being generated by the 'British' Broadcasting Corporation.

No doubt mindful of the broadcaster's incessant and very vocal criticism, the Prime Minister made an approach to Sir James Dyson. Could his engineering and design company manufacture urgently required ventilators? The entrepreneur readily agreed to assist. Dyson personnel started to work round the clock in order to produce the much-needed equipment that would sustain those suffering from severe illness. In the meantime, Sir James wrote to the Treasury. The tycoon wished to clarify the tax status of employees who would arrive in the UK from overseas to lend their expertise to the project. Not receiving a reply and up against the clock, Sir James went back to Boris Johnson who assured him that he would personally look into the taxation issue; time was very much of the essence.

That might have been the end of the matter. A champion of British engineering had answered an SOS from a government faced with an unprecedented medical emergency and which was under pressure from a hyper-critical media. Not quite. As far as the BBC was concerned an opportunity to kill several birds with one story had just serendipitously arisen: two high profile figures – Boris Johnson and Sir James Dyson – both of whom it held responsible to varying degrees for the UK's decision to leave the EU in 2016. Nor did the fact that PM and business tycoon were working together in order to save lives cause the broadcaster a moment's hesitation.

A BBC news article soon appeared headlined: 'Boris Johnson told Sir James Dyson he would 'fix' tax issue.' With its implicit suggestion of favours for friends, the broadcaster was attempting to stir up beliefs about Tory party links to big business, that the rich and powerful use their influence to their advantage with the Conservatives – a scenario it usually terms as conspiracy theory. However, as Dyson would stress, his company had invested £20 million in the project – money that it would not seek to reclaim. Ensuring that employees were not hit with punitive tax demands was hardly a net gain for anyone – least of all Dyson.

Nonetheless, the broadcaster went on to print a series of text messages exchanged between PM and entrepreneur: 'The PM messaged Sir James saying: '[Chancellor] Rishi [Sunak] says it is fixed!! We need you here.' The BBC news article also printed a message in which the Prime Minister had said: 'I am First Lord of the Treasury and you can take it that we are backing you to do what you need.' In the same article, presumably in order to imply it had been broken, the broadcaster went on to extensively quote from the Ministerial Code.[1]

Despite BBC innuendo it appeared the vast majority of observers did not discern anything sinister in the messages. Faced with thousands of potential deaths due to lack of suitable equipment, the Prime Minister was cutting corners which nobody – not even Tony Blair – could object to. 'I find it hard to get worked up about this,' said the former Prime Minister when offering his thoughts on the BBC's sleaze story. 'If you're in the middle of a huge crisis, people are going to be using every means they can.' Another article published on the BBC website that same day headlined with: 'No apology' from PM in Dyson row.' Browsing that article it might be inferred that Mr Johnson had erred in some way, done something wrong, which was precisely the impression corporation activists were hoping to plant in the minds of the BBC audience. In reality, the only 'row' was that concocted by a broadcaster intent on taking Boris Johnson's scalp any way it could.

'Texts…seen by the BBC'
There was no stopping the broadcaster. The following day it would print yet another article insinuating dark deeds afoot. Applying one of its health-checks to Sir James by labelling him a 'prominent supporter of Brexit'[2] and at the same time revealing, albeit inadvertently, why the entrepreneur had always been on the BBC wrong-think list and thus a legitimate target for its disinformation, the article includes the following passages discussing Dyson's relocation from Singapore back to the UK:

This week he [Dyson] was also involved in a controversy over texting Prime Minister Boris Johnson about tax issues.

The texts - seen by the BBC - show Mr Johnson saying he could 'fix' tax issues relating to Dyson staff who came to the UK to work on the pandemic.[3]

There are two things to note here: firstly, like the supposed row any 'controversy' continues to exist solely in the heads of politically-motivated BBC activists. Secondly, although the BBC wishes its audience to believe it had gained access to secret and therefore illicit text messages, ('seen by the BBC') Sir James had – wisely as it would transpire – disclosed the content of the messages to officials enabling them to make an assessment viz any perceived impropriety. Consumers of BBC 'news' outraged by what they took to be the stench of corruption implicit in the broadcaster's reporting were simply being misled. There was not, nor ever had been, anything underhand about either the texts or the relationship between Sir James and the Tories.

But all of this nudge-nudge, wink-wink innuendo was nothing compared to BBC reports which had started circulating on its vast television and radio platform. The excitable broadcaster had a problem: tantalisingly close to nobbling its pair of reviled Brexiteers, as ever the facts were not its friends. Mr Johnson and Mr Dyson were doing everything in their collective power to expedite a process that would save lives, a collaboration which had come about not least because of incessant criticism from the BBC. Notwithstanding, the impartial broadcaster had the scent of blood in its finely attuned nostrils. There must be some way of scoring a mortal blow against both men. How? If reality doesn't fit the agenda, simply create your own reality. And so, the BBC did just that.

After Sir James had been contacted by the BBC's political editor Laura Kuenssberg, the broadcaster began referring to him as a 'prominent conservative supporter.' It transpires that the corporation had been doing some digging. In 2009 Sir James had been invited to speak on the topic of British engineering at the Conversative Party annual conference; he'd accepted a similar invitation from the Labour government in 1998. No matter, it seems that the broadcaster was intent on painting Sir James as a political ally of the Prime Minister thereby cementing its favours-for-friends narrative which it hoped would seriously wound Mr Johnson and his government, perhaps even prove to be the catalyst which would propel Sir Keir Starmer and Labour into Number 10 Downing Street.

In order to further bolster its false story of Tory cronyism, the BBC next invented a story that Sir James – whom it was now habitually and falsely referring to as 'a prominent conservative supporter' – had donated money to the party. He had done no such thing; what he had done was contribute £11.5k to the Wiltshire Engineering Festival via his local MP who happened to be a Conservative. The festival encourages children to learn and study engineering.

'She [Kuenssberg] and the BBC' fumed Sir James, 'made this grotesque mischaracterisation to justify their 'sleaze' story which would otherwise simply not have stood up.'[4]

In an article written for *The Telegraph* ('BBC twisted the truth over my links to the Tories') the tycoon had no choice but to address the broadcaster's falsehoods. A shaken Dyson said it was untrue that he tried to 'extract favours from the Prime Minister.'[5] The businessman summed up the broadcaster's efforts thus:

'The BBC's characterisation of me as a prominent Conservative donor, or supporter, leveraging a position of power to extract favours from the Prime Minister, is completely untrue.'[6]

'We would like to put the record straight'

On 12 May, three weeks after it had falsely informed the world that Sir James Dyson was a 'prominent conservative supporter' and had implied he had used that position to sweeten up a more than willing Prime Minister, faced with actual reality Auntie had no option but to offer a grovelling apology. In order to appreciate the extent to which the broadcaster attempted to mislead it's worth quoting from the statement at length:

> We accept that Sir James Dyson is not a prominent
> Conservative supporter as was stated... The James
> Dyson Foundation made a charitable gift to support the
> Wiltshire Engineering Festival for school children. We
> accept that this does not signal affiliation to any political
> party and we would like to put the record straight.

In other words, every item of BBC reporting had been false: Sir James is not nor has he ever been a 'prominent conservative supporter.' Nor has he ever made political donations to the Conservative Party. Could things possibly get any worse for the broadcaster? 'Sir James' continues the statement 'also raised concerns about the accuracy of other aspects of our reporting:'

> We wish to make clear that Sir James contacted Number 10
> in response to the Prime Minister's direct request to him for
> assistance in relation to the urgent need for ventilators and
> incurred costs of £20m which his company voluntarily
> absorbed in trying to assist in the national emergency. His
> text messages to the Prime Minister were also later sent to
> officials. We are sorry that these facts were not always
> reflected in our coverage, and we apologise for not doing so.

Thus, every single aspect of the broadcaster's original Tory-Dyson sleaze hit piece had been either flat out false or conceived in such a way as to give the audience a false impression of events. In order to further mislead its audience, the broadcaster had simply omitted all the facts referred to in the above paragraph – facts 'not always reflected in our coverage.'

The BBC's unethical behaviour, particularly the manner in which it had disseminated false information about a respected businessman and his company had been conceived for a specific purpose: to enable it to pursue its anti-Boris Johnson campaign. In some ways, Sir James Dyson – the reputation of himself and his company – had merely been collateral damage. It's not the first time an innocent party had found itself in the crosshairs of BBC shenanigans; Petro Poroshenko had also been subject to the broadcaster's slander when it had falsely asserted that Ukraine's then president had attempted to bribe lawyers acting for then president Trump.

Unimpressed by BBC behaviour and an apology that as well as being belated had been forced out of the broadcaster, the final word was left to Sir James: 'To justify its claim that I am a prominent Conservative supporter,' concluded Sir James from the Dyson website, 'the BBC shamefully twisted our charitable gift to school children to suit their political narrative.'[7]

Though the broadcaster had finally been forced to admit the truth – that it had invented a Tory sleaze story where none existed, misleading in the process an admittedly ever decreasing audience - the damage had already been done; the clarification was not published or announced on any BBC news channel, but was quietly added to the Corrections page of the BBC website where few if any of those who had been originally misled would encounter the actual facts.

Noting how the broadcaster had casually dismissed its actions apparent in phrases in which it stated it had been 'happy to set the record straight' *The Telegraph* also reminded readers of just how unethical BBC behaviour had been:

> This was more than a slight error so easily dismissed. The essence of the story was that Sir James had access to the Prime Minister personally because he was a friend and a Tory donor. Stripped of that central point there was no story.[8]

Indeed, without BBC falsehoods there would have been no story. Unlike Poroshenko, Sir James did not sue for defamation but could so easily have done so. In its determination to unseat Boris Johnson as British Prime Minister in the hope of reversing Brexit, the BBC had concocted and then promoted a series of falsehoods about the entrepreneur it assumed would wound Johnson - maybe mortally. Disinformation at its most cynical.

The Telegraph ended its piece in anticipation of the report into BBC conduct by the broadcaster's allies at Ofcom and which it was certain would have to follow. The paper is still waiting.

SUMMARY

The BBC claimed Sir James Dyson was a prominent Conservative supporter and implied he had used his links with the party for favour. Sir James has no especial links with the party. The false story was an attempt by the BBC in fact to attack Prime Minister Boris Johnson.

'1,162 died from coronavirus in a single day in the UK'

BBC Radio 4 Today: 8 January 2021

Throughout the coronavirus 'pandemic' of 2020-21, the British government was on what appeared to be a mission: to convince the population it was at grave risk of becoming infected and thereafter dying from Covid-19. Convince is the key word. For, despite what the government said, the evidence did not appear to support warnings which were always dire and which had been largely based on modelling devised by the likes of Professor Neil Ferguson, an academic notorious for his erroneous predictions e.g. Ferguson predicted as many as 150,000 deaths could result from the 1994-96 outbreak of Mad Cow disease; as of 2022, less than 200 have actually died.

Despite the appalling track record of Ferguson and his Imperial College employers, their predictions are *still* used to inform government health policy. Such was the case during the so-called coronavirus pandemic. Should lockdown restrictions be lifted, Ferguson predicted 100,000 Covid cases per day would follow throughout 2021. Not long after making this erroneous prediction the academic admitted (once again) he had been wrong.[1]

In his defence Ferguson may have been under pressure to supply ministers with statistics that supported what appeared to be a pre-planned government narrative: a deadly pandemic was about to sweep through the country, protection from which could only be obtained through vaccination. However, reality hardly supported such catastrophic predictions. For the vast majority of people Covid-19 infection resulted in moderate or mild symptoms; as with all causes of mortality, frequency of deaths due to Covid increased with age. Despite these obvious provisos, the Boris Johnson government adopted an approach whose aim appeared to lie in exaggerating the threat. A document written at the very start of the pandemic by the Scientific Pandemic Influenza Group on Behaviours (SPI-B) and dated 22 March observed that:

> A substantial number of people still do not feel sufficiently personally threatened; it could be that they are reassured by the low death rate in their demographic group...the perceived level of personal threat needs to be increased among those who are complacent, using hard-hitting emotional messaging.

If mass vaccination was to occur as seemed to be the government plan from the start, it could only proceed provided the population felt sufficiently threatened. The problem was that with such a negligible death rate people in fact felt 'reassured.' For once the government was correct: people had started to look around and the conclusion reached did not tally with the apocalyptic messaging coming from various sources such as Ferguson, Health Secretary Matt Hancock and Chief Scientific Adviser Sir Patrick Vallance who would go on to erroneously predict 4,000 deaths per day would occur during a second wave.[2] What mattered was to create fear where none existed, to exaggerate, mislead. In order to achieve this end would require 'hard-hitting, emotional messaging.' As part of its recommendations as to how this state of fear would be achieved, the SP1-B group advised ministers to 'use media to increase sense of personal threat.'

As to why any government would indulge in such dishonest behaviour, that was a question for those claiming to hold power to truth. Later, the government would be accused of using 'covert psychological strategies' in order to terrify people into compliance.' Critics of this type of psychological manipulation would also make the accusation that the entire country had been left in 'a state of heightened anxiety.' Concerns such as these however did not feature in the output of the corporate-legacy media. It was left to independent voices, many of whom found themselves under attack from the mainstream media for daring to oppose the government's extreme response to Covid. Although it also claims to be independent, the BBC had nothing whatsoever to say about a situation which had been deliberately manipulated and which had left countless numbers of people both physically and psychologically damaged.

As a crucial resource of international wealth and power the state broadcaster would not have to be asked twice to play its part in this deception; the corporation had in fact been primed and ready to go for some time. As expected, and despite the emergence of worrying anomalies (e.g. bizarre footage of Chinese citizens seemingly collapsing upon contact with the virus[3]) BBC coverage to this point had been wholly credulous and lacking in even basic journalistic enquiry.

But playing dumb was merely the tip of an especially unethical iceberg. In line with government expectations, the BBC was *actively manipulating* its audience's emotions, striving to create an entirely false reality as remarked upon by Mark Woolhouse, Professor of Infectious Disease Epidemiology at the University of Edinburgh: 'I heard [the official Covid] argument caricatured as; everyone died... BBC News backed up this misperception by regularly reporting rare tragedies involving low-risk individuals as if they were the norm.'[4]

Indeed, one of the broadcaster's favourite tactics aimed at stoking fear was to search exhaustively for a Covid 'denier' who had subsequently supposedly died of the virus. This way it could promote a story of ignorance which had resulted in death. Although such cases were vanishingly rare, the dogged broadcaster pursued them with zeal in order to give the false impression that these cases were in fact widespread. One such example of this form of BBC astro-turfing was a story published on 28 January 2021 titled: 'Covid deniers blamed over Shrewsbury man Gary Matthews' death.'[5] That the broadcaster should act in this duplicitous manner should have come as no surprise. From the very start it had dutifully amplified every story of the deadly Wuhan plague while studiously ignoring any evidence that cast doubt on an official narrative which told of wet markets and viruses 'jumping' from marine life to humans.

As could be discerned from the response of a British government determined to manufacture a crisis where none existed, there appeared to be more to the supposed pandemic than met the eye; had the whole thing been planned as growing numbers of critics were starting to suggest? That's a question for future criminal courts to ponder; the role of facilitators such as the BBC will also need to be addressed.

What is certain is that just when the British state required that its citizens be bombarded with information that would increase their levels of anxiety, the 'British' Broadcasting Corporation began making some fundamental 'errors' in its reporting of the pandemic. Recall that SPI-B had speculated that the public was not worried about coronavirus because of the low-death rate. If that perception could be changed, then presumably the level of anxiety would increase in line with government requirements. And so, BBC reports began to make a catalogue of mistakes. There are far too many to list here, but some of the most egregious deserve mention.

Following disclosure from health minister Robin Swann, an item broadcast on BBC Radio 5 Live towards the end of 2020 duly claimed that hospitals in Northern Ireland were admitting 'four to five hundred [Covid] patients a day.'[6] If so, then the country was facing a health crisis on an unprecedented scale. Only it wasn't true. As so often happens when establishment narratives require a little bit of enhancement, the BBC had got the wrong end of the stick. Mr Swann had in fact revealed that between 400 and 500 Covid patients were being *treated at that time* i.e. it was a cumulative not daily total. If the BBC was to be believed *3-3,500 patients per week* were being admitted to Northern Ireland hospitals with Covid – a clearly ludicrous proposition not borne out by any reality. Subsequently, a BBC clarification was quietly issued on the broadcaster's website, but not until *three months* after the misleading claim had first aired.

Irrespective of the facts, BBC misinformation was already having the desired effect. Research by Kekst CNC had found that half of respondents thought Covid had killed 1 per cent of the UK population or over 600,000 people; the actual figure was 44,000. A third of respondents thought up to 10% of the population had been killed by Covid which would equate to about 6.6. million deaths.[7]

'We should not distort known facts'
What was being witnessed in BBC reporting was a well-worn practice whereby false information is published to a mass audience prior to subsequent modification. Timing is key; sneaking a correction out three months after a falsehood has been broadcast is part of a carefully considered strategy whereby the lie has already been established as true in the minds of the BBC viewer/listener by the time a correction or retraction arrives. Crucially, the more often lies are repeated the likelier BBC consumers will be to accept their validity. According to a psychological theory known as the Illusory Truth Effect, repetition is indeed a highly effective tool when it comes to promoting false narratives; bombarding the target audience with repeated falsehoods really does work. Not only this, but research has shown that when confronted with the truth beliefs can be so ingrained that individuals will continue to hold on to the original falsehood.

Take for example BBC coverage of that old chestnut known as Russiagate. Research (Majin 2021) showed that in just a single month – July 2018 – BBC online published 183 stories which included the words 'Trump' and 'Russia.'[8] Four years on and a worryingly high percentage of BBC consumers continue to swear that Mr Trump was a Russian spy. The original lie or half-truth does indeed appear to retain some sort of primacy as observed in the research of De keersmaecker and Roets (2017) who remark that: 'The influence of incorrect information cannot be simply undone by pointing out that this information was incorrect.'

In an edition of BBC Radio 4's *Today* programme broadcast on 8 January 2021, its 6 million listeners were informed that '1,162 people had died from coronavirus in a single day' – just the sort of statistic to stoke the kind of panic demanded by the government. However, the figure was in fact the number of deaths which had occurred *within 28 days of a positive test,* a statistic itself that incorporated deaths recorded *with Covid...*

As to how such an elementary mistake could have occurred that's for readers to decide. BBC editorial guidelines state that, 'All BBC output...must be well sourced, based on sound evidence, and corroborated.' The guidelines also state that:

> The BBC must not knowingly and materially mislead its audiences. We should not distort known facts, present invented material as fact or otherwise undermine our audiences' trust in our content.

> We should normally acknowledge serious factual errors and correct them quickly, clearly and appropriately.[9]

The 'clarification' was issued on 2 June 2021, *five months* after the original misinformation had been aired.

Just weeks later, an edition of BBC Newsnight broadcast on 27

January ran a story about care home deaths.[10] The programme announced that 3,615 people had died of Covid in English and Welsh care homes 'in the last week.' This figure represented an increase from the previous month of 157%. According to Office of National Statistics' data, care home death for the period in question were in fact as follows:[11]

Week ending	Total deaths
8 Jan	1,384
15 Jan	1,734
22 Jan	2,389
29 Jan	2,523

The mistake had been made because 'wrong figures' had been used in the broadcaster's calculations. The BBC correction was quietly issued on 7 July – almost *six months* after the original falsehood aired.

In October 2021 *Newscast,* a podcast produced by BBC 5 Live, asserted that two-thirds of hospitalised over-80s were unvaccinated. The programme also observed that as 94% of over-80s were vaccinated, and only 6% were not, this represented an 'extraordinarily disproportionate' figure. Once again, the broadcaster had got its sums badly wrong. A listener to the programme immediately spotted the 'error.' Of the 1,533 over-80s hospital admissions in the relevant week, only 134 were unvaccinated. Thus, the proportion was less than 10% - not even close to 66% ('two thirds') as reported by the BBC. Upon receipt of a complaint BBC *Newscast* had no option but admit its 'mistake.'[12]

Misleading the public with regards to the unvaccinated had become a key BBC objective. The idea was to imply that this group were suffering far worse outcomes than those who had taken the shots, that getting vaccinated was the sensible thing to do, the right thing to do. The broadcaster was not alone: Pfizer shareholders and executives heartily agreed. So too did Bill Gates.

No sooner had *Newscast* been exposed than in an interview with an intensive care doctor for BBC Radio 4 *Today*,[13] Martha Kearney asserted that: 'The vast majority of the people you're having to treat are unvaccinated.' To which the doctor replied: 'It's true that the majority of patients in intensive care are unvaccinated.' Kearney went on to claim that 30 percent of critical care beds were occupied by Covid patients and that 'three-quarters' of them had not been vaccinated. In fact, data from the Intensive Care and National Audit Research Centre revealed that 48% of intensive care patients were unvaccinated while 51% had been vaccinated.

Meanwhile, a report on BBC One Scotland managed to also gets its wires crossed.[14] The impact of the pandemic on the NHS so the programme stated, had resulted in 'more than 50,000 staff' being absent over a week. NHS Scotland employs 147,000 staff, so if the BBC was to be believed almost 33% of its employees were absent because of Covid. In fact, just over 7,000 staff had been absent over the time period in question, under 5%.

And so the 'mistakes' keep happening, but always of course in the same direction: that which favours and/or promotes the establishment narrative, in this case that of the government and its Big Pharma partners.[15] We'll end this section with yet another BBC blooper – this time going against a favourite BBC wrong-thinker, Israel.

An edition of BBC Newsnight broadcast on 20 April 2021 got into all sorts of problems when attempting to portray Israel's Covid response. The BBC's own correction, which followed four months after the programme had aired, needs no comment from us: 'We conflated the vaccination rates for Israel's Palestinian citizens and Palestinians in the occupied territories when we said the roll-out rate was half a percent.' Just 0.5%? Wow. Was not this more proof of Israeli oppression? The correction continues: 'In fact, within Israel it was then estimated to be around 67%.' To put the icing on an especially misleading BBC anti-Israel item the correction concludes: 'We also said the 'Palestinian population has not been inoculated at anywhere near the rate of the Israeli population. To be clear, this was because of vaccine hesitancy.'

If you'd formed the impression after watching BBC Newsnight that Israel's treatment of the Palestinians during the Covid crisis was proving to be less than equitable, several months after this misleading item aired the broadcaster set the record straight: a couple of sentences buried deep inside its news website.

And just as this book is going to press in summer 2022, up pops the BBC to ask: why eight percent of the population remain unvaccinated against Covid-19?[16] The idea is of course to suggest the unvaccinated are a minority, outliers, abnormal etc. According to data published by the UKHSA the figure is in fact 29.8%.[17] To a BBC audience primed on antivaxxer content, the misleading figure no doubt *sounds about right*; it accords with previous BBC disinformation. When you have truthiness, who needs facts?

SUMMARY

The BBC has made a catalogue of 'mistakes' reporting Covid. It always over-reports, but never under-reports number of infections, hospitalisations, deaths etc. The only exception is unvaccinated rates, which it under-reports.

'A pandemic of the unvaccinated'

Ros Atkins on…Compulsory Covid vaccinations:
bbc.co.uk: 11 December 2021

Ros Atkins on…is a series available on BBC News Channel in which the show's eponymous host presents an analysis of a current affairs issue. Titles in the series include: 'Migrant Channel crossings,' 'Tree planting and climate change,' 'The No. 10 Christmas party denials' and 'Rising tensions with Russia.' While the programme claims to approach topics even-handedly, in reality Atkins promotes the BBC-establishment narrative while undermining and/or dismissing opposing voices and arguments.

In December 2021 Atkins turned his attention to Covid-19, specifically the issue of compulsory vaccinations – a development his BBC employers were attempting to normalise on behalf of both the British state and the world's most powerful pharmaceutical companies. Compulsory vaccinations would make Pfizer & co mega tons of cash. The People's Vaccine Alliance (PAV) estimates that Big Pharma had already been making $93.5 million per day from its Covid shots[1] - a figure which would increase exponentially should vaccination become mandated.

That the British state broadcaster should be promoting the interests of rampant corporatism is of course entirely consistent with its affiliations. Big Pharma is a cornerstone of what has been referred to as international corporate-political power. But BBC enthusiasm for vaccine mandates is not entirely linked to corporate profiteering. Some commentators suggest that compulsory vaccinations will facilitate the introduction of digital ID. According to npr, several thousand Swedes have already had microchips inserted into their hands allowing users to 'swipe' their hands against digital readers.[2] Digital ID, warn critics, could lead to a radical, top-down authoritarian system of government and un-precedented encroachment into civil liberties.

Clearly, such a system could only work provided every citizen actually has a digital ID. Could this explain the measures used by the Boris Johnson government through 2020 and 2021 as it went to quite extraordinary lengths to coerce UK citizens to get 'jabbed?' Might it also explain BBC and legacy media sustained attacks on viable Covid treatments such as Hydroxychloroquine and Ivermectin? As will be discussed later in this book, emergency authorisation of the experimental Covid injections was granted on one proviso: that no alternative treatment existed.

However, following hundreds of thousands of adverse reactions to the vaccine (and thousands of potential deaths), the drive to 'vaccinate the planet' in the immortal words of BBC Media donor Bill Gates soon began to stall. In response, the British state broadcaster upped the ante. It turned its firepower on what it impartially referred to as 'antivaxxers' - several million men and women who had so far resisted state coercion to get 'jabbed.' The compulsory tax-payer funded BBC deployed a number of tactics aimed at marginalising a group estimated to number 5-6 million, most prominently ridicule and shaming.

'We have to get the world vaccinated'

So we come to Oxbridge graduate Ros Atkins' take on com-pulsory vaccination. So-called vaccine hesitancy threatening to derail pharma-government plans, by winter 2021 the globalist-affiliated asset known as the BBC was diligently pushing the idea of vaccine mandates into the public forum. Atkins' job was simply to further this agenda. The facts stacked against him, fulfilling his brief would necessitate recourse to propaganda.

Ros Atkins on...Compulsory Covid vaccinations begins with three contributors opining about the necessity of Covid vac-cinations. Atkins 'experts' duly offer up the same message: *here, at the end of 2021, Covid has become a 'pandemic of the unvaccinated.'* The point is made by Dr Tom Frieden and Professor Sebastian Stehr. A third contributor, Dr John Swartzberg of UC Berkeley, declares that, 'We have to get the world vaccinated.' Coincidentally, it's precisely the same sentiment shared by Bill Gates who, since 1999, has made some 54 donations to...UC Berkeley, the largest coming in at $32 million. It is often the case that BBC doesn't mention affiliations of its various 'experts' when to do so would reveal potential conflicts of interest. Not only does the programme's host not bother to reveal this information, but the fallacious 'pandemic of the unvaccinated' claim goes unchallenged.

Platforming individuals who agree with its thesis while denying a platform to those who disagree - a crude but effective propaganda technique - is a tried and trusted BBC tactic. Having little or no exposure to experts who take a different view, an audience can be misled into believing a consensus exists. Social media awash with reports of fully vaccinated individuals catching Covid, the veracity of the claims peddled by Atkins's show was highly questionable. Meanwhile, data from the UK's Covid 19 Surveillance Report also seemed to contradict the assertions of Atkins' cherry-picked experts:

Cases presenting to emergency care resulting in overnight inpatient admission, between week 49 and week 52[3]			
Vaccinated	%	Unvaccinated	%
5,925	59	4,056	41

Death within 28 days of positive COVID-19 test by date of death between week 49 and week 52[4]			
Vaccinated	%	Unvaccinated	%
2,081	72[5]	809	28

This pattern whereby the vaccinated were being admitted to hospital and dying from Covid in significant numbers had been observed for some time – before, during and after Atkins' December broadcast.

Next up the broadcast presents various politicians who spread two related but baseless claims: 1 – Covid can only be contained via lockdowns and 2 – that to avoid locking down the answer is vaccination. Missing from this false dichotomy is any mention of successful public health strategies used by countries such as Taiwan who, thanks to its 'timely and vigorous response,' *The Lancet* observed, 'allowed [it] to avoid the national lockdown used by New Zealand.'[6] Also missing is any consideration of natural immunity, nutrition and lifestyle choices. Indeed, listening to this segment of Atkins' programme one could be forgiven for thinking that lockdowns are effective when it comes to preventing virus spread. They are not; the literature is extensive and unequivocal.[7]

Hence, the BBC is pushing a particularly egregious falsehood, one it must know to be wholly false: the choice is between lockdown or vaccination. Lockdowns being so reviled, the assumption is of course that the 'choice' will be vaccination.

The show goes on: all intelligent people agree that compulsory vaccinations are a good thing. But what about the other side – why do some people refuse to get vaccinated? BBC propaganda, as mentioned, relies heavily on the tactic of omission. Hence, not once in his broadcast does Atkins discuss the ethical implications of mandating a vaccine that has been linked to a range of adverse side effects including death. To do so would do irreparable harm to the BBC narrative. And there is absolutely no question about it, Covid vaccines *have* caused innumerable suffering to otherwise healthy individuals. BBC presenter Lisa Shaw is one of many individuals who died as a direct result of receiving a Covid vaccination. On top of which a growing body of evidence clearly demonstrates just how unethical mandating Covid vaccines would be: according to VAERS, as of 31 December 2021 there had been 21,382 US deaths linked to Covid vaccination.[8]

'Mandating vaccination is not a new idea'
Yet who could possibly object to mandatory vaccinations wonders Ros Atkins. Time to ask the public…

A young woman is worried that vaccine mandates could suppress freedom. 'This assessment,' responds Atkins, 'is not shared by the president of America, Joe Biden.' Juxtaposing an ordinary member of the public (wrong-thinker) with a plethora of authority figures such as presidents and hand-picked professors (right-thinkers) though risibly transparent, remains a favourite BBC tactic.[9] Well, who are *you* going to believe?

Next, Atkins tells his audience that mandating vaccines is not a new idea. In order to tackle smallpox, mandates were used widely in 19th century Europe. According to the Effectiviology website, *false equivalence* is: a 'logical fallacy that occurs when someone incorrectly asserts that two or more things are equivalent, simply because they share some characteristics, despite the fact that there are also notable differences between them.'[10] Smallpox is generally acknowledged to have a mortality rate in the region of 30%. For example, the outbreak which occurred in Iceland in 1707 is estimated to have killed just over one quarter of the island's 50,000 residents.[11] However, a fatality rate of 50-70% was estimated in the outbreak which ravaged News South Wales in 1789.[12] Clearly, smallpox is considerably more virulent than Covid 19.[13] Not only this, Covid 19 mortality rates increase with age. The frail and elderly are much more likely to die from Covid than younger cohorts. Atkins' comparison is thus rendered completely invalid.[14]

In yet another blatant example of cherry-picking, the broadcast goes on to quote a poll by German newspaper *Der Spiegel* in which 72% of respondents are in favour of mandatory vaccination.

This is the same publication which in 2018 confessed that one of its star reporters, Claas Relotius, had 'falsified his articles on a grand scale.'[15] Issues of integrity aside, Atkins' producers had simply searched for a poll that supported the programme's fervent support for compulsory vaccinations, a task that had taken them to Hamburg, to a pro-establishment newspaper with a history of publishing false stories.

Atkins' researchers could just as easily turned to a poll conducted by ITVs popular daily magazine programme *Good Morning Britain*, which had been conducted the week before *Ros Atkins on...*came to air. The poll, which was subsequently deleted on or around 7 December, and had at the time of its deletion over 42,000 votes, asked viewers:

With Omicron cases doubling every two days, is it time to make vaccines mandatory?
YES: 11 %
NO: 89 %

Instead, Atkins chose to highlight a similar online poll carried out on behalf of *Der Spiegel* by a company called Civey.[16] The poll consisted of a single question: 'should there be a general obligation to vaccinate against the corona virus in Germany?' To emphasise just how inexact polling is, one week after Atkins' broadcast a US poll by Convention of States Action and Trafalgar Group found 69% opposed to vaccine mandates.[17]

To finish this misleading piece of BBC propaganda, the host, attempting to imply that mandatory vaccination is a normal state of affairs, claims that, 'Many health care workers are told they have to get a flu vaccine.' This is not the case in the UK where, according to *The British Medical Journal*, 'The UK Department of Health recommends annual influenza vaccination for healthcare workers, but uptake remains low.'[18]

Before the programme ends, there is time for one final misleading statement. 'So yes,' confidently declares the host summing up, 'the number of unvaccinated people is a major factor in the threat this pandemic poses.' It's an assertion unsupported by data. If anything, the reverse seems to be true. For example, two weeks before Atkins took to air, *Newsweek* reported that Covid cases were 'surging' in the 5 most vaccinated states in the US: Vermont, Rhode Island, Maine, Connecticut and Massachusetts.[19] Analysis from Florida reveals a similar pattern. As of December 2021, 94% of Dade county's population was classed as vaccinated. Between 31 December and 6 January, it recorded 3,796 new cases of Covid per 100,000 of its population – by far the highest throughout the entire sunshine state.[20] Much the same pattern was observed in Scotland. 'Case rates have been lower in unvaccinated individuals,' reported The *Herald,* 'than the single, double, or even triple-jabbed since Omicron became the dominant variant in Scotland.'[21]

At the time of writing in June 2022, the latest Covid data has been made available. According to the UK Health Security Agency, in March 2022 a whopping 92% of deaths from Covid occurred in the vaccinated population – 82% amongst those who had received three doses.[22]

Omission through to false equivalence, cherry-picking data and platforming on-message contributors, in its almost 6 minutes running time Ros Atkins' analysis had used a variety of propaganda tactics to promote his employer's narrative and thereby mislead BBC consumers. Of the information not omitted, ignored or hidden, virtually everything seen and heard on *Ros Atkins on...Compulsory Covid Vaccinations* was either flat-out wrong or based on seriously flawed data and statistics.

Atkins and his producers had done their very best to fulfil their brief, but it had not been good enough. For this was a classic example of what happens to those who pursue narrative rather than truth, those working to a set brief. Atkins and his team had fallen headlong into a trap waiting to ensnare those ideologically (and financially) wedded to narrative: they had worn blinkers. But here's the real sting in the tail: such deception might ordinarily be expected to result in some kind of penalty: investigation, suspension, fine and even closure of organisation etc. That's what could happen to *some* institutions – those without protection.

Indeed, the broadcaster didn't even blink. Immune to sanction, censure or reflection, it merely set off on its next 'anti-vaxxer' narrative with renewed vigour.

SUMMARY

The BBC promoted the claim there was an ongoing pandemic amongst those not vaccinated against Covid. According to official data the opposite is true: infections and hospitalisations are significantly higher among the vaccinated.

'Wouldn't harm a fly: The Christian convert'

'Liverpool bomb: Suspect seemed a genuine Christian, says church worker:'

bbc.co.uk: 16 November 2021

One image in particularly accompanied the glut of BBC stories which began circulating on Remembrance Sunday 2021: a small group of people posing inside Liverpool's Anglican Cathedral, amongst them the bishop himself and an individual by the name of Emad Al Swealmeen. Reticent to the point of muted when it comes to divulging religious affiliation in certain circumstances, on this occasion the broadcaster wanted its audience to be in absolutely no doubt at all regards Al Swealmeen's faith. The Iraqi-born asylum seeker was a Christian, a recent convert to the religion. Television, radio, online - in virtually every item which followed the broadcaster never missed an opportunity to emphasise one aspect of Al Swealmeen: his Christianity.

So exactly who was Emad Al Swealmeen and moreover why was the state broadcaster taking such obvious pains to point out his supposed religion? Accounting for the BBC's uncharacteristic candour is simply a matter of relating what occurred in Liverpool on that Sunday, 14th of November.

Clocks about to strike 11am Al Swealmeen had seemingly blown himself up in a taxi which he had directed to the main entrance of The Liverpool Women's Hospital. Investigators were unsure if the hospital had been targeted or whether the intended target had been a nearby Remembrance Sunday ceremony. There was however one aspect they were sure about:

'Had it detonated in different circumstances we believe it

would have caused significant injury or death,' said police about a device packed with ball-bearings and which could thus have caused 'significant injury and death.'

The would-be suicide bomber's background soon became known. Posing as a Syrian, in 2014 Al Swealmeen had sought and been denied asylum in the UK. In 2015 he had undertaken the five-week Alpha 'crash course' on Christianity and was baptised at Liverpool's Anglican Cathedral, in the immediate aftermath of which the thirty-two-year-old renewed his application for asylum. Soon after that the cathedral 'lost touch' with its convert.

The bomber had clearly chosen the time to commit the atrocity with care. At 11am on Remembrance Sunday the whole of the United Kingdom falls into contemplative silence as it remembers those who died during war. It is a moment of national unity. Thus, as a way to express contempt towards Britain, its people and traditions there can be fewer more effective ways than shattering the peace and harmony of Poppy Day, a moment when old and young alike gather.

Its 2019 recital having attracted 10,000 people, Liverpool's Anglican Cathedral was once more expecting to host one of the largest events of its kind in the country. 'Military personnel, veterans and families of the fallen from recent conflicts,' announced the cathedral 'will join civic dignitaries from across the Liverpool City Region to gather inside the Cathedral for the service Sunday 14 November 2021.'[1] The service was due to start at 10.40 am. Clearly an attack at an event of such magnitude would have catastrophic consequences.

The significance of the day together with the bomber's background and modus operandi, question began to be asked upmost most of which was one question in particular: had Al Swealmeen's conversion been genuine? Rumours had long since circulated that failed asylum seekers were using the church as a means to circumvent the immigration system. An advice sheet produced by the Church of England titled 'Supporting Asylum Seekers – Guidance for Church of England Clergy' further fuelled suspicions. The 10-page document gives hints and tips to clergy as to how they can assist the asylum claims of religious converts. It includes advice about writing letters of support; it also offers advice such as ensuring church leaders and as many supporters as possible attend court appearances etc. Sections of the document include sub-headings such as: 'if a claim is refused, can we mount a personal campaign?' The following paragraph might have come straight out of Broadcasting House:

> Some journalists have suggested that asylum seekers are only claiming to have become Christians, in order to be baptised and use this to secure leave to remain in Europe. In responding to these claims, the antiimmigration rhetoric of a number of media outlets must be acknowledged. Their stories featuring asylum seekers and refugees are used to support a broader political narrative about British identity, rights and values, as was particularly evident in the run up to the EU referendum.

'Used to make cakes for the church'
Despite the plethora of evidence which pointed towards the true identity of the bomber and his motivations which circulated throughout Monday 15th November, the day after the incident, for its part the BBC continued to promote its 'Christian convert' narrative. After all, here was that most rare and precious of commodities: a Christian terrorist on UK soil. Sticking to its preferred narrative, the 'British' state broadcaster told its audience the story it wanted them to hear. 'Liverpool bomb: Suspect seemed a genuine Christian, says church worker,' so headlined one BBC article published on 16th November which related how, during his 'conversion,' the terrorist suspect had lodged with a Christian couple. In common with the corporate-establishment

media, the BBC quoted this sponsor extensively – easily surpassing their counterparts in terms of the space it allocated him. In a sub section of the article titled 'Wouldn't harm a fly'[2] the BBC allocated the sponsor plenty of room to wax lyrical about the wannabe suicide bomber who had spent 8 months under his roof:

> During that time we saw him really blossoming as regard to his Christian faith. Every night we used to pray, my wife and him...and studied the scriptures and we had a great time together.

> And I was in no doubt by the time that he left us at the end of that eight months, that he was a Christian.[3]

Another BBC article of 16 November also allocated generous coverage to the same sponsor, repeating the quote about his 'blossoming faith' and adding that 'He wanted to be a Christian. And he liked what he heard about salvation by faith.'[4]

Rather than raising the type of questions a true journalist might wish to investigate regarding Al Swealmeen's convenient and expeditious conversion, the BBC developed a tripartite mantra: 1) Al Swealmeen was a genuine Christian convert 2) He had previously been sectioned under the Mental Health Act and 3) Muslim people now faced hatred.

While the broadcaster stuck grimly to its narrative-driven guns, in the 24 hours since the incident real journalists had thankfully been researching not only Al Swealmeen but the church's somewhat dubious role in assisting asylum claims. 'Liverpool explosion: Bomber Emad Al Swealmeen tried to 'game the system' by claiming he was Christian,' so reported *The Times* on 16 November. A Home Office source told the paper that by converting to Christianity, the dead man had indeed 'gamed the system' – and moreover that it was a common tactic used by

Iranian and Iraqi asylum seekers. Home Secretary Priti Patel confirmed that Al Swealmeen had exploited what she called Britain's 'broken asylum system.'

Indeed, Tuesday 16th November saw a flood of information emerge regarding Al Swealmeen and bogus conversions. It soon became apparent that Liverpool's Anglican cathedral had been facilitating the religious conversions of suspiciously high numbers of asylum seekers. One asylum appeal, quoted widely in the non-liberal media, had observed that: 'The number of Iranians attending the cathedral was 'improbably large' for them all to be genuine converts.'[5] Also quoted widely was an assistant bishop of Liverpool who had no recollection of Al Swealmeen's conversion given it would have been 'one of hundreds' he had conducted.[6]

Not that these revelations unduly disturbed the BBC's set 'Christian convert' narrative. Once more highlighting the bomber's previous mental health issue, a BBC article of 17 November went on to inform its audience what a lay reader at Liverpool's Emmanuel Church had said about an individual it continued to refer to as 'Christian convert Al Swealmeen, 32.' According to this witness, the bomber 'used to make cakes for the church and sell them.'[7]

On the same day – 17 November – clearly spooked by the sheer quantity of actual journalism happening around it and in order to preserve its precious Christian terrorist narrative, the broadcaster went on the offensive. In an article titled 'Liverpool bomb: Church not aware of converts abusing system,' the BBC made a valiant but ultimately doomed attempt to cling onto a cherished narrative that was on the point of disintegration.[8] After informing readers that in Iran (Al-Swealmeen was Iraqi) Christians face 'intensive oppression' the article solicits the denials of the same Liverpool church officials likely complicit in assisting bogus asylum seekers attain their objectives.

Thus, BBC audiences would have been no doubt assured to

learn that according to the cathedral it had 'developed robust processes' to safeguard against bogus conversions. They would have been further assured to hear from its home affairs adviser who the broadcaster quotes as stating that baptism was taken 'extremely seriously' and never performed 'as a means to dodge the law.' And if all that was not enough to convince the BBC consumer of both Al Swealmeen and the church's sincerity, the article quotes a certain Benedict Ryan who pooh-poohs the suggestion that the church would collude with bogus asylum seekers, adding that there were 'many genuine Christian converts who sought asylum.'[9] Meanwhile, listeners to the BBC Radio 4 *Today* programme heard from Rev Sally Smith who claimed only a 'very, very small minority' of conversions were done to boost asylum claims. Smith also told the broadcaster there was 'no way' that she would assist asylum seekers whom she suspected were not genuine Christians.

As ever with a BBC narrative, the facts were not its friends; in fact, they were actually turning out to be pretty hostile. While Auntie repeated its tripartite mantra ensuring the omnipresence of the image of Al Swealmeen and the bishop, independent journalists – those pursuing facts rather than promoting a narrative – had started unearthing ever more interesting information about religious conversions and the motivations behind them. A former Dean of Liverpool, The Reverend Pete Wilcox, had made an observation back in 2016 which though omitted by the broadcaster from its raft of stories was widely reported elsewhere: 'I can't think of a single example,' had said Wilcox, 'of somebody who already had British citizenship converting here with us from Islam to Christianity.'[10]

The more information that emerged, the further from truth the broadcaster's 'Christian convert-terrorist' narrative became. It just went from bad to worse. For it soon emerged that investigators were working on the theory that Al Swealmeen had in fact *reverted back to Islam* in the months before the attack[11] – a course of action entirely commensurate with the known facts. Indeed, further enquiries by security services revealed that Al Swealmeen had been praying at his local mosque 'all day, every day' since April 2021, the period when he had started to construct his homemade device.[12] It was theorised that the attack had likely been an act of penance to atone for apostasy. 'Methodology wise,' confirmed a security analyst in an interview with *The Telegraph*, 'this attack is entirely jihadist.'[13] Thus, within 48 hours of the incident, there was little if any doubt remaining as to the identity and motivations of the would-be suicide bomber.

BBC credulity has already been remarked upon. Moreover, its naivety can be turned on and off like a light switch as and when required as was the case with the Liverpool suicide bomber. To appreciate the extent of its credulity consider for one moment the sheer quantity of dots the broadcaster failed to join up, so wedded to its Christian terrorist narrative had it become:

- Al Swealmeen was an Iraqi Muslim
- His claim for asylum had been rejected
- He then 'converted' to Christianity
- After his 'conversion' he promptly left the church
- Concerns raised about fake conversions from Islam
  to Christianity in (some) media
- He (prematurely) exploded a bomb close to a cathedral
- Act took place on British day of Remembrance
- Act took place at almost exactly 11am
- Plot bore hallmarks of jihadist terror attack

OK, so even the hapless inspector Clouseau might have picked up on this many clues, but apparently not BBC activists. Just consider for a moment the level of dishonesty required, when faced with all this information, to persist with a narrative stating that the suspect was in fact a 'Christian terrorist.' Why then would this publicly-funded organisation wish to mislead its dwindling audience in this way? Why would it take so many pains to invert reality? Clearly, its conduct is calculated. That image of the suspect and the bishop was used again and again in order to promote not truth, but the preferred narrative of the broadcaster and its ideological partners. It's only when placing BBC behaviour in a wider context its motivations can be appreciated; only when the BBC's role as a wealth and power proxy is acknowledged do actions such as these begin to make any kind of sense.

'We just loved him'

On 18th November the BBC produced a summary of the affair. 'What we know so far' is predictable for what it chooses to omit: There is no mention of Al Swealmeen's mosque attendance in the months leading up to the incident. Naturally, the ubiquitous Liverpool cathedral image of bishop and bomber rubbing shoulders, with its implication that the bomber was indeed a practising Christian, *is present*. A section entitled 'What is known about the bomber?' once more cites Al Swealmeen's sponsors. 'We just loved him,' they apparently told the broadcaster adding that the would-be suicide bomber was a 'lovely guy.'[14]

Weeks after a potential catastrophe had been averted the inquest into the incident became available. For the most part the report repeats what was already known about the botched attack. However, there was additional information which counter terrorism police had discovered when searching Al Swealmeen's rented flat and upon which coroner Andre Rebello commented:

> When premises were searched both a Holy Koran
> and prayer mat were present and it was fairly evident
> that he carried out the religious duties of someone who
> is a follower of Islam, notwithstanding the reported

conversion to Christianity.[15]

Despite its best efforts to imply the Liverpool bomber had been a genuine Christian convert and in the face of overwhelming contradictory evidence, publication of the inquest conclusions finally put to rest the BBC narrative. Or did it?

Having been bombarded with article after article in which the bomber's sponsors had told of Al Swealmeen's deep interest in the Christian faith and his devotion to bible study not to mention that oft produced Liverpool cathedral image which accompanied the majority of BBC stories, it's highly debatable whether the average BBC consumer would have been convinced by the conclusions of a mere inquest. And just to limit the impact they might have had, the coroner's remarks about Al Swealmeen's true faith were tucked away right at the very end of the broadcaster's own report into the inquest; no expansion, no comment, no headlines and absolutely no contrition whatsoever.[16]

Its 'Christian convert' narrative in bits, all of a sudden Emad Al Swealmeen's *actual* religion mattered not a jot to the 'British' Broadcasting Corporation.

SUMMARY

Despite overwhelming contrary evidence, the BBC consistently reported that the Liverpool bomber Emad Al-Swealmeen had been a genuine Christian convert. The bomber was in fact a follower of Islam and had almost certainly been intent on causing carnage outside the city's Anglican cathedral on Remembrance Sunday.

'Why people are using a horse drug'

'Ros Atkins on…why people are using a horse drug'
bbc.co.uk: 16 Sep. 2021

When in September 2021 US podcast host Joe Rogan announced via Instagram that, just three days after contracting Covid-19, he'd made a spectacular recovery from the infection, far from exhibiting intrigue or even relief the corporate-legacy media instead went ballistic. Rogan, they stormed, was promoting what it termed 'medical misinformation.' Yet all he had done was to simply describe the treatment protocol which had proved so efficacious for him, a reality that did not deter the corporate media; the attack on him only intensified. A BBC segment platformed a member of The Brooklyn Institute for Social Research who duly accused the podcaster of spreading 'harmful information.'[1] How then to explain this bizarre response? After all, if Rogan had indeed recovered from the illness, then a possible solution to the global 'pandemic' could be close at hand; thousands of lives could be saved in the same way. However, rather than journalistic curiosity the mainstream media chose to *attack* the podcaster. A campaign began to have the fifty-four-year-old thrown off Spotify, the platform which hosts his popular podcast.[2]

The reason for the witch-hunt soon became clear: Rogan had mentioned he had taken Ivermectin. That a cheap, off patent alternative to mass vaccination existed was not a narrative the pharmaceutical industry necessarily wished to hear.[3] Indeed, moves were already afoot to ensure that Ivermectin – like Hydroxychloroquine before it – would present absolutely no

140

impediment to mass vaccine rollout and the stupendous profits awaiting manufacturers such as Pfizer and Moderna.

Joe Rogan's testimony was thus the last thing Pharma needed. For it had come at a moment when the Federal Drug Agency (FDA) and its pharmaceutical partners were congratulating themselves on a campaign to demonise the very same drug which had potentially saved Rogan's life. Indeed, the Instagram message had come in the aftermath of an infamous tweet issued by the FDA[4] towards the end of August which read: 'You are not a horse. You are not a cow. Seriously, y'all. Stop it.'[5]

Horses? Cows? But what did it all mean?

According to a communique issued the previous day in a Mississippi poison control health alert 'at least' 70% of recent calls to its office had been related to ingestion of a livestock formulation of Ivermectin. As well as being used to treat parasitic infections in humans, as with several other prescription drugs a variety of Ivermectin exists to treat animals. Thus, it appeared that in order to treat Covid-19 some US citizens were taking the form of Ivermectin used in veterinary medicine, presumably due to difficulty obtaining the human variety.

Whatever the veracity of these claims a potentially huge spanner had been thrown into the works of the FDA and its Big Pharma partners. More and more evidence was accumulating with regards to the efficacy of Ivermectin in relation to treatment of mild to moderate Covid-19 infection – *in humans*.[6] 'Ivermectin has many big, powerful enemies,' observed Dr Bruce Boros, a retired cardiologist based in Key West, Florida and member of the non-profit Front Line Covid Critical Care Alliance (FLCCC).[7]

In response to this growing body of evidence and seemingly desperate to discredit Ivermectin, the FDA had appropriated the Mississippi alert. Enlisting the assistance of the entire corporate-legacy media, the agency had been then able to incorrectly label the drug a 'horse de-wormer.' Suddenly, the Noble prize-winning drug used to successfully treat diseases such as dengue fever, Zika, Ebola and eastern equine encephalitis *in humans*, overnight became associated with horses. By all accounts the FDA was delighted by this gross distortion of reality.

Rolling Stone magazine was just one of many 'liberal' publications which took up the FDA's dishonest ball and ran with it. An article on 3 September claimed that gunshot victims were being denied treatment at Oklahoma hospitals which had been overwhelmed by patients who had overdosed on 'horse de-wormer' i.e. Ivermectin.[8] The false claim was naturally amplified all over the legacy media. As for the BBC it headlined with: 'Don't take horse de-wormer for Covid, doctor pleads.'[9] It soon emerged however that the original alert had been incorrect. A correction issued by the Mississippi health department clarified that the 70% figure did not relate to all calls to poison control, but *only* to Ivermectin. In fact, there had been six calls in total relating to Ivermectin. And four of those calls had related to livestock issues.[10] Retractions and corrections swiftly followed. 'An earlier version of this article,' so read the 13 September edition of *The New York Times*, 'misstated the percentage of recent calls to the Mississippi poison control center related to ivermectin. It was 2 percent, not 70 percent.'[11]

Though its fake anti-Ivermectin hit-piece had been thoroughly debunked, the legacy media's ruse was, as anticipated, bearing fruit. The drug became increasingly difficult to obtain. 'It's not safe to dispense,' declared the Vermont board of Pharmacy that autumn.[12]

Meanwhile, stung by the dishonesty of the legacy media, Joe Rogan sought answers from his latest podcast guest, Dr Sanjay Gupta of CNN. In its similar role to the BBC – that of establishment gatekeeper – CNN had naturally led the assault on Rogan.[13] It was time for the network's medical consultant to answer some very awkward questions. Why asked the host of

Gupta had CNN insisted that he had taken a 'horse de-wormer?'

> They lied and said I was taking horse de-wormer. It was prescribed to me by a doctor...does it bother you that the network you work for out and out lied about me taking horse de-wormer?'

To which Gupta could only reply: 'They shouldn't have said that.'[14]

'Donald Trump retweets'
All of which brings us to BBC activist Ros Atkins. In a piece broadcast during the height of the assault on Rogan, Atkins presented a segment on the BBC news website titled: 'Why people are using a horse drug.' As ever, Atkins' broadcast is overflowing with claims which are highly misleading – not least the 'horse drug' headline as well as evidence which has, of course, been specifically selected to bolster whichever establishment narrative the BBC just so happens to be pushing. It comes as no surprise that his sources are *The New York Times*, *Washington Post* and, oddly, *The Chicago Sun Times* of which more later.

The same *New York Times* 'correction' re its reporting of the Mississippi health alert story having been published three days prior to Atkins' piece does not prevent the host from kicking off with a similarly sensational claim of his own: a '245% increase'[15] in poison cases between July and August 2021 in the US. 'These are people,' the host goes on to assert, 'who have taken Ivermectin and become ill.' Ivermectin, it ought to be noted, is considered an especially safe drug in terms of side effects. An exhaustive study into the drug's safety profile had found 'infrequent and usually mild to moderate side effects.' The report also concluded that it was noteworthy that 'no deaths have seemingly ever been reported after an accidental or suicidal overdose of ivermectin.'[16] If the 'poison' alluded to by Atkins is indeed Ivermectin – then it can only be the animal formulation of the drug and as with any drug in existence e.g. paracetamol - if taken in large enough quantities can become toxic. Further, when Atkins says 'ill' there is no way of knowing what exactly this means; mild or severe, the host isn't saying. Blurred vision has been reported in rare cases of excess ingestion of Ivermectin. The vast majority of viewers would just have to trust Atkins and the BBC that substantial numbers of people had been 'poisoned' by the Nobel-Prize winning medicine.

Amongst other things what the BBC was doing here was deliberately conflating the two formulations of ivermectin – animal and human in the hope that BBC audiences would start to equate 'poison' with *all forms* of Ivermectin.

The rest of the broadcast treads a familiar path. Doctors such as Pierre Kory who present results of Ivermectin efficacy have, according to Atkins, been interviewed by 'conservative news outlets...' In stark contrast, the broadcaster ensures medics who might contradict its strictly-controlled anti-Ivermectin narrative are never seen or heard on any BBC platform. According to the programme's host, Kory is one of several medical personnel 'promoting' Ivermectin despite their 'lack of credibility.' Dr Kory's extensive twenty-eight-page CV is available online.[17] Likewise, his colleague at FLCCC, Dr Paul Marik's *ninety-page* CV is also available to view at the organisation's website.[18]

And so it continues: a combination of ever more dubious claims promoted on behalf of pharmaceutical giants along with attempts to smear highly-qualified physicians daring to present evidence of Ivermectin efficacy. As ever with the broadcaster, its smears follow a set formula: link the target to an accepted wrong-thinker; play the man not the ball. Thus, along with the aforementioned 'conservative news outlets' Atkins also links doctors associated with Ivermectin advocacy to what he calls 'Donald Trump retweets.' Arguably the host's best adjacency smear is one provided by a headline from *The Chicago Sun Times,* a publication rarely, if ever, cited by the BBC: 'Angry QAnon backers demanding Ivermectin.' As will be seen in a forthcoming chapter, QAnon is one of the broadcaster's most valued go-to bogymen which just might help explain inclusion of the hitherto obscure *Chicago Sun Times* in this BBC broadcast.

Conservatives, Donald Trump supporters and QAnon 'backers' – the list of wrong-thinkers supporting Ivermectin tells its own story, well doesn't it? As misleading as the broadcast has been so far, its next claim manages to even top this.

'Turning to Ivermectin despite a lack of evidence'
The attack on a Nobel Prize winning medicine responsible for treating such debilitating conditions as river blindness has been and continues to be as unprecedented as it is relentless. To suggest there is a war against Ivermectin would be no exaggeration. Certainly, those parties lobbying against the drug are immensely powerful. That the 'British' Broadcasting Corporation is playing a vital role on behalf of those same interests is wholly commensurate with the thesis outlined at the start of this book.

But what about Atkins' assertion that there is no evidence to support the claims made by the likes of Dr Kory and many other physicians around the world who have also successfully used Ivermectin to treat Covid-19 patients? Evidence of the drug's efficacy chronicled throughout the world from Japan through to Peru, from India through to Mexico, in a programme full of baseless claims and slurs, this one takes some beating.

Ever since Ivermectin had been shown to inhibit SARS-COV-2 in vitro,[19] demonstrating powerful anti-viral properties, its efficacy to treat mild and moderate Covid-19 infection has been proven in study after study after study. It was duly observed that countries wherein the drug was routinely used as part of other therapies had significantly lower incidence rates of Covid than average e.g.

Africa where use of the drug is widespread to combat parasitic infections.[20]

'Why it works so well in COVID-19,' observed Dr Paul Marik 'is that Ivermectin has shown very high activity fighting both the SARS-CoV-2 virus as well as the inflammation produced in all stages of COVID-19. It works pre-and post-exposure, the early symptoms phase and late-stage disease.'[21] In the face of such overwhelming evidence the objective of the BBC along with the medical establishment has been nothing if not predictable: to discredit the studies and the personnel conducting them.[22] There have been a number of strands to the attack, encompassing but not limited to contributions from:

- Students running online 'news' websites e.g. Grftr
- Individuals with links to Big Pharma such as the UK's Chief Scientific Officer Patrick Vallance and Jonathan Van Tamm, its Deputy Chief Medical Officer.[23]
- Medics such as the WHO-appointed[24] and Gates-affiliated Dr Andrew Hill, who, after having confirmed Ivermectin's efficacy, went onto perform a mysterious U-turn.[25]

Corporate media 'health correspondents' and their colleagues had also set out to purposely discredit a safe and highly effective Covid-19 treatment. As noted, the emergence of an alternative to mass vaccination would ruin the £billions of profits anticipated - $32 billion apiece for Pfizer and Moderna in 2021 alone.[26]

At the time of writing, 81 Ivermectin studies have been logged (including 31 Random Controlled Trials) from 27 countries which have involved almost 130,000 patients.[27] The evidence is clear and unequivocal: used in mild to moderate cases of Covid-19 infection the drug has consistently demonstrated a high level of efficacy. What follows is a brief overview of the conclusions reached by a sample of researchers:[28]

Worldwide (Kory *et al,* 2021)
'Meta-analyses based on 18 randomized controlled treatment trials of ivermectin in COVID-19 have found large, statistically significant reductions in mortality, time to clinical recovery, and time to viral clearance.'

Dominican Republic (Morgenstern *et al,* 2021)
'In 28 days of follow-up, significant protection of ivermectin preventing the infection from SARS-CoV-2 was observed.'

Worldwide (Yagisawa *et al,* 2021)
'Results of 42 clinical trials, including approximately 15,000 patients have been subjected to a meta-analysis. 83% showed improvements with early treatment, 51% improved during late-stage treatment, and 89% prevention of onset rate noted. This confirms the usefulness of ivermectin.'

Brazil (Kerr *et al,* 2022)
'In this large PSM study, regular use of ivermectin as a prophylactic agent was associated with significantly reduced COVID-19 infection, hospitalization, and mortality rates.'

Mexico (Lima-Morales *et al,* 2021)
'The results of our study indicate that the combination of Ivermectin, Azithromycin, Montelukast, and Acetylsalicylic acid, significantly increases the likelihood of full recovery within 14 days after the onset of symptoms.'

Peru (Chamie-Quintero *et al,* 2021)
'These sharp major reductions in COVID-19 mortality following Ivermectin treatment thus occurred in each of Peru's states, with such especially sharp reductions in close time conjunction with Ivermectin treatments in each of the nine states of operation.'

Pakistan (Afsar *et al*, 2020)
'Ivermectin use is associated with reduced duration of febrile illness in COVID-19 in outpatient setting, thus potentially saving precious lives, reducing direct load on healthcare facilities and preventing high cost of management in a community setting.'

Egypt (Aref *et al*, 2021)
'Local use of ivermectin mucoadhesive nanosuspension nasal spray is safe and effective in treatment of patients with mild COVID-19 with rapid viral clearance and shortening the anosmia duration.'

Africa (Tanioka *et al*, 2021)
'In areas where ivermectin is distributed to and used by the entire population, it leads to a significant reduction in mortality.'

Argentina (Mayer *et al,* 2022)
'ICU admission was significantly lower in the ivermectin group compared to controls among participants.'

India (Azeez *et al*, 2021)
'Ivermectin has a significant clinical benefit as a preventive drug against COVID-19 for hospital personnel in settings with limited resources.'

'A drug that's for horses'
Having told his audience that (Ivermectin) 'isn't just about people making demands of doctors, or going to a pet shop to buy de-wormer…' the BBC broadcast ends with host Ros Atkins warning that a 'lack of trust in science is to blame for people seeking 'a drug that's for horses…'

Into 2022 and just how many deaths could have been prevented using Ivermectin shall never been known. As for the 'British'

Broadcasting Corporation it was business as usual. In January that year a report on the BBC website told how inmates in Arkansas prisons were taking legal action against the state because they had been prescribed 'the horse deworming drug Ivermectin to treat Covid-19.' According to the broadcaster:

> Anti-vaccine activists and conspiracy theorists have been promoting the drug as an alternative to vaccination.[29]

It is doubtful whether the likes of Dr Pierre Kory, Dr Paul Marik, Dr Bruce Boros, Dr Tess Lawrie and the countless thousands of medics who have conducted trials and successfully used the drug to prevent serious illness and death would use lazy slurs such as 'anti-vaccine activists' or 'conspiracy theorists' to describe themselves. Their business is saving lives. The business of the Big Pharma-allied, Bill and Melinda Gates Foundation-affiliated BBC on the other hand... that's for the reader to decide.

SUMMARY

The BBC reported that in order to treat Covid people were turning to Ivermectin, what it describes as a horse dewormer. It is in fact a versatile and exceptionally safe drug used to treat humans and which is on the WHO'S list of essential medicines. Trial after clinical trial indicates Ivermectin is a highly efficacious treatment for mild to moderate Covid infection.

'How false science created a Covid miracle drug'

BBC online article: 6 Oct. 2021

In October 2021 the BBC appointed what it termed its very first 'specialist health disinformation reporter.' Upon her appointment the activist declared that her role would help to fight against 'people who want to push an agenda, gain influence or *even make money…*'[1]

Since the start of the coronavirus 'pandemic' and with £billions of government funding available to combat it, the BBC activist was right to express concern about money. According to reports, Pfizer and Moderna were set to share $93 billion from Covid vaccine sales in 2022.[2] Big Pharma were not the only ones salivating. Enterprises of all kinds – some old and many brand new - were standing by just waiting to take advantage of the type of hysteria that could be so easily whipped up by unscrupulous actors with platforms enabling them to reach millions of unsuspecting people. With this in mind it might be worth digging a little deeper into the relationship between Bill Gates' interests and those of the 'British' state broadcaster. 'We've forged a close relationship with the BBC,' revealed Microsoft's Chief Scientific Officer Eric Horovitz when discussing Project Origin - a venture whose aim is to curate information and news as per establishment requirements.[3] Project Origin is part of the BBC-led 'Trusted News Initiative' whose members as well as Gates' Microsoft includes a who's who of globalist wealth and power proxies e.g. Facebook, Google, Reuters, Twitter, *The Wall Street Journal, The Financial Times* etc.[4]

Money, according to the song, makes the world go round. Just ask the 'British' Broadcasting Corporation. From its compulsory television licence fee along with various commercial interests, the broadcaster collects an estimated income of £5 billion per year. As staggering as this figure is, according to the BBC it's barely enough to cover its outgoings which include an eye-wateringly massive salary and pension scheme valued at £17.3 billion.[5] Every penny – *dollar* – counts. Especially welcome then must be the contributions to BBC finances from the Bill and Melinda Gates Foundation. Between 2015 and 2020 the foundation made three donations to the corporation totalling $3.5 million. But that was small fry compared to the $53,270,980 donated to BBC Media Action in the form of 15 separate grants.[6] 'BBC Media Action,' observes journalist Karen Harradine in a piece about the Gates' extensive funding of the corporate-legacy media, 'claims that it reaches more than 100 million people a year. That's a lot of people exposed to BBC propaganda on climate change, Covid-19, vaccines and Israel.'[7]

'Does this amount to buying access and influence?'
On the subject of donations, once upon a time the BBC had investigated the top 10 Conservative Party donors. Although not at liberty to directly accuse the party of accepting cash from those seeking favours, the broadcaster chose instead to imply as much when asking: 'Does this [i.e. making donations] amount to buying access, and influence?'[8] The biggest donation uncovered by the broadcaster had been one of £2.5 million from the manufacturer JCB. The air was heavy with implication; why would any business give so much money away if not with the expectation of some form of future pay-off? Why indeed.

As for BBC Media Action donor Bill Gates, amongst other investments the billionaire has multiple stakes in a range of entities involved in the manufacturer and promotion of vaccines; as well as holdings in Pfizer and BioNTech, he funds the vaccine alliance GAVI and, after the US government, is the second largest benefactor of the World Health Organisation, the body that has worked tirelessly to support the roll-out of Covid-19 vaccines. In an interview with CNBC recorded at Davos, the Microsoft founder revealed that he expected 'over a 20-1 return' from his investment into vaccine research and development. 'Decades ago,' he wrote 'these investments [vaccines] weren't sure bets, but today, they almost always pay off in a big way.'[9] In December 2019, Gates took to Twitter: 'What's next for our foundation?' he tweeted: 'I'm particularly excited about what the next year could mean for one of the best buys in global health: vaccines.'[10]

The timing of Gates' various pronouncements were nothing if not fortuitous.[11] Should such an event as, say, a global pandemic happen to occur, the wealth of the billionaire and his cohorts would increase to unimaginable levels.[12] When, on 11 March 2020, the Gates-funded WHO declared a 'global pandemic,' the Microsoft founder's excitement expressed just a few months earlier seemed entirely justified; for the solution to the 'pandemic' had already seemingly been agreed: mass vaccination. Mr Gates had backed a winner – a huge winner. There was just one potential fly in this staggeringly lucrative ointment. Section 564 of the Federal Food, Drug, and Cosmetic Act states that the Federal Drug Agency:

> may authorize unapproved medical products or unapproved uses of approved medical products to be used in an emergency to diagnose, treat, or prevent serious or life-threatening diseases or conditions caused by CBRN[13] threat agents when certain criteria are met, **including there are no adequate, approved, and available alternatives**.[14]

Clearly, as long as drugs such as Hydroxychloroquine and Ivermectin existed Covid vaccinations could never be granted the status of emergency use authorisation [EUA] required to enable mass rollout.

'I and other health experts'

On 12 April 2020 Mr Gates was 'interviewed' by BBC Breakfast News wherein the controversial broadcaster allocated him an extraordinary *seventeen minutes* of airtime.[15] Even more remarkable was the deferential manner of the BBC activist with whom he spoke who, rather than speaking truth to power, merely provided a series of cues which enabled Gates to expound his vaccine advocacy. Lavishing praise on a Ted Talk given by his guest in 2015 whereby Gates had uncannily predicted future pandemics, the BBC host observed that, 'They (presumably governments) didn't listen to you in 2015.' Gates shrugged. So flattering were the 'questions' the Microsoft founder could have written them himself.

When encouraged to talk about the importance of a global response to Covid, Gates readily agreed that it was 'critical':

> because the tools that are going to reduce deaths, the
> thing that will get us back to the world that we had before
> coronavirus is the vaccine and getting that out to all 7 billion
> people…

In response to another BBC cue, Gates appeared to imply he held medical qualifications when responding that 'I and other health experts were saying that this [coronavirus] is the greatest potential downfall the world faced.' And so the 'interview' went on. Here are just a sample of pertinent questions the BBC forgot to ask its billionaire donor:

- What medical qualifications do you hold?
- How much BioNTech stock did you purchase in Sept 2019?

- How much profit will you personally make from Covid vaccines?
- How are you able to predict 'pandemics' with such accuracy?
- Does holding stock in vaccine manufactures while being the second largest funder of WHO represent a conflict of interest?

These are the questions a *journalist* would have asked. However, as noted in the introduction to this book, BBC employees are NOT journalists; their job is to protect (global) wealth and power from scrutiny, which is precisely what the BBC activist did here. Not once during this extraordinary 17-minute promo did the BBC reveal that it had received substantial donations from the Gates Foundation.[16]

Whilst the broadcaster readily provides promoters of Covid vaccines with a massive platform, it is not so accommodating when it comes to alternatives to vaccination.[17] It was hardly surprising then when BBC 'Reality Check' launched its latest attack on one of the most efficacious of those alternatives - which brings us neatly enough to the BBC article: 'Ivermectin: How false science created a Covid 'miracle' drug.'

'The BBC can reveal'
A key strategy for those wishing to mislead the public is a practice known colloquially as cherry-picking. Given that it involves the selection of items which support an argument and the rejection of those items which do not and which may contradict it, cherry-picking is an especially deceptive practice. As such it has been used by propagandists throughout the ages. With that in mind it's back to the BBC claim of 'false science' – and what a claim. The corporation was about to go out on a limb, but why?

The answer was simple: the broadcaster was now looking for any opportunity to discredit Ivermectin. Here was a cheap, off-patent drug with the potential, lest we forget, to thwart the dreams of Gates, Pfizer, Fauci and others in one foul swoop, and by doing so deny them $billions.

In its quest the broadcaster had seized upon – prematurely as it would turn out – a paper which had appeared at the end of September in the online version of the journal *Nature Medicine*.[18] The paper's authors had seemingly been searching for faults with the growing number of studies reporting Ivermectin efficacy – all but a full-time task. One Egyptian study in particular had caught the group's attention. 'The BBC can reveal' so went an article which followed hard on the heels of the paper's publication, 'there are serious errors in a number of key studies that the drug's promoters rely on.'[19] *A number of key studies…* The BBC article was immediately noticed by Dr John Campbell host of a popular YouTube channel devoted to health matters.[20]

Suppressing the irritation he clearly feels to be presented with such amateur skulduggery, Dr Campbell highlights a whole raft of problems with the BBC article and the paper upon which it is based. Starting off by remarking that the 'BBC… used to be a really good organisation,' Campbell draws attention to the fact that the authors of the corporation's article appear to have no medical qualifications whatsoever. Indeed, the authors are what the broadcaster calls 'disinformation' reporters.[21] They have no medical training at all; nor do they appear to have experience of conducting medical research. It's an inauspicious start and it doesn't improve. Dr Campbell points out the 'paper' which the BBC activists have carefully selected to further its attack on Ivermectin is not an academic paper at all; it is in fact a *2-page letter* – 'basically an opinion piece' in Dr Campbell's immortal words. Indeed, its two pages present no data, results or analysis; nor is the piece peer-reviewed. It is, as Dr Campbell rightly points out, nothing more than an opinion piece with just a handful of references. Yet this is the 'evidence' upon which a couple of BBC 'disinformation' activists are purporting to debunk a hugely efficacious Covid-19 treatment. Risky, but backed up by massive wealth and power, any risk becomes negligible.

Dr Campbell next turns his attention to the opinion piece's authors and in particularly its lead author, a certain Jack M Lawrence, 'presumably,' observes an incredulous Campbell, 'a professor or senior academic… well, no actually, he's a student.' [long pause]. The BBC relying so heavily on an article whose lead author is a student, 'some may find surprising' notes the Dr with admirable understatement. In response to the broadcaster's attempts to aggrandise the credibility of this disparate student-led group of anti-Ivermectin activists, Campbell observes that: 'This international group of scientists is in fact a Twitter group.' The lead author of the opinion piece, Jack Lawrence, is indeed a student 'currently pursuing a master's degree in biomedical science' according to a bio on Grftr.news, a website he founded. The now seemingly defunct website devoted much energy to attacking a US political pundit called Tim Pool for holding, so it seems, conservative opinions on some matters.[22]

Regarding his much-vaunted (by the establishment media) 'paper' Lawrence was unsurprisingly promoted by the pro-vaccine, anti-Ivermectin *Guardian*, like the BBC a trusted proxy of international corporate-political power. While the student's 2-page opinion piece had not been subject to even minimal academic scrutiny, not least from the BBC, the work he was criticising *had been* – as Lawrence himself admits in his article:

Thousands of highly educated scientists, doctors, pharmacists, and at least four major medicines regulators missed a fraud[23] so apparent that it might as well have come with a flashing neon sign. That this all happened amid an ongoing global health crisis of epic proportions is all the more terrifying.[24]

What escaped established medical protocols, peer-review and the scrutiny of 'thousands of highly educated scientists' had not apparently escaped the eye of a precocious student. But what had these highly qualified and experienced professionals missed exactly? For as Dr Campbell rightly observes Lawrence's 2-page letter, notwithstanding the complete lack of evidence to support its opinions, is characterised most strikingly by its vagueness. Two of its meagre seven references cite a study by Elgazzar *et al* which had been included in a comprehensive meta-analysis of Ivermectin papers by Bryant *et al*[25] and appears to be the main peg upon which the student-led Twitter group was pinning much of its hopes.[26] What both the letter and BBC article fail to mention is that Lawrence's accusations of fraudulence are *emphatically denied* by the paper's lead author. So much for that - had not the BBC article spoken of fraud committed in a 'number of key studies?' Locating these important studies would prove nigh on impossible.

As remarked upon in a rebuttal letter written by a trio of medical researchers, the Elgazzar study was not withdrawn by the authors, but upon receipt of a complaint from the student-led Twitter group.[27] Professor Elgazzar subsequently confirmed he had not been offered a right to reply. Nonetheless, re-analysis excluding the Elgazzar paper from Bryant's original meta-analysis still showed a substantial reduction in mortality.[28] These results were confirmed by independent analysis which found Bryant's results were 'still strongly supported (91.2%) in the absence of Elgazzar 2020.' The authors further conclude that their analysis: 'based on the statistical study data, provides sufficient confidence that ivermectin is an effective treatment for COVID-19.'[29] So much for 'false science.'

Lawrence though was not the sole author of the opinion piece. He was part of what the BBC described a team of 'independent scientists.' One of the team was a certain Gideon Meyerowitz-Katz an epidemiologist aka as 'Health Nerd' on Twitter.

According to his bio on the same platform he is a 'well-known research trouble-maker.'[30] No doubt owing to his evangelical promotion of vaccines and equally strident attacks on Ivermectin, Meyerowitz-Katz's blog on Medium contains the following disclaimer: 'Because I know people will say silly things, I have never been paid by any pharmaceutical companies, hold no interests in drugs of any kind, and am funded entirely by the Australian state and federal governments.'

An anti-Ivermectin activist without compare, Meyerowitz-Katz has coincidentally become somewhat of a favourite BBC talking head.[31] Even less surprising is the conclusion to a paper concerning the pros and cons of lockdown on which Meyerowitz-Katz was lead author.[32] 'It appears clear' so went the paper's conclusion 'from evidence to date that government interventions, even more restrictive ones such as stay-at-home orders, are beneficial in some circumstances and unlikely to be causing harms more extreme than the pandemic itself.' However, the vast majority of research suggests lockdowns have caused immeasurable harm.[33] According to some commentators, lockdowns were purely used as a coercive measure to increase vaccine uptake, which may or may not explain Meyerowitz-Katz's erroneous conclusion.

'More than a third of 26 major trials'

Dr Campbell ends his BBC rebuttal mystified and not a little perplexed. In another exclusive BBC 'reveal' its article claims that, 'more than a third of 26 major trials of the drug for use on Covid have serious errors or signs of potential fraud.' The article goes on to claim that 'None of the rest show convincing evidence of ivermectin's effectiveness.' It also quotes Dr Kyle Sheldrick,[34] part of the Twitter group, whom it refers to as 'one of the groups investigating the studies' - an investigation which had 'not found a single clinical trial claiming to show that ivermectin prevented Covid deaths that did not contain "either obvious signs of fabrication or errors so critical they invalidate the study.'"

Presumably, Dr Sheldrick's extensive 26-study investigation would be pretty easy to locate; had it not after all blown apart the case for Ivermectin as per BBC reporting? So, in which academic journal would this dynamite study be found?[35] No trace of this landmark study is found at Sheldrick's own blog. In fact, it's not even mentioned... [36] Having himself searched in vain for the evidence which supports the BBC's bold assertion Dr Campbell concludes that it 'simply does not exist.'[37] Not only had he been unable to locate the vague studies referred to in the broadcaster's anti-Ivermectin hit-piece, he observes that in using the 2-page opinion piece the BBC is guilty of 'quoting unpublished evidence.'

And so the mystery of BBC 'Reality Check's' source material remains unsolved. The investigation which found not one out of 26 'major studies' supported Ivermectin use is strangely elusive, apocryphal, which might just explain the dearth of references in the BBC article.[38] Turns out the broadcaster's Ivermectin 'debunk' had in fact been cherry-picked – nothing weightier than a 2-page op-ed authored by a student and a favourite BBC anti-Ivermectin activist.

SUMMARY

The BBC claimed that an analysis of 26 Ivermectin studies had found no evidence of efficacy re Covid-19. Such a study does not exist. It also claimed that another analysis had reached a similar conclusion. The analysis in question turned out to be a 2-page op-ed written by a student. The existence of cheap and effective alternatives to treat Covid-19 would seriously effect mass vaccination and therefore pharmaceutical profits.

'Groups such as QAnon have campaigned against the statue carved by Gill'

'Man damages BBC headquarters statue with hammer'
bbc.co.uk:12 January 2022

At a little after 4.00 pm on the evening of 12 January 2022 a person was seen to scale the BBC's headquarters located at Portland Place, London. Armed with a hammer, the intrepid individual hoisted himself up above the building's main doors onto a plinth which housed a ten-foot sculpture known as 'Ariel and Prospero' and against which he began to hack. The sculpture, which features Prospero stood behind the naked boy Ariel, was the work of Eric Gill and had been commissioned by the BBC in 1933. A cause of controversy from its inception, the artist always claimed he had given the broadcaster exactly what it had wanted.

In an article entitled, 'Man damages BBC headquarters statue with hammer,' the broadcaster duly reported the incident. Having reported that the individual had shouted 'paedophilia' while he attempted to deface the statue, the broadcaster then made the following bizarre claim:

'In recent years, groups such as QAnon have campaigned against the statue carved by Gill, who died in 1940.'

QAnon?[1] Exactly why would the broadcaster mention this particular entity – a psy-op that operated throughout the majority of Donald Trump's tenure as US president and which promptly disappeared with Joe Biden's election victory of 2020? That's one question. There are more: has this loosely affiliated collection of largely US-based individuals really been 'campaigning' to have Gill's statue removed from Broadcasting House in London? And more yet: why highlight QAnon and not mention any of the actual campaign groups that have been petitioning to have the statue removed throughout the years? And most perplexing of all: why did the broadcaster plant QAnon in the heads of its audience in the first place?

To answer these questions necessitates a quick dive into the activities of that group of BBC activists called 'disinformation' reporters. Although QAnon had long since left the stage (The last Q drop occurred on Dec. 8, 2020) by the time of the incident at Portland Place and had always been at the very most a fringe movement,[2] the BBC 'disinformation' team maintains an impressive daily output of all things QAnon. Why should this be? The answer is fairly simple: QAnon has become establishment shorthand for 'crazy, conspiracy theorist.' Thus, organisations like the BBC can and do habitually attempt to link various protest groups and establishment sceptics/critics with QAnon e.g. anti-lockdown protests. In doing so the broadcaster is able to achieve several things at once: divert attention from the issue in hand and, having done so, focus it onto specially-created bogeymen such as QAnon. Instead of honing in on wrong-doing etc. public anger will be diverted onto a mythical threat.

'Oh I have many, many more. Tons.'

Recently BBC 'disinformation' reporters have been working non-stop in order to link those expressing legitimate concerns about the safety of Covid vaccinations to QAnon. Linking those concerned about Covid vaccines – a diverse and substantial number of people from around the world – with an (all-but defunct) group that was largely US-based and made up of what the broadcaster would term 'red-neck Trump supporters' has a single, transparent aim: to discredit critics and sceptics of vaccines and vaccine policy.

In order to manufacture links, the broadcaster utilises a number of tactics. Extrapolation – using a tiny sample to guess larger trends – can, in the wrong hands, be an especially deceptive tactic. It works like this: charged with advancing a narrative, the BBC activist will simply trawl Internet message boards such as 4chan until he/she locates a suitable outlier. Claims made by the outlier – the more fantastical the better – will then be amplified by the broadcaster and presented in such a way as to suggest these claims are representative of a wider group. For example, in September 2020 a BBC 'disinformation' reporter claimed that a female protesting against child trafficking and whom she immediately linked to QAnon, told her that 'Prince Charles ate babies in tunnels.'[3] The BBC consumer is subtly being encouraged to dismiss the anti-trafficking protest based on this carefully selected – likely fabricated – single, unverified anecdote: *these people are weirdos. Ignore them* – that's the BBC message.

Extrapolation is in fact a favourite BBC tactic. Following an anti-lockdown protest in April 2021 which had taken place on London's Oxford Street, noting how the broadcaster had characteristically used a single QAnon banner to illustrate its report, a social media user made the following perceptive comment:

> One banner represents the views of everyone protesting in London today - truly desperate, barrel-scraping smears from the BBC's 'disinformation unit.'

To which the head of BBC 'disinformation' replied somewhat testily and revealingly: 'Oh I have many, many more. Tons. Quit trying to smear our work - you'll fail.'[4]

In an article entitled, 'How Covid-19 myths are merging with the QAnon conspiracy theory,' the broadcaster's 'anti-disinformation unit' goes onto claim that: 'The merger between QAnon and Covid-19 conspiracies is also apparent in a number of emails received by the BBC.'[5] The article's sub-text is familiar enough: bad actors (i.e. the poor and disenfranchised) are conspiring against the rich and powerful. They must be stopped.[6]

In reality, significant numbers of people (parents, physicians etc) have expressed concerns about Covid vaccines of whom few, if any, have any affiliation with or indeed interest in QAnon. Intent on building its narrative however, the BBC focuses on the outlier or the quack – whosoever will enable it to invert reality on behalf of the powerful interests on whose behalf it operates, in this case the pharmaceutical industry and powerful pro-vaccine organisations such as GAVI and WEF.

All of which brings us back to the BBC claim that QAnon has been campaigning to remove Ariel and Prospero from its head-quarters. Let's start with Eric Gill, the object of ire for the man who took a hammer to the statue.

Mr Gill became notorious after his diaries revealed he had sexually abused two of his daughters, his sister and the family dog. However, long before the abuse revelations surfaced when the sculptor's diaries came to light in 1989, Gill's work had caused controversy. According to the *Daily Herald* his depiction of Ariel's 'organ' had caused young maidens to 'blush.' Indeed, local MP for St Pancras between 1931 and 1945, George Mitcheson, called the work 'objectionable to public morals and decency.'

It seems the overtly sexual nature of this and other works by Gill disturbed certain tastes. Groups such as Minister And Clergy Sexual Abuse Survivors (MACSAS) campaigned to have sculptures created by him such as Westminster Cathedral's 'Stations of the Cross' removed from the Catholic church. 'Survivors couldn't pray at the Stations of the Cross,' said campaigner Margaret Kennedy in 1998. 'They were done by a paedophile. The very hands that carved the stations were the hands that abused.'[7]

Following 2012 revelations concerning Jimmy Saville which unmasked the BBC presenter-cum-DJ as a prolific paedophile, focus returned once more to Gill's notorious 'Ariel and Prospero' statue adorning the entrance of Broadcasting House. Would the broadcaster consider removing the statue? Short answer, no. Meanwhile, in 2014 calls were made for Gill's statue of St Michael the Archangel to be removed from St Patrick's Catholic Church in Dumbarton. 'I find it detestable,' a local campaigner told *The Lennox Herald*, 'that art by such a man can be happily displayed publicly.'[8]

While the broadcaster remained obdurate as well as indifferent, momentum began to build. A series of petitions began to appear online at sites including Change.org and 38degrees. Petition titles indicated a shared goal: 'Remove statue by Eric Gill outside the BBC' and 'Remove Eric Gill Statue from BBC building' and 'Prospero and ariel sculpture removed from the BBC' and 'Remove a statue outside the BBC sculptured by a known paedophile Eric Gill' etc.

Revulsion towards public displays of Gill's work was also shared by groups campaigning against sexual abuse of children. The chief executive of The Survivors Trust, an organisation which supports survivors of childhood rape and sexual violence, had this to say about Ariel and Prospero: 'It's an insult to allow a work like this to remain in such a public place. It is almost mocking survivors, it is intolerable.'[9] These sentiments were echoed by Peter Saunders, the chief executive of the National Association for People Abused In Childhood. 'There's a strong argument that this statue should be removed, said Saunders. 'These symbols are in people's faces. The statue, he went on to add, 'was especially inappropriate in light of the recent Jimmy Savile scandal.'[10]

With such a controversial history attached to Ariel and Prospero, how peculiar that the BBC would attempt to associate a US fringe group QAnon with the long history of protest. All the available evidence suggests that sectors of the public have long since been offended by Gill's works and have been urging the

BBC to remove the statue for several decades, urgings it has steadfastly resisted. Even stranger, the BBC article fails to mention The National Association for People Abused In Childhood or The Survivors Trusts, organisations, as noted, that have actually called for the removal of the statue from BBC premises. It was however a ruse that appeared not to fool too many people. A contributor to a Mumsnet forum commented thus:

> I can't help feeling the fuss around QAnon has been very useful for these apologists and enablers, Feeling concerned about a potential safeguarding issue? What are you, some kind of QAnon crazy person?'[11]

So what about those (British) QAnon campaigns alleged in the BBC article? Search the Internet all day long and you will find not even the faintest trace of a group anywhere in the UK describing itself as or allying itself with QAnon. That's because such a group does not, nor ever has, existed. But the 'British' Broadcasting Corporation want such a group to exist so badly it has conjured one up from nowhere i.e. its very own British QAnon.

If no such group exists, it therefore follows that there is no 'campaign' whose objective is to force the BBC to remove Gill's infamous statue. Clearly, this BBC claim is 100% pure disinformation.

'British QAnon-adjacent 'save the children' followers'

Having unearthed this piece of blatant and highly troubling piece of BBC disinformation, the logical step is to submit a formal complaint to the broadcaster. Let's then observe the mechanisms which kick in when the broadcaster is caught red-handed spreading lies. This is the BBC stage 1 response (in its entirety) to our complaint (CAS-7060615-P3K4C7) which simply asked the broadcaster to provide verifiable evidence of the existence of the

(British) QAnon group and its 'campaign against' the statue:

> We've been conducting research online and since 2020 our
> journalists have been seen messages referencing the Gill statue
> in QAnon-themed groups, accounts and channels online.

Note the reference to 'QAnon-themed groups' and 'messages seen
referencing' the statue. There are innumerable online forums such
as Mumsnet where the Gill statue is 'referenced' on a regular
basis; these are not 'campaigns' nor would they claim to be. It's a
common occurrence down at Broadcasting House: in order to back
up an original falsehood, the BBC is obliged to invent ever more
implausible claims. A vicious circle.

Of course, at this juncture the corporation could simply have
opted to tell the truth. But that would have opened up a whole new
can of worms: why divert attention away from the substance of the
protest? That was an explanation to be avoided, one that would
have led into even deeper quagmires. Instead, the broadcaster is
compelled to tie itself up in even greater knots. It is worth quoting
the stage 2 response in full:

> Your original complaint said the article was misleading
> because you could not find any evidence of campaigning.
> Campaigning also refers to engaging in activism and it comes
> as no particular surprise that you couldn't find this evidence on
> Google because it concerns discussions on QAnon-themed
> groups, accounts and channels

> However, our anti-disinformation team point out that there
> were at least two specific protests organised by what they
> describe as British QAnon-adjacent 'save the children'
> followers in front of the Gill statue in 2020 demanding its
> removal. Our reporter Shayan Sardarizadeh points out that he

was present at one while doing research for this article:[12]

Hearsay and anecdote a-plenty, but not a shred of verifiable evidence to support the BBC claim. Next, we move on to the third and final stage of the BBC complaints procedure: the broadcaster's Executive Complaints Unit (ECU).[13] This is the second paragraph of its response:

> You objected to a statement that 'In recent years, groups such as QAnon have campaigned against the statue.' This was a reference to demonstrations by groups such as Freedom for the Children UK which have organised demonstrations against Gill's work, who they accuse of being a paedophile. This kind of accusation is a key feature of the Qanon conspiracy theory, which originated in the USA. Demonstrations in the UK against Gill have featured the hashtag #Saveourchildren and 'WWG1WGA' – a QAnon slogan meaning 'where we go one, we go all.'

Notice the immediate pivot to a group called Freedom for the Children (FFC). This is a group (in the loosest possible sense) that occasionally campaigns against paedophilia – especially amongst those who use their influence to evade justice. Freedom for Children then is not (British) QAnon. Nor has it ever claimed to be. But the ECU needs to manufacture a link and badly. The 'logic' used appears to go something like this: *FFC have organised demonstrations against Gill's work. They accuse the notorious paedophile of being a paedophile. Accusing paedophiles of being paedophiles is a 'key feature' of QAnon. Ergo FFC is QAnon...*[14]

British Broadcasting Corporation Broadcast Centre, BC2 B4, 201 Wood Lane, London, W12 7TP
Telephone: 020 8743 8000 Email: ecu@bbc.co.uk

Executive Complaints Unit

Mr ████ ████
Via email

Ref: CAS-7060615

9 March 2022

Dear Mr ████

"Man damages BBC headquarters statue with hammer", BBC News Online

Thank you for contacting the Executive Complaints Unit about an article about damage to the statue of Prospero by Eric Gill on the exterior of Broadcasting House. As you know, the BBC Complaints Team has informed you it does not intend to respond further to your complaint. It now falls to the Executive Complaints Unit to decide whether you were given a reasonable response to your original complaint and whether the BBC Complaints Team was correct in deciding that further investigation of your complaint wasn't justified. This is in line with the BBC Complaints Framework and Procedures[1] which sets out the process for handling complaints.

You objected to a statement that *"In recent years, groups such as QAnon have campaigned against the statue"*. This was a reference to demonstrations by groups such as Freedom for the Children UK which have organised demonstrations against Gill's work, who they accuse of being a paedophile. This kind of accusation is a key feature of the Qanon conspiracy theory, which originated in the USA. Demonstrations in the UK against Gill have featured the hashtag #Saveourchildren and "WWG1WGA" – a QAnon slogan meaning "where we go one, we go all".

Analysts on extremist groups regard this activity as an extension of the Qanon conspiracy theory into British life. The phenomenon is explored in more detail in another BBC article, "What's behind the rise of Qanon in the UK?", which was mentioned in the response you received from the Complaints team. As Qanon is a movement without boundaries, relying on social media connectivity, it is not misleading to style the protestors in the demonstrations against Gill, and whose slogans replicated

---

[1] http://www.bbc.co.uk/complaints/ and click on the link for BBC Complaints Framework (bottom right)

Qanon memes, as Qanon activists. Accordingly I do not think the statement, though it could have been phrased more specifically, was misleading.

In my view the decision by the Complaints Team was reasonable and appropriate in the circumstances and the decision not to engage in further correspondence with you was justified. There is no provision for further appeal against this decision within the BBC but it is open to you to approach the broadcasting regulator, Ofcom for its opinion. You can find details of how to contact Ofcom and the procedures it will apply at https://www.ofcom.org.uk/tv-radio-and-on-demand/how-to-report-a-complaint. Ofcom acknowledges all complaints received, but will not normally write back to individual complainants with the outcome of its considerations.

Yours sincerely

If making accusations against paedophiles automatically qualifies one for membership of QAnon, then the organisation is quite possibly much larger than even the BBC presumes.

The response then goes on to state that anti-Gill demos in the UK have featured certain hashtags – apart, that is, from all the many anti-Gill protests and campaigns that have *not featured* such hashtags. We know that the BBC scans any protest crowd for a flag or banner presenting WWG1WGA or QAnon and it was natural enough that the ECU would grasp at such an obvious straw, but as for #SaveOurChildren the hashtag occurs in various contexts including campaigns against abortion and the vaccinating of children. When a Bangkok child pornographer was caught through adverts on Twitter, #saveourchildren once again resurfaced.[15] That's because it is a generic hashtag widely used on social media; the ECU is implying it is somehow specific to the both the fictional British QAnon and the fringe US group with whom the broadcaster is attempting to link it. It is not.

That the supposed links have been manufactured by BBC 'disinformation' reporters and how they go about achieving this objective is naturally not considered by the ECU. So, here then is a step-by-step guide to how the broadcaster habitually attempts to frame anti-paedophile protests as QAnon:

Step 1 - BBC 'disinformation' activists attend a protest in order to locate an outlier who will enable it to discredit entire protest.

Step 2 - Select protester, ask: 'Have you heard of QAnon?' Continue until eliciting an affirmative. Next:

Step 3 - Politely ask leading question e.g. 'Would you agree that eating babies is evil?' etc.

Step 4 - Ensure a QAnon banner is photographed. If no QAnon banners can be found, head of BBC 'disinformation' has 'tons' which can be used *in loco*.

Step 5 - Anti-paedophile rally reported by BBC as 'QAnon protest' attended by 'conspiracy theorists' who say that 'eating babies is evil' etc.

A number of troubling questions arise in light of this behaviour, most concerningly: why should this publicly-funded institution expend so much time and energy attempting to discredit anti-paedophile protests? According to the National Society for the Prevention of Cruelty in Childhood, a child is sexually assaulted every *seven minutes* in the UK.[16] Shockingly, it is a phenomenon that appears to becoming more, not less widespread. Meanwhile, allegations of high-powered paedophile rings continue to surface.[17] All of which makes the broadcaster's (strenuous) efforts to portray anti-paedophile protests as 'QAnon' even harder to explain.

If ever there was an activity that justified round-the-clock exposure – hyping up even - then surely it is that which concerns the sexual abuse of children? *It really is about time you stopped exposing child sexual abuse and turned your artillery instead on those who expose this vile practice* - said nobody, ever. For what possible reason would the broadcaster have for trying to discredit anti-paedophile protests? And yet, the BBC takes pains to do just that. As ever, the question is: Cui bono?

'No provision for further appeal against this decision'
Imagine if you chanced upon a bar brawl one day. Imagine too if one of those involved happened to be wearing a Manchester United football shirt, or Scunthorpe United – it matters not. While an unethical operator - especially one operating an agenda – would no doubt take the opportunity to portray the incident as being caused by Man United or Scunthorpe 'soccer hooligans,' real journalists would reject such a simplistic smear. Ethical reporters would seek to find out the cause, to ascertain as a minimum how many, if any of the participants, share the subject's affiliation to the soccer club. Was this a brawl over football or did one of the brawlers just happen to be wearing a favourite shirt? Though essential in the establishment of truth, it's not the sort of question that would trouble a propagandist looking for a cheap hit.

'As Qanon is a movement without boundaries,' continues the judgement, 'relying on social media connectivity, it is not mis-leading to style the protestors in the demonstrations against Gill, and whose slogans replicated Qanon memes, as Qanon activists.' And with this neat piece of extrapolation so ends the response: 'There is no provision for further appeal against this decision within the BBC.'

Having exhausted the BBC complaints procedure, complain-ants can, if they so wish, head over to BBC-friendly regulator Ofcom. Just how friendly is Ofcom to the broadcaster? This friendly: during 2020-21 some 462,255 complaints were made against the BBC, no doubt coming in equal measures from 'both sides' and incontrovertible proof therefore that the broadcaster is 'getting it just about right.' Receipt of under 10,000 complaints per year – now that *would be* cause for concern. Of the 185 complaints which ended up at Ofcom, the regulator investigated a grand total of...zero.[18] Even though the 'British' Broadcasting Corporation had been unable to provide a single shred of verifiable evidence to support its assertion that (British) QAnon had been 'campaigning' to have Prospero and Ariel removed from Broadcasting House – Ofcom, the broadcaster's fellow wealth and power proxy, duly ignored the complaint.[19] Even when it loses, thanks to its powerful connections, in the end, the broadcaster is always sure to win out.

SUMMARY

The BBC claimed that a group called 'British QAnon' has been campaigning to have a statue removed from its London HQ. No such group of that name exists, nor any such campaign with that objective. However, plenty of anti-child sex abuse groups have asked the BBC to remove the statue, none of whom are or have been affiliated to QAnon. The broadcaster has always refused to remove a statue which survivors of child sexual abuse find so offensive.

'The director of a large NHS trust has contacted the BBC'

Various BBC news and online reports: 16-17 April 2020

The coronavirus outbreak of spring 2020 caught many countries unaware. Given the global scale of the crisis, hospitals the world over suddenly required extra gowns, goggles, masks and gloves etc. known collectively as Personal Protective Equipment (PPE) and used, as the name implies, to protect front-line staff from injury or infection. Such was the scale of the 'pandemic' it soon became apparent that demand far outstripped supply. With National Health Trusts crying out for equipment, accusing the government of incompetency would no doubt prove a temptation far too great for an anti-Boris Johnson organisation to resist. Predictably enough, the BBC churned out story after story attacking the government's response to the shortage.

Perhaps then it should have come as no surprise when, on 16 April 2020, yet another story of PPE shortages broke across the corporation's immense media platform. The story led the main BBC 10 o'clock bulletin. Titled 'NHS boss: I've hardly any gowns, can I call Burberry?'[1] it featured prominently on the BBC news website too where the opening paragraph read:

> The director of a large NHS trust has contacted the BBC asking for the phone numbers of Burberry and Barbour because he doesn't have enough gowns.

Keep that claim in mind: in his or her desperation, a very senior figure in the NHS had actually decided to contact the BBC in order to obtain some telephone numbers (yes, really).

From the outset something didn't quite ring true about this BBC scoop; would a senior NHS boss – anybody for that matter – really act in this way? Social media seemed to think not. 'If I need to find a telephone number,' remarked one account, 'I consult Google or 192.com, not the BBC. But hey, that's just me.' Indeed, the broadcaster's story, fresh out of the bag, was met by a good deal of online scepticism as well as copious amounts of mockery: 'NHS cutbacks worse than thought,' wryly observed another user, 'they can't even afford secretaries…'

Throughout its many renditions, the BBC stressed certain aspects of its story:

- An approach had been made to the BBC
- The approach had been made by an 'NHS trust boss'
- The trust in question was 'large' i.e. a major trust
- The trust was about to run short of PPE

On the morning of 17 April, BBC Radio 4's flagship *Today* programme had begun by placing the story right at the top of its schedule declaring that, 'The boss of an NHS trust has asked the BBC to put him in touch with a fashion company making protective gowns because he fears he is about to run out.' The BBC news machine was allocating maximum publicity to this story. As ludicrous as it sounded, the broadcaster was sticking with its claim that its high-powered contact had seemingly been incapable of finding a telephone number for him/herself. Instead, the person in question had turned to the BBC.

It didn't take long for this story of a desperate NHS boss's plea to spread into the public forum. Soon enough this shocking story of government incompetence was being shared all over the Internet. LBC radio presenter James O'Brien told his 650,000 Twitter followers that the NHS boss had shone a light on a 'shambles.'

'The BBC is not disclosing his name or the trust he runs'

A more detailed account was provided via the BBC's online version of the story. 'The BBC is not disclosing his name or the trust he runs,'[2] asserted the article pre-empting a question that would inevitably arise. Thus, the broadcaster knew both the individual's name *and name of his trust*. Extensively quoting its source, readers are informed the individual who had got in touch had a 'huge concern': his trust had less than 24 hours' supply of PPE! Referring to the mystery contact as an 'NHS Trust Director' though raised yet more red flags. As several commentators remarked, NHS Trust bosses are not called 'Directors.' Their official title is Chief Executive. Hardly out of its box, the BBC narrative was unravelling at a rate of knots. If Auntie was to be believed, an 'NHS Trust boss' while unable to locate the telephone number of Burberry *had* managed to locate details for the BBC whom he contacted in order to obtain a telephone number readily available via multiple resources.

'Here's how to decide whether a source should be trusted'

Who exactly were the BBC engaging with? A high-status professional who just so happened to be confirming BBC anti-government talking points - that's who. Serendipity, or something like it. For instance, in response to claims that there was in fact no shortage of PPE, the BBC's contact dismissed government denials as 'fantasy.'

In the midst of its attack, the article let slip an interesting piece of information which seemed to contradict the story the broadcaster had told thus far: the 'NHS Trust boss' and the BBC had apparently been engaged in sustained dialogue as evidenced in what it termed an exchange of 'messages[3] and phone calls.' But had not those dramatic BBC headlines implied the broadcaster had received an urgent call, out of the blue, that a 'desperate' NHS boss had called the corporation in order to obtain a telephone number, just hours to spare before disaster struck? Mission accomplished, presumably the desperate boss would have thanked the BBC before immediately calling Burberry and Barbour... O what tangled webs we weave, when we set out to deceive. Fabrication is a fraught business. As a minimum, basic elements of the fable need to be agreed upon. Clearly, there had been several interactions between broadcaster and contact. And if that aspect was true of a BBC story that was getting ever more specious the longer it went on, there had therefore been plenty of time for editors to check the veracity of their source, to confirm that he was who he claimed to be i.e. an 'NHS Trust boss' if indeed that's what he was claiming to be.[4]

Verification is an important part of a (real) journalist's work. In an article titled 'Think like a journalist: How to check a story' BBC Bitesize offer the following advice to aspiring journalists:

> Here's how to decide whether a source should be trusted: Who is telling this story, what do you know about them? They may have a reason for sharing or might have made mistakes.
> Journalists make sure they have at least two sources to verify a story.

Whatever the BBC was selling many of its consumers weren't buying. Social media incredulity together with lashings of mockery continued throughout Friday 17 April, the day of the scoop. In typical style Auntie dismissed complaints submitted through its online complaints portal with a brief press release:

> Earlier on Friday we reported that a boss of an NHS trust had contacted the BBC with concerns about the provision of gowns for staff during the coronavirus crisis.

However, in its attempt to pretend nothing was amiss, once again, a key aspect had been confirmed: the BBC had been approached by its contact, not vice versa. His reason for contacting the BBC is also confirmed:

> He had asked the BBC for the phone numbers of Burberry and Barbour - two companies which have become involved in making gowns - because he was concerned about supply shortages.
>
> We should clarify that the person concerned is not the boss of an NHS trust but is part of a network of organisations helping to source personal protective equipment for some NHS trusts.
>
> The mistake was caused by a misunderstanding of the person's role in the fight against the pandemic.[5]

Covering up lies is a risky business. While they may mask an immediate issue, take the heat off momentarily, lies are like sticking plasters - they can and do fall off. Notice how this reply – standard BBC fire-fighting - only helps increase suspicion: what possible 'mistake' could account for the BBC portraying their contact as the boss of a large NHS trust when in reality he was no such thing? No explanation is provided simply because there isn't one to give – at least not a *plausible* one. To have provided a rationale would have involved spinning an even greater yarn.[6] Wisely, the broadcaster chooses to avoid digging itself any deeper into the hole.

The problem for the BBC is that the truth would pitch them into even deeper trouble: *We made this story up to attack Boris Johnson and his Conservative government, to make them seem inept.* The truth really would have put the broadcaster in serious trouble. Double, triple down then - hope it all blows over. The bland BBC statement with its classic non-admission left many observers underwhelmed. 'They didn't just report this story,' remarked Baroness Hoey, 'they led their news bulletins on it all morning and now they slip out a short press release. They should apologise on air.' The former MP closed her statement with a hashtag: #happenstoooften.[7]

Also dissatisfied with the BBC's brisk dismissal, some complainants escalated the issue to the Executive Complaints Unit (ECU), a BBC department which, though it might appear to be charged with arbitration, in common with all entities that mark their own homework, is simply a mechanism convened to enable the broadcaster to have the last word.[8]

Unlike its colleagues in BBC Complaints, the ECU must be at least *seen* to take issues seriously. Above all else, in stark contrast to the entire corporation of which it is part, the ECU must provide a rationale for decisions taken. And therein lies an Achilles heel: for a broadcaster whose reporting promotes the narratives of the rich and powerful while actively suppressing information that might counter these narratives, the requirement to actually defend its output can only mean one thing: yet more artfulness, yet more truthiness.[9] Lies, tis said, oft' beget more lies.

'A slick and quick communicator'

Which brings us neatly to the actual ECU judgment – the final word on the issue – and much of which revolves around the actions of Simon Browning, the BBC Business reporter who broke the original story and whose Linkedin profile reads: 'I'm a slick and quick communicator who can build creative narratives when under huge pressure.'

Early on in its analysis, the ECU describes the mechanism by which business reporter and 'NHS Trust boss' allegedly came to be in contact: 'An organisation which promotes UK manufacture, which he [Browning] had dealt with often before, suggested he contacted the source in connection with a shortage of PPE in a particular area of the NHS.' Yet BBC headlines had clearly stated that it was an NHS boss *who had contacted it* – presumably because it made the story seem more urgent, more dramatic. In the ECU version of events, this key aspect of BBC reporting isn't true: the broadcaster it was who had contacted the source.[10] Oddly, the ECU does not make a point of commenting on or even acknowledging this contradiction – which is wholly commensurate of course with its objective: to get its colleagues out of jail.

And the absurdities just keep on coming: if a third-party had indeed suggested that Browning contact the source, presumably this 'organisation which promotes UK manufacturing' would have also surely mentioned the source's job role. Presumably, the BBC's slick and quick reporter would have then gone on to contact the source at his actual place of work – not at an NHS Trust - large or even small, but at his *actual place of work…* And if that is so, the BBC must have known right from the start this was no 'NHS trust boss.'[11] Which leads to yet another oddity: recall that BBC News stated it would not (in the name of journalism) be revealing the name of the source or *name of the Trust* he ran… The broadcaster had indeed known all along the name of the fictional NHS Trust their contact did not actually run. Tangled webs indeed.

And the ECU response to these glaring contradictions? Crickets. Nada. It's yet another problematical issue that not only remains unresolved in the ECU report, but not even remarked upon. The 'judgement' continues in much the same vein: it simply ignores every contradiction and illogicality, breezes past anything which unmasks the broadcaster's duplicity. In the ECU's defence, it is only doing its job – one which involves inventing rationales *retrospectively*. Tying itself up in knots is merely an occupational hazard.

It just gets better. Browning, the report admits, contacted the source 'a week before the story broke.' After initial contact, according to the arbitrator, Browning and his contact had 'several phone conversations.' In other words, the broadcaster did indeed have plenty of time to establish the identity of its source prior to 16-17 April when the dramatic headlines came pouring out of Broadcasting House – a whole week in fact. Given the BBC would go on to splash its scoop all over its vast platform, the requirement to confirm key aspects such as credibility of its *only* source was greater than ever.[12] Alas, no. Basic checks were not carried out. The broadcaster did not confirm any details with the 'large' NHS trust i.e. name of its 'Director,' or the current, desperate state of its PPE supplies etc. How remiss.

'Entirely natural in the circumstances'

It eventually emerged, *after* the story had broken, that the BBC contact was a certain Paul Durrands. At the time of his interactions with the broadcaster, Mr Durrands was (and still is) the Chief Operating Officer with a company called Oxford Academic Science Network (OASN) a role which apparently sometimes involved PPE procurement.[13] After reading about Burberry (and Barbour) manufacturing protective gowns via the BBC news website, according to the ECU's ever more bizarre version of events Durrands, desperate apparently to procure PPE himself – though not desperate enough to go straight to Burberry - would have, at some point, asked Browning for the contact details of the aforementioned manufacturers:

'So, although the source could undoubtedly have obtained information about contacting those companies elsewhere,' reads the ECU judgment, 'it was entirely natural in the circumstances that he should have asked the business reporter.'

Hence the ECU, like its colleagues in BBC news, is asking us to accept a rather incredible proposition: although it engaged in several exchanges with Durrands over a period of a week, Browning and the BBC business team did not once confirm his credentials. And, moreover, that during all of these interactions, hanging in the air like some implausible plotline from a theatrical farce, the erroneous assumption regarding the true nature of Mr Durrand's job role as a (large) NHS Trust Director – a job title of dubious provenance.[14] A careless comment, dropped name, if Durrands had mentioned the merest snippet concerning his *actual work* at OASN during his many interactions with the broadcaster, the BBC scoop would have been killed stone dead...

By now the ECU is having to strain credulity to its limits. Note how the story has radically changed: from a desperate 'NHS trust boss' urgently calling the BBC (via switchboard?[15]) to obtain readily available telephone numbers, the story has transformed into something entirely different: now it is *the BBC contacting the source* - who was not, it transpires, an NHS trust boss - and who had, for reasons unclear, decided to ask a BBC business reporter for the numbers of Burberry and Barbour during one of several conversations with him. Even so, the ECU fails to explain why a BBC reporter would have these telephone numbers so readily available – assuming the numbers were not committed to memory, it can only be assumed Browning would have had to access the information via smart phone or laptop... an act of research apparently beyond that of his source – a presumed high powered NHS executive. Thus, the original BBC story telling of an urgent telephone call has transformed into something entirely different – the source apparently asking (not 'contacting') Browning for the numbers during one of several chats.

In some ways the question of precisely how contact details were obtained is immaterial, a diversion the ECU is more than happy to pursue. The point is that breathless BBC report after report implied that an important figure in the NHS had got in touch with the BBC specifically to obtain Burberry's (and Barbour's) contact information – an action which showed just how desperate the PPE shortage had become and the inadequacy of the

Johnson-led government. The original BBC story had thus been false on just about every level – pure disinformation. Hence the ECU steers its report into what must have appeared safer waters.

Picking its way carefully through a misinformation minefield of its colleagues' making, the report next attempts to explain what went wrong; just how had this farcical case of mistaken identity arisen? The piece de la resistance! It's certainly worth the wait:

Browning, it transpires, had apparently been told (presumably by the third party) that Durrands 'oversees an NHS trust' and had also heard the source himself refer to 'my trust.'[16] There was however one important phrase Browning *had not heard* his contact utter during all their conversations and that was: ''Oxford Academic Science Network' – his actual company and where he holds a senior position... And there the ECU seems content to leave the matter. As might be expected of a senior executive, Mr Durrands is readily searchable on the Internet e.g. via his Linkedin profile, upon which is clearly displayed his role at OASN.[17]

There was also the question of BBC claims that their source ran not just any old trust, but a 'large' trust - information it could not have ascertained from Durrands who did not work for a trust, small or large. Given that Durrands had somehow managed to avoid discussing his actual job role, how then did the BBC discover this information?[18] It's yet another road down which ECU does not wish to travel: a cynic might surmise that 'large trust' sounds more impressive than 'small trust' and therefore makes the story of PPE shortages that much more dramatic and urgent. It also makes the government appear much more negligent.

Piecing together the evidence we can, with a high degree of certainty, posit a version of what actually happened in the week leading up to those incessant BBC headlines of 16-17 April 2020 asserting the corporation had been contacted by an 'NHS Trust boss': In order to attack the Boris Johnson government over PPE shortages, the BBC contacted an individual from a private procurement company whom it assumed would be able to provide ammunition to further that quest. To increase the impact of its story the broadcaster attributed an important role to its contact – that of 'NHS Trust boss' and 'Director.' Didn't the individual have experience of sourcing PPE? And anyway, 'private procurement company' does not invoke anywhere near the level of sympathy conjured up by 'NHS.' While the motives of a private company might be suspect, who could doubt the probity of the National Health Service?

The BBC never had been contacted by an 'NHS Trust boss.' It was pure misinformation calculated to pile even more pressure on a beleaguered Tory administration and maybe, just maybe result in the corporation getting the scalp of Boris Johnson. And so, as predicted, in running cover for BBC Business, instead of pursuing truth, the broadcaster's arbitration department merely weaved some extra layers of deceit into a typically tangled BBC web.

That the founding member of the 'Trusted News Initiative' had consistently told falsehood after falsehood, initially in order to unseat a democratically-elected Prime Minister, then to cover up those lies, is shocking enough. But arguably more shocking is the response of Boris Johnson and his 'Conservatives' to this persistent and cynical dishonesty. There wasn't one.[19]

SUMMARY

The BBC claimed it had been contacted by a senior NHS boss desperate to locate business telephone numbers. In fact, it was the broadcaster who had contacted a private company in order to enable it to criticise the government response to PPE shortage - a tactic it hoped would pile pressure on the Boris Johnson-led administration.

'We can just refer her [sic] to our line again'

Internal BBC e-mail: 25 May 2021

We have already encountered activists in the mould of Ros Atkins, Justin Rowlatt and Daniel Sandford within the pages of this book. All three have a great deal to say about issues of the day – Trump, Brexit, Covid etc. Nor do they pull any punches. Indeed, as with fellow BBC colleagues the trio hardly bother to hide their own opinions; with good reason - they don't need to. For despite reporting that is always strident, always partial and conceived to mislead, a very sobering fact remains: none of this trio of activists will ever face more than superficial scrutiny regarding the veracity of the information they present via their respective BBC platforms – a withering social media comment at the very worst, a vague idea that 'right-wingers' are not impressed.

Being effectively unaccountable means activists are therefore free to spread counter factual information about rising climate-related 'death tolls,' 'Brexit hate crimes,' 'pandemics of the unvaccinated' or 'horse de-wormers' etc. In one of his mono-logues Atkins even declared that 'Neo-Nazis are not the threat Putin describes.'[1] Seriously. Replete with similarly dubious assertions as well as omissions and 'errors' galore, it is just as well that the broadcaster's output is never properly scrutinised.[2] And so, safe in the knowledge they are insulated from scrutiny, Atkins, Sandford, Rowlatt and colleagues can therefore make whatever wild assertions they choose – with just one proviso: claims must promote the correct narrative. Power without accountability then, a truly alarming predicament.

Before taking some examples of BBC practice, it is worth assessing the means by which the broadcaster engineers this state of affairs. So just how does the BBC manage to avoid having to justify its output? The answer involves two strands. First and foremost, as remarked upon throughout this book the corporation is a vitally important asset of what has been described as a system of global power - more than enough to assure total immunity.[3] For the less curious citizen it boils down to a much simpler equation: reputation.

At least a proportion of the British public assumes its national broadcaster is somehow straight, above board. It's just the way things are and always have been, an assumption that appears to be self-evident – what 'everybody' thinks. How then does such an erroneous notion become so ingrained? Easily. For the wily broadcaster utilises various safeguards that enable it to circumvent meaningful scrutiny i.e. Samira Ahmed's online feedback programme BBC Newswatch, BBC Complaints, the Executive Complaints Unit (ECU) and, when all these cards have been played, the broadcaster knows it can rely on its very good friends at Ofcom to ensure the matter goes no further. The objective of these partisan agencies viz BBC output is one and the same: to give the illusion of oversight, to reassure the public that the broadcaster is adhering to certain standards, that its news reports, documentaries etc. are the result of rigorous procedure. if an organisation can present itself as beyond reproach, why should its word not be taken on trust? *We are independent, impartial and honest* etc. Given enough reverence, a situation could arise whereby criticism, far from welcomed, is actually considered a serious breach of etiquette, simply not done - at least not by those who stand within the golden circle of influence: politicians, civil servants, celebrities etc. Thus, a mythology is born.

Safeguards then are vital to how the BBC rolls. Without them the broadcaster would be cruelly exposed. Never explain, never apologise, imagine Ros Atkins having to justify why he conflated smallpox and Covid-19 compulsory vaccination mandates, or Justin Rowlatt compelled to explain why official statistics regarding decreased climate-related deaths are 'slippery.' Nothing to gain and everything to lose embarrassment could only result if BBC personnel were obliged to explain their proclamations. That's where BBC Complaints and the ECU come in: to stymie. Using deflection, obfuscation, protraction and various other tactics, the vast majority of the 500,000 complaints the BBC receives annually are snuffed out long before they ever reach Ofcom or the attention of the activist in question, their stings expertly removed. Cocooned between the ivory towers of Broadcasting House and blue-tick Twitter the average BBC activist may likely never experience even mild pushback, never get called out – at least not to the face. Even if it did happen, pushback would hardly emanate from within the golden circle, rather from those outside it – 'trolls' or 'Russian bots' or both.

However, in order to head off criticism as well as comply with self-evaluation culture the broadcaster occasionally offers a few scraps of what resembles contrition, but is nothing of the sort: *Yes, we do make occasional errors but they're minor, Hey, we're only human!*[4] Herein lies a crucial part of the broadcaster's ploy: make (small) admissions, make them seldomly and quietly:

North West Tonight: BBC One, 20 July 2022
We reported on councillors in Liverpool voting on whether to scrap the position of elected mayor in the city. By mistake we showed pictures of the former Lord Mayor instead of the elected mayor. We are sorry for this error.

For every trifle such as this one published, many more serious complaints are headed off, forestalled. The illusion of robust oversight is however established.

'The BBC... has no view or position itself on anything we may report upon'

The above statement is a favourite BBC stock phrase with which those who complain about bias, accuracy etc, will be invariably met. If any statement could ever be described as a textbook example of Goebbels's Big Lie this would surely be a strong favourite. Despite the obvious absurdity of such a claim, BBC fire-fighters recycle it with impunity. Corporation activists will even claim to have no opinion whatsoever about former US president Donald Trump – a figure reviled by just about every single one of the BBC's 20,000 + political activists. Nor is this an unusual phenomenon. *Psychology Today* reports that the 'mental distress' which is felt when being untruthful is only transitory, doesn't last long.[5] Thus, the BBC activist can happily mock, deride and lie about the ex-president one minute and the next minute - without even the merest of qualms - claim to have no opinion on the same individual.

The stock phrase cited at the start of this section was duly presented by the broadcaster in response to a complaint made by a viewer following an edition of BBC Newsnight broadcast 3 June 2019.[6] During an interview with Liz Harrington, a spokeswoman for Donald Trump, presenter Emily Maitlis made a claim about the then president: 'He's not liked at all here [i.e. in the UK].' The complainant pointed out that at the time Mr Trump actually had a 21% approval rating in the UK. Therefore, the BBC claim was factually incorrect. That's as maybe, but the reality that the president enjoyed a fair amount of support in the UK and beyond contradicted a key BBC (and of course globalist) narrative, and into which the broadcaster had invested considerable effort in establishing: Trump was loathed all over the world.

Audacious and deceitful in equal parts, the BBC response, when it came, should have surprised no-one. Its Complaints faculty merely replied that in her misleading comment Maitlis had been 'reflecting the mood of certain politicians such as Sadiq Khan and Jeremy Corbyn.' Only the presenter had made no such acknowledgement. At no point had Maitlis said she was reflecting the opinions of two Labour politicians - one of whom had a history of needle with the US president. To the complainant's assertion that the presenter's comment had been motivated purely by political bias and institutional malice towards Trump, BBC Complaints replied that: 'The BBC as an organisation has no view or position itself on anything we may report upon...'

Eventually the complaint reached the ECU. How would the broadcaster worm its way out this one? 'You consider that the presenter's comment about the president's popularity was misleading,' declared the BBC arbitration service, 'but the evidence of opinion polling would tend to support what was said.' The judgement continues; 'A YouGov poll published this year found that only 21% of respondents had a positive opinion of the President with 67% holding a negative opinion.' Which is precisely what the complainant had *already pointed out*...

Thus, 33% of those polled had either a positive or neutral opinion of the US President. In other words, over 21 million people in the UK either potentially supported Trump or did not have a strong view either way. Clearly, Maitlis had misled the audience of Newsnight. Her statement that Trump was 'not liked at all' in the UK had been demonstrably false, but far from acknowledging as much BBC Complaints had stonewalled the complainant at every juncture. As expected, the ECU had gone on to put the finishing touches to an archetypal piece of BBC deception, inverting reality, laughing in the face of those forced to fund its activities i.e. the British public. And so, yet another issue had been 'resolved' by the mechanisms devised and operated by the same organisation under fire: happily, once again the broadcaster had found itself not guilty... It happens day in, day out.

'Do you wish us to just ignore?'

Under the surface of BBC behaviour such as that just described lurks an unmistakable undercurrent: contempt; not only contempt for truth and integrity, but contempt towards ordinary tax-payers manifest so clearly in the complaint just remarked upon. After all, to swear that night is day and vice versa while claiming to be 'honest' requires ample amounts of arrogance but arguably even greater levels of scorn. What such behaviour does *not* require is respect. The following case of questionable BBC practice begins back in 1986. Not only does it illustrate how the broadcaster attempts to avoid scrutiny, it also reveals Auntie's attitude towards the general public – in this case a bereaved mother, and a little while later, a real journalist attempting to establish truth.

Late on an October afternoon in 1986 two nine-year old Brighton schoolgirls, Nicola Fellows (10) and Karen Hadaway (9), seemingly vanished into thin air. Earlier in the day the friends had been spotted playing in and around the vicinity of Wild Park - an area located to the north of the town and which the girls' parents had declared to be off limits. That same evening the youngsters had still not returned home. The missing girls' mothers joined fellow residents from the estate in Moulsecoomb where the girls lived, searching the local parks well into the night. Their bodies were discovered the following day hidden away in park undergrowth; they had been sexually assaulted and strangled. A local man was acquitted of the murders in 1987, but found guilty following a retrial in 2018.

Five years after the murders a BBC reporter called Martin Bashir claimed to be in the process of researching the case for Public Eye, a BBC documentary series. Promising Mrs Hadaway items would be tested for DNA, the reporter managed to requisition the outfit her dead daughter had been wearing that dreadful day - school sweatshirt, T-shirt and underwear. However, the clothing would never be returned. Karen Hadaway's clothes disappeared and along with them potentially vital evidence. Nor would the BBC produce a documentary about what had become known as the 'Babes in the Woods' murders. What had become of the clothing? Mrs Hadaway petitioned the BBC but without success. Met by indifference and obfuscation the distraught mother described the corporation's response to her requests for clarification as 'shameful.'

Not until 2004 would the BBC finally address Mrs Hadaway's concerns. This change of heart was not due to the distress caused to the murdered girl's mother by BBC stonewalling over the years, but rather because police had recently launched Operation Salop, a cold case review of the Babes in the Woods murders. Russell Bishop, the chief suspect was up for parole. Subsequent to the 1986 murders Bishop had served a prison term for the attempted murder of another young girl and detectives were anxious that he should not be released. Advances in forensic testing could yield new clues.

Having dismissed Mrs Hadaway's requests for several years, but with a police reinvestigation imminent, the broadcaster at last took action: it supposedly launched an internal review, to little effect. According to an investigation undertaken by *The Mail on Sunday* neither the dead girl's relatives nor members of the Public Eye documentary team were approached by the broadcaster. 'The acting director-general of the BBC at the time Mark Byford,' went the article, 'has also admitted no 'formal investigation' was held into the missing clothes.'[7] Martin Bashir and colleagues from Public Eye concurred: all denied having been contacted during the broadcaster's 2004 review. Dorothy Byrne, a former Channel 4 executive, said the BBC's failure to launch a major inquiry 'exposes utter contempt for a grieving mother and the police.'[8]

For its part, the BBC begged to differ. According to its version of events a full investigation *was* launched in 2004. Claims to the opposite effect were 'incorrect.'[9] Meanwhile, police frustration grew. So too did that of the dead girl's family. How could the BBC possibly have 'lost' such a crucial cache of evidence? And why was it taking so long to make an admission?

It was not until 2021 that the broadcaster owned up. Following another hunt for the missing clothing BBC Director General Tim Davie finally apologised to the grieving Mrs Hadaway and instructed Martin Bashir to do likewise, which he did via a short handwritten letter. The loss of Nicola's clothing was, wrote the reporter, 'a matter of deep regret.' Mrs Hadaway was however left distinctly unimpressed. The BBC had consistently ignored her requests and had it not been for external pressure may have continued to do so indefinitely. Too little too late, Mrs Hadaway was disgusted with the way Bashir had not only failed to fulfil promises, but also at his and his employer's subsequent amnesia regarding the whole affair; in short, the BBC had, as ever, sought to grind the process to a halt in the hope that the bereaved parent would, like many complainants before and since, become disillusioned, go away; the broadcaster had eventually done the right thing, but only under duress. It had taken 35 years to arrive at this point.

As unedifying as BBC behaviour had been, there was more to come in the shape of a rather revealing coda to the affair. Mrs Hadaway's local newspaper, *The Brighton Argus*, had naturally enough been involved with the case from the start, breaking the story in its evening edition of Friday, 10 October 1986, under the poignant headline: 'Little playmates vanish in the fog.' The paper had duly reported on updates including an interview Mrs Hadaway conducted for BBC *Women's Hour* in Spring 2021 in which she called for an investigation into the behaviour of Mr Bashir and which would eventually lead to Tim Davie's official apology.

In the immediate aftermath of Mrs Hadaway's interview a reporter with the Argus contacted the BBC. Would there now be an investigation into Mr Bashir and events precipitating the lost clothing? It would appear that the reporter, Jody Doherty-Cove, was met with something less than candour for he was obliged to resend his request to the BBC Press Office. The reporter's surprise can be imagined when, just minutes after sending his request to the broadcaster, he received the following response:

> It's the journalist from the Argus again. We can just refer her to our line again or do you want us to just ignore?[10]

Oops! Rarely do BBC machinations reveal themselves, but the mask does occasionally slip and when it does…

Mr Doherty-Cove had been mistakenly copied into this internal BBC email. Nor was this just an everyday case of misgendering, a serious enough matter itself – at least within the corridors of Broadcasting House. This was in fact a rare glimpse into the behaviour of *the real* BBC. As such here was a sobering reminder of the huge gulf that exists between the carefully curated image of probity/sobriety and the reality of actual BBC culture: deceit, cynicism, contempt etc.[11] For here was an organisation once again preparing to dismiss Mrs Hadaway's enquiry in the same way it does to the hundreds of thousands who complain about its ethics every year. The contempt is all too apparent: *shall we feed her a stock phrase* ('our line') *or shall we just ignore her* (in the shape of Doherty-Cove's approach) *as per the last 35 years*? But there is of course a third option not considered by the BBC Press Office: treat the bereaved mother with respect, be honest…

Mr Doherty-Cohen was also less than impressed by BBC antics: 'It's astonishing,' he wrote on social media, 'the BBC feels it can ignore important questions from the local press about how and where a murdered schoolgirl's clothing was lost by Martin Bashir.'[12]

'Lessons must be learnt'

What made this behaviour even more shocking was the fact that the day before the BBC Press Office had sent out its email, the media had reported the outcome of the Dyson enquiry which had investigated Bashir's infamous 1995 BBC *Panorama* interview with Princess Diana. At a time in her life when she had been especially vulnerable, the ambitious reporter had tricked the princess into taking part in an interview in which she poured out her heart – a dialogue which many believed precipitated a chain of events which ultimately led to her death.[13] In his 127-page report Lord Dyson had excoriated the BBC. One of the report's most shocking findings related to BBC culture. Dyson observed that the corporation had neither sanctioned or reprimanded Mr Bashir but had covered up the 'deceitful behaviour' used by its reporter to secure the sensational interview. Amongst other things Bashir had faked bank statements in order to gain the trust of Earl Spencer; he had also intimated to Diana that the royal family were 'out to get her' – whatever had been necessary to persuade the princess to grant the interview.

The subsequent BBC cover-up had gone right to the very top of the organisation. Then Director General Tony Hall, the individual who had been a driver behind the so-called Trusted News Initiative, had played a leading role in the cover-up. 'You should be very proud of your scoop,' Hall had written in a note to Bashir at the time of the Diana interview. Misgivings arising soon after the interview with regards to the manner in which it had been obtained, in an internal BBC review conducted in 1996 Hall cleared Bashir of any wrongdoing.[14] The reporter's dealings with Diana were adjudged to have been 'absolutely straight and fair.' Lord Dyson would call Hall's supposed review 'flawed and woefully ineffective.'

In an emotional statement Prince William summarised better than anyone else the sheer extent of BBC malfeasance on display:

BBC employees lied and used fake documents to obtain the interview with my mother, made lurid and false claims about the royal family - which played on her fears and fuelled paranoia - displayed woeful incompetence when investigating complaints and concerns about the programme and were evasive in their reporting to the media and covered up what they knew from their internal investigation…she (Diana) was failed not only by a rogue reporter, but by leaders of the BBC… (the Panorama interview) established a false narrative which for over a quarter of a century has been commercialised by the BBC and others…

The timing of the Dyson report could not have come at a less opportune moment for the BBC. One day after its publication and while Tim Davie had been hastily writing to tell BBC staff that 'lessons must be learnt' from Lord Dyson's withering conclusions - presumably in terms of probity, honesty and integrity - the BBC Press Office had indeed been musing how best to deceive Mrs Hadaway, how to stymie her quest for truth, whether to fob her off with an empty stock phrase or to simply ignore her altogether.

SUMMARY

From Savile to Bashir the BBC has a long track record of covering up the unethical behaviour (and even criminality) of its employees. This is because its privileged position depends on propagating an image of probity. As long as it remains a vital asset of global wealth and power its many scandals will continue to be brushed under the carpet by the same establishment whose interests it serves.

'[Donald Trump] long-time fan-boy of Putin'

Ukraine crisis:
The West fights back against Putin the disruptor:
bbc.co.uk, 6 March 2022

IT has already been suggested elsewhere in this book that the United States has long since aimed to emerge as the dominant military and economic power in Eurasia. Geo-political dominance presupposes control too over the region's economic sphere. Take the case of Russia. This vast nation just so happens to be one of the world's leading producers of oil and gas. The combined value of its natural resources has been valued at almost $850 billion.[1] Russia also has 1,400 tons of gold. These are prizes avaricious western eyes have coveted ever since the Cold War. In the event of say a coup, access to these plentiful resources – their distribution via government contracts and cronyism etc. - would be decided by entities connected to and part of the Washington consensus, with a few crumbs leftover for British contractors. No doubt fortunes would be made overnight. But there's a fly in this potentially lucrative ointment: Vladimir Putin, an official whom the BBC habitually refer to as a 'strong man' i.e. one opposed to US-(UK) hegemonic power. Dealing with the Russian president has become an obsession up at Capitol Hill. Naturally, the offensive includes the participation of the BBC, some of whose contributions to the cause have already been encountered in our earlier analysis of *Russia with Simon Reeve*.

'Our propaganda may effect soviet policy'
As an important asset of international corporate-political power,

the BBC has indeed played (and continues to play) a vital role in what is a silent war against the Russian state. The corporation has been engaged in anti-Russian subterfuge for quite some time as former BBC Director General Hugh Greene acknowledged when discussing the rationale behind the broadcaster's Russian output: 'Listeners to our broadcasts can help to form a soviet public opinion not unfriendly to the west,' remarks Greene, 'and thus by a gradual process our propaganda may effect Soviet policy.'[2]

So what of those avowals of objectivity and impartiality, cries that the BBC is an independent purveyor of news and most certainly therefore not an adjunct of the British (US) state? What about them? The broadcaster has an oven ready reply to such concerns: 'Our editorial standards do not require absolute neutrality on every issue' so reads paragraph 1.2 of the BBC's Editorial Standards. In other words, the BBC grants itself liberty to take sides when it suits, which is most, if not all of the time: Brexit, Assad, Trump, Boris Johnson, mass migration, climate, fracking, transgenderism and, not forgetting, all things Russian.

Thus, the article that appeared on the broadcaster's website in March 2022 was merely the latest part of the anti-Russian propaganda campaign referred to by Greene. Titled, 'Ukraine crisis: The West fights back against Putin the disruptor' such is the abundance of disinformation in this BBC front page report, it is impossible to choose a single item upon which to focus.

As the title implies, this is an analysis of the Ukraine-Russia crisis which began in February of the same year, but which had been brewing for years - ever since the 2014 US[3]-UK and EU backed 'colour revolution' (a euphemism for coup) and which dethroned the democratically elected president Viktor Yanukovych. Not that the BBC was troubling itself with such minor details as western directed insurgency when it began pumping out pro-Ukraine, anti-Russian propaganda by the truck load that same February.[4]

Virtually any sentence in this hagiography to US imperialism could be cited, but we'll confine ourselves to just eight examples of its dubious claims and outright falsehoods:[5]

'Putin has been trying to engineer...the destruction of the liberal international order.'

'He has been determined - successfully at times - to weaken America, and hasten its division and decline.'

As acknowledged in these two sentences, the 'liberal international order' is of course just another way of saying the Washington Consensus. The US capital is the most powerful city in the world. Thus, it is the place where the socio-economic objectives of the wealthiest and most powerful (US) entities coalesce into the narratives promoted by the BBC and its fellow wealth and power proxies. Should a 'strongman' resist this neo-liberal agenda then he or she will duly be portrayed as a pariah (demagogue, unhinged, evil etc.) – whatever it takes to trigger the average consumer of mainstream disinformation into fury and indignation.

Those aware of the United States' (and UK's) nebulous activities around the world which have included funding various so-called rebel factions in order to facilitate regime change in places such as Iraq, Libya, Syria, Afghanistan, Chile, Nicaragua etc. will no doubt see the irony of analysis which paints the US (CIA) and UK (MI5/MI6) as benign powers and *Russia* as a threat to peace and security.[6]

Such sweeping generalisations about Putin's determination to 'weaken America' are unsupported by even a shred of evidence. NATO's rapid expansion towards the Russian border suggests the *precise opposite* is in fact true: it is the United States which is determined to 'hasten' Russian 'division and decline.' It was a prominent member of the Democrat party named Adam Schiff who openly boasted to the US senate in January 2020 about US plans to conduct a proxy war against Russia: 'The United States aids Ukraine and her people so we can fight Russia over there, and we don't have to fight Russia here.' This plan to further expand US hegemonic power at the expense of a sovereign nation does not seem to trouble the 'British' Broadcasting Corporation that much.

Next the article arrives at the Russia-Ukraine conflict and US condemnation:

'The Kremlin argued... it was hypocritical for Washington to complain about this violation of international law after Bush had invaded Iraq.'

Occasionally the broadcaster will be forced to admit a truth as with this statement. In order to undermine the truth, it will then seek to discredit by attribution to a wrong-thinker – in this case the Kremlin, but it could just as easily have been Nigel Farage, climate 'deniers' or Narendra Modi. Of course, it wasn't just the Kremlin that noted the gross hypocrisy of the world's most rapacious imperial power acting as judge and jury regarding Russian manoeuvres in neighbouring Ukraine. But that's precisely the impression that the broadcaster hopes to leave in the mind of its audience.

'America... no longer wanted to police the world'
Projecting the BBC narrative onto a wrong-thinker is a fairly standard mainstream media tactic. Thus, the broadcaster purports in this next example to know Putin's innermost thoughts, Putinsplaining. Attributing its own narrative onto a target enables the broadcaster to create any fantasy required in order to consolidate its narratives regards the Russian president's ulterior and very dark motives:

'But Putin knew that America, after its long wars in
Afghanistan and Iraq, no longer wanted to police the
world.'

As for the suggestion that America no longer wanted to 'police the
world,' once again this a claim without any foundation. In an
article titled 'Why is the US the world's police force?' exhibiting
just a tadge more geopolitical knowledge than the BBC, *The
Boston Review* remarks that, 'For political elites, the appeal of the
UN was that it provided the United States and Britain with a way
to police the world while avoiding the appearance of empire-
building.'[7] Use of US and UK so-called soft power has always
been the key to expansionism and ultimately plunder. The
unfounded claim that the United States has suddenly given up its
premier geopolitical role is patently absurd, but not entirely
unexpected in this erratic BBC op-ed.

'In 2013...Bashar al-Assad the Syrian dictator used chemical
weapons against his own people.'

'By helping Assad carry out his murderous war, he extended
Moscow's sphere of influence in the Middle East when the
United States wanted to extract itself from the region.'

The 'murderous' war referred to here is in fact the US-UK-funded
civil war initiated and prosecuted largely by Islamist groups and
Al-Qaeda offshoots, the aim of which is the overthrow of the
Syrian government and its replacement by a US-UK approved
client regime.

The chemical weapon claim is yet another staple of anti-Assad
western propaganda, an attack that even the pro-west Human
Rights Watch organisation refers to as 'alleged.'[8] In 2013 the
Damascus suburbs of east and west Ghouta reportedly came under

attack. Dozens upon dozens of dead children were subsequently pictured lying in a morgue, victims according to the New York-headquartered UN of a chemical attack carried out by the Assad government. However, analysis published by the non-partisan International Institute for Peace, Justice and Human Rights confirmed what many had begun to suspect: the attack had almost certainly been staged to justify 'humanitarian intervention' in order to advance western powers' regime change agenda. Authored by ISTEAMS President and International Coordinator Mother Agnes Mariam, in what it terms the 'criminal use of children' the report raises a chilling prospect: how did the dead children lamented over by the western media actually die and by whose hand?[9] The 'British' Broadcasting Corporation appears to neither know nor even care.

> 'Putin even sought to influence the outcome of the 2016 presidential election in the hope that Hillary Clinton, a long-time nemesis, would be defeated and that Donald Trump, a long-time fan boy, would win.'

According to Facebook, accounts which 'likely operated out of Russia' bought the grand total of $100,000 worth of ads during the 2016 US presidential election – a drop in a huge ocean wherein tens of millions of dollars are spent.[10] According to the exhaustive Mueller report and much to BBC disappointment, there was no collusion between the Trump campaign and Russia. Despite the oft-peddled meme that '17' US agencies had found evidence of Russian interference the world still waits for the evidence to be presented in a way that can be independently verified. As for the 'evidence' cited by wealth and power proxies such as the BBC, one word springs to mind: 'thin.' For example, according to Wikipedia's summary Russia stood accused of 'arousing con-servative voters' in the run-up to the 2016 US election. This was apparently achieved by adding the meme 'Blue Lives Matter' to social media posts. It gets even better; what the online encyclopaedia describes as a Russian oligarch was 'detained on a recent trip to the United States, but it is unclear if he was searched.' If that fails to convince there's this: 'in December 2016, two unidentified senior intelligence officials told several U.S. news media outlets that they were highly confident that the operation to interfere in the 2016 presidential election was personally directed by Vladimir Putin...' And so forth.[11]

At this juncture it is worthwhile taking stock of the position taken by wealth and power proxies which include the likes Wikipedia as well as the 'British' Broadcasting Corporation viz the 2016 US election. The broadcaster's logic must run something like this:

A long time 'fan-boy' of Vlad Putin, American businessman Donald Trump visited Russia in 2013 to judge a beauty contest. While there Trump was secretly filmed with prostitutes in scenes the BBC claimed were 'of a sexual nature.' Putin had caught the billionaire in a honey trap. The idea, appears to run BBC thinking, was to acquire material with which to blackmail Mr Trump when he became US president. While not one political pundit inside or outside the United States envisaged Trump even running for let alone winning the presidency, one soothsayer apparently had: Putin.[12] It worked! Donald Trump became US president just as the Russian president had predicted. Brace for the dirty dealings about to occur... anytime soon... Ok, so the Trump administration imposed tough sanctions on Russia throughout its tenure, much tougher than the previous Obama regime, but so what? And If Putin did not use his leverage gathered in the hotel room – key parts of which had been 'verified' by the BBC – what of it? Had not Trump and Putin said polite things about one another when leaders of the world's two most powerful countries? If that's not proof of something fishy,

201

then what is? Besides, if the conspiracy theory has not quite happened, there's always 2024... No doubt Trump and Putin are plotting together how to win the next US election as we speak.

That's one explanation. Of course there is another less farcical explanation than the one proffered by the BBC and which may help explain the outcome of the 2016 election: having become disillusioned with career politicians in the mould of the Bushes, Clinton's etc. and with the United States in seemingly terminal social and economic decline, substantial numbers of Americans decided to vote for a successful, well-known businessman during the 2016 cycle – especially in areas of the country (e.g. the rust belt) which had been negatively impacted by decades of political ineptitude. Republican supporters voted for a Republican candidate and maybe a few independents joined them. Admittedly, it's a theory not quite as colourful as that hawked around by the BBC and Wikipedia. With its Muscovite setting and its high-class prostitutes, bugged hotel rooms, spying and shadowy kremlin villains, the broadcaster's version of events has less to do with reality and rather more in common with the plot of a novel. John le Carré springs immediately to mind.

'George Herbert Walker Bush... Cold War warrior'

As far as the BBC assertion that Donald Trump was (is) a Putin 'fanboy' his administration's record of sanctions between 2016 and 2020 has already been remarked upon several times. This false BBC assertion probably emanates from a letter sent by Mr Trump to the Russian president in 2007 congratulating him on being named *Time* magazine's 'Person of the Year' (yet more Putin 'fanboys' presumably). 'As you probably have heard,' wrote Mr Trump in his brief missive 'I am a big fan of yours.'

As noted, BBC disinformation often starts with a grain of truth. Was the New York property mogul really a fan of the austere Russian leader, literally? Back in 2007 when the letter had been penned the Trump organisation was just one of many US entities that had been seeking or already had investments in Russia – a market known to be volatile but potentially very lucrative for the astute. His had not been the only US enterprise hoping to grab a piece of the action. At the time of the Russia-Ukraine conflict it was revealed that The California State Teachers' Retirement System, the second-largest pension fund in the U.S, held Russian investments with a market value of $32million.[13] Similarly, at the outbreak of the conflict *Business Insider* reported that four members of the US Congress had recently invested money into Russian companies.[14] And with Starbucks, McDonalds and the rest of corporate America heavily invested in Russia too, the point is that the country of Putin has always been a favourite destination for the dollar. It's called business.

Indeed, Trump's letter came at a time when an associate, Felix Sater, had been exploring real estate projects on the property tycoon's behalf in the Russian capital.[15] Was Mr Trump then really a Putin 'fanboy' as per the BBC claim? Or was this perhaps an attempt – albeit a rather unsubtle one - to curry favour with those who could further his business interests? Whisper it, but could the letter have been a prime example of flattery?

It is however worth mentioning that by not adopting an overtly hostile attitude towards Russia, sanctions notwithstanding, the Trump presidency had represented a serious setback to an international wealth and power cabal which has long sought conflict with Russia in order to weaken and ultimately eliminate it as a military rival. 'Trump did not condemn Putin during the campaign,' reported Forbes 'and expressed a hope (shared by many across the political spectrum) of improved relations.'[16] In the topsy-turvy world of BBC political activism that Trump did not aggravate Russia as per Washington imperatives could only mean one thing: he had to be a Putin 'fan boy.'

With the following paragraph this BBC panegyric to US

corporate wealth and power truly had peaked. It can only be imagined how Simon Reeve – he of the delicate stomach – might have reacted to this little gem:

'Joe Biden, like George Herbert Walker Bush, is a Cold War warrior, who has dedicated his presidency to defending democracy at home and abroad.'

Although BBC admiration for the architect of the illegal Iraq war which killed, maimed and displaced millions of Iraq citizens is obvious enough, not least by its oleaginous reference to 'George Herbert Walker Bush,' the countless number of dead, displaced and injured might not necessarily agree with a depiction that could truly said to be the inspiration of an actual fanboy organisation.

And on this obsequious note to US imperial hegemony, we must bid adieu to yet another model of BBC impartiality.

SUMMARY

A BBC article which appeared on the front page of its news website made a number of false, misleading and baseless claims about Russia and Putin – the latest stage of the broadcaster's anti-Russia campaign which has been in motion since the end of the Second World War.

You will own nothing
and be happy

Although this is a book replete with BBC quotations, the title of this, its final chapter, is *not* a BBC soundbite. Although the seven-word phrase that heads this chapter has oft been quoted and re-quoted, for reasons that will become clear it's one that the broadcaster itself is not especially fond of repeating. Unable to label it and the dreadful idea it represents a 'conspiracy' and thus unable to palm it off as the work of conservatives or even the dastardly QAnon, the famously bombastic broadcaster falls mysteriously silent when it comes to this particular meme. Before we observe how Auntie misleads by omission, some background.

Following release of a video which went viral in Autumn 2020, an organisation calling itself the World Economic Forum (WEF) gained the sort of worldwide prominence that seemingly only social media can facilitate. *8 Predictions for the World in 2030* had first aired back in November 2016, and contained, as the title suggests a series of forecasts. According to the WEF, by 2030 the United States will no longer be the world's superpower; people will consume meat only as a treat; a billion people will have been displaced by climate change and a better job will need to be done of integrating these climate refugees.

But the prediction that really grabbed attention was one which proclaimed the following: 'You'll own nothing and be happy.'[1] This assertion was quickly followed by another: 'Whatever you want you'll rent and it will be delivered by drone.' A Political and social system bereft of private property rights and ownership is generally classified as Communism i.e. total state control. Little wonder that upon its re-release the video sparked a huge social media backlash.[2] It seems that the vast majority of people are happy with things as they stand i.e. owning their own assets. Such was the mockery and disdain aimed its way the WEF promptly deleted the video from its social media account.

However, another WEF soundbite continued the theme: 'Welcome To 2030: I own nothing, have no privacy and life has never been better. I don't own anything. I don't own a car. I don't own a house…'[3] In the light of this persistent message many (non-BBC) commentators mused over an obvious question these unsettling proclamations raised: if not ordinary people, then *who* would own assets – the rich and powerful perchance? The Party of Orwell's dystopian nightmares? *Somebody* would have to. Nor is Schwab's vision a passing fancy. 'As humanity moves towards a post-carbon future,' announced the WEF in spring 2022, 'people must accept that things like eating meat and property ownership is simply unsustainable, says Klaus Schwab.'[4]

In 2020 the WEF's founder had co-authored a book which detailed more of the organisation's theories. Taken together the video and the book' - *The Great Reset* - seemed fairly innocuous, the utopian ramblings of an undoubtedly egocentric academic. For the WEF proposal was nothing short of a radical transformation of society as we know it – a blueprint which attempts to govern how people live their lives in accordance with principles dreamt up by Professor Schwab. Not to worry, for the Swiss-German octogenarian's eccentric theories would soon fall by the wayside, or would they?

Since the early 1970s Schwab has been assiduously building an extensive network of 'exclusive' influence that stretches round the globe and whose membership includes presidents and prime ministers past and present, royalty and various other heads of state, business/finance leaders as well as media figures. What then happens at Davos, the annual event hosted by Schwab at his organisation's Swiss HQ? The answer is that nobody really knows. 'It's forbidden,' noted *Quartz* writing about the 2014 Davos forum, 'to report or tell others who said what during this week's event.'[5] Indeed, much of what is agreed at the summit is done so implicitly, thereby evading scrutiny. Movers and shakers return home to promote and/or implement an agenda created not by democratic procedure, but one tailored to the economic (and ideological) objectives of a tiny, but powerful group of individuals.

'It's a big club and you're not in it,' famously quipped the American comedian George Carlin once upon a time referring to 'elite' alliances such as Davos. Happily, it appears that the BBC *is* a member of that club.[6]

'Checks and balances which underpin our democracy must not be forgotten,' so warns the infamous WEF video at its conclusion. But a wealthy and powerful plutocracy plotting a course for humanity in conjunction with a private organisation commandeered by a Swiss technocrat is about as far away from democracy as it is possible to get. And a system which approximates to medieval serfdom, albeit a hi-tech version – where the little people 'own nothing' – while the rich and powerful presumably control everything with the implication that decisions are made by this same tiny 'elite,' would be the very antithesis to democratic society.[7]

As the scope of WEF influence became apparent in the aftermath of the video's release, unease naturally increased. With his *Star Trek*-style tunics, Germanic lisp and egocentricity, Schwab might have looked and sounded like an archetypal James Bond villain, but there the similarities begin and end. Unlike cinematic pariahs the WEF works hand-in-hand with governments, *not* against them. Schwab's dreams are not dismissed as the ravings of a madman, far from it; they form the cornerstone of the Davos agenda and are therefore received with utmost solemnity by royalty, prime ministers and CEOs of the world's biggest corporate enterprises. In other words, the WEF, an unelected quango of the rich and powerful, is not only at the heart of public policy around the globe, but is actively *driving it forwards*. Indeed, back in a January 2019 press release the UK government announced it had formed a new partnership with the WEF, 'to ensure innovators have the environment needed to create and support the industries, products and services of the future.'[8] As far as such policies are concerned many, if not all, revolve around net zero and sustainability. In a letter sent to attendees prior to the 2020 Davos summit, Schwab co-authored a letter 'inviting' participants to set a target of achieving net zero greenhouse gas emissions by 2050.[9]

Space prevents anything more than a cursory appraisal of this unelected think-tank; suffice to say its tentacles reach far and wide. There is however room for one final thought which sums up the scope of its power, real or imagined: the Covid-19 pandemic Schwab described as 'a rare but narrow window of opportunity to reflect, reimagine, and reset our world.'

To *reset* our world...[10]

While the idea of the rich and powerful deciding what the poor and disenfranchised can and can't do, what they can and can't say, might be abhorrent to some, it might not necessarily trouble the sort of mind that blames the little people for Brexit...

'Light on specific detail'

All of which brings us to a BBC article: 'What is the Great Reset - and how did it get hijacked by conspiracy theories?' Written by as many as *five* BBC 'disinformation' activists the article is, as its title suggests, a less than subtle attempt to underplay concerns about Professor Schwab's secretive organisation and its agenda.

'Believers' the article begins 'spin dark tales about an author-itarian socialist world government run by powerful capitalists and politicians.'[11] Unlike the BBC activists who penned this article it's quite possible the 'believers' had read WEF articles such as this headlined: 'Universal basic income is the answer to the inequalities exposed by COVID-19.' With the kind of spooky prescience exhibited by Gates and co, this particular article was published on 17 April 2020 – when Covid had barely just begun and well before the reckless fiscal policies of government had been assessed. And anyway, apart from politicians and capitalists, who else would run government – children? Pets?

Davos itself is indeed attended by some of the world's most powerful individuals, many of whom are associated with equally powerful trans-national organisations such as the IMF, WHO, UN, EU, World Bank etc – an embryonic world government some might argue in all but name.[12] Moreover, in a speech given in 2017 at John F. Kennedy School of Government, Harvard, Schwab boasted that: 'What we are very proud of now is that we penetrate the (global) cabinets (of countries).' The problem for wealth and power gatekeepers like the BBC is Herr Schwab's vanity; he rather likes to brag.

So, a hyper-capitalist, quasi-governmental organisation that wields substantial influence over democratically-elected governments is proposing universal basic income. 'Dark tales' indeed. But the BBC article also has an internal logic failure: that powerful capitalists wish to lord over a society run along socialist principles is a 'contradiction' the article triumphantly asserts. Given that the rulers of socialist and communist states have always been rich and powerful 'capitalists,' this BBC gotcha (i.e. supposed incongruity between socialism and capitalists) does not quite succeed in the manner its quintet of activists seem to think.[13] Indeed, it might be argued that the *very essence* of a socialist/communist state is that whereby the poor have next to nothing while the 'elite' leadership lives in relative luxury.

Nor does the article improve. The Great Reset shouldn't be

taken too seriously state the BBC activists because it's 'light on specific detail' and thus it's 'difficult [sic] see precisely what the Great Reset might mean in practice.'[14] Nothing to see here. While the BBC might have feigned innocence, Gordon Brown seemed to know exactly how the reset would unfold calling it an: 'all-consuming industrial revolution right across the board, the speed of change a thousand times faster than during the first industrial revolution effecting all services, all products, all countries, all industries, all people.'[15]

Mr Brown went on to add some further observations about a phenomenon that the BBC wish its own believers to think is merely the muddled thoughts of a crusty old German academic:

It's going to lead to job destruction…massive technological change... It's going to force governments to change their minds about how they operate and all this has been set out by Klaus Schwab in the speech he made in Abu Dhabi to the summit of the agenda council.

Job destruction…affecting all people…force governments…set out by Klaus Schwab – the words of a true disciple and former British prime minister no less. That's as maybe, but BBC consumers had been reassured that any suggestion that Brown and co were telling anything approximating to truth was just another 'conspiracy theory.' Unfortunately for a corporation doing its very best to gatekeep for this hugely powerful institution, Schwab can't help but gloat over his own influence in world affairs. In the same speech in which he boasted that his organisation penetrates global cabinets, Schwab cited Canada, France and Argentina as examples of countries where (at least) 'half' the cabinet were WEF Young Leaders i.e. under his influence.

The BBC article goes on to coyly agree that there are questions for unelected individuals such as Schwab to answer in relation to the scope of his influence. Alas, while the 'British' Broadcasting Corporation shows no signs itself of asking those questions, the WEF does face criticism from, according to the BBC: '*Conservative* (our italics) political figures and outlets.' Yes, indeed it's those pesky conservatives trying to hold unelected million/billionaires like Gates and Schwab to account. Don't they ever give it a rest?

Eventually the article references a video released by the WEF, but not *that* video – not the one that attracted so much online mockery and criticism, the one that declared that the little people 'will own nothing.' Instead, the broadcaster switches focus to what it terms 'a flashy launch video' narrated by Prince Charles. And it's *this video* the broadcaster implies sparked so much interest in the WEF. The article also attempts to attribute interest in Schwab's agenda to a video of Canadian Prime Minister Justin Trudeau mentioning a great reset which, according to the broadcaster 'went viral' on 15 November 2020 – just two days prior to the pressure becoming so much on the WEF that on 17 November, it deleted *8 Predictions for the World in 2030.*

'In the hands of a diverse group of online activists,' continues the article now in full damage limitation flow, 'the Great Reset has been transformed - from a call to encourage people to think about a sustainable future, to a sinister plot against humanity.' The Great Reset is thus merely 'a call' to 'encourage' people to 'think.' Despite BBC portrayal of a benign verging on insignificant organisation, The World Economic Forum's objectives could not be clearer: to radically transform the world in which we live. Soon enough leading politicians around the world had begun using a phrase associated with Schwab's Great Reset aka The Fourth Industrial Revolution: *Build Back Better.* At times, the rhetoric of WEF alumni sounds eerily like that of their mentor, the same brand of utopianism that a quintet of BBC wealth and power gatekeepers class as 'vague:'

211

'We must grasp the historic opportunity before us: to learn the lessons of this awful pandemic and build back better,' espoused Boris Johnson listed under the category of 'People' on the WEF website. *'Above all, we will embrace the instincts and know-how of the wealth creators,* [italics ours] those in the private sector who invest money and take risks on new ideas that lead to new jobs, new industry and some of the greatest advances humanity has ever known.'[16]

Back with the article the broadcaster has progressed to making light of 'conspiracies' revolving around Schwab while confirming many misgivings about the multi-millionaire's unelected think-tank - albeit unwittingly. Still studiously ignoring the actual promo that caused uproar, the BBC article observes that, 'In a video from January, the WEF acknowledged that the messaging around the Great Reset didn't quite go to plan.' To clarify: the 'flashy' WEF video referenced by the BBC in its article *did* go to plan. It went exactly according to plan. In fact, it went so well to plan, it is still available to view online and elsewhere (comments disabled, naturally). The video that actually did not go to plan and apparently unknown to the BBC - *8 Predictions for the World in 2030* – as noted, the think-tank pulled on 17 November 2020 after massive public pushback.

By linking the WEF acknowledgment with the wrong video, it seems the broadcaster is indeed anxious not to mention the phrase that sent chills down people's spines: 'You will own nothing and be happy.' Perhaps that's because unlike with The Great Reset whichever way they might try to spin it, there's no easy way for BBC activists to deflect away from the core message of communism and the suffering entailed under authoritarian top-down political systems of that ilk. Critics ('conservatives' and Fox News hosts according to the broadcaster) fear that if ever implemented, The Great Reset would result in an even greater disparity between rich and poor and the hollowing out of the democratic system.

And so, in order to mislead its audience about the WEF agenda, the infamous phrase is wisely omitted from the BBC article.

SUMMARY

When the powerful and influential WEF released a video which promised a form of technocratic Communism was on its way, public outrage forced the organisation to delete the video in question. The BBC however claimed the furore had been caused by an entirely different WEF video - a ruse that allowed it to omit mentioning the sinister phrase which had sparked the huge public backlash.

Bibliography

Afsar, N. *et al* (2020) 'Ivermectin Use Associated with Reduced Duration of Covid-19 Febrile Illness in a Community Setting,' *International Journal of Clinical Studies & Medical Case Reports*, Volume 13- Issue 4, pp. 1-9.

Aref, Z. *et al* (2021) 'Clinical, Biochemical and Molecular Evaluations of Ivermectin Mucoadhesive Nanosuspension Nasal Spray in Reducing Upper Respiratory Symptoms of Mild COVID-19,' *International Journal of Nanomedicine*:16 4063 4072.

Azeez, T. *et al* (2021) 'Chemoprophylaxis against COVID-19 among health-care workers using Ivermectin in low and middle income countries: A systematic review and meta-analysis.' *Indian Journal of Pharmacol*. 2021 Nov-Dec;53(6).

Belgonia, E. and Naleway, A. (2003) Smallpox vaccine: the good, the bad, and the ugly, *Clinical Medicine & Research*, Apr;1 (2):87-92.)

Brzezinski, Z. (1997) The Grand Chessboard: American Primacy and its Geostrategic Imperatives: Basic Books.

Briggs, A. (1985) The BBC: The First Fifty Years: OUP.

Bryant, A. *et al* (2021) 'Ivermectin for Prevention and Treatment of COVID-19 Infection: A Systematic Review, Meta-analysis, and Trial Sequential Analysis to Inform Clinical Guidelines.' *American Journal of Therapeutics*, 28, e434–e460.

Chamie-Quintero *et al*: (2021) 'Sharp Reductions in COVID-19 Case Fatalities and Excess Deaths in Peru in Close Time Conjunction, State-By-State, with Ivermectin Treatments,' SSRN.com, 21 Jan. 2021.

Chaudry, R. *et al* (2020) 'A country level analysis measuring the impact of government actions, country preparedness and socioeconomic factors on COVID-19 mortality and related health outcomes,' *EClinicalMedicine* 25 (2020) 100464.

Chua, G. T. *et al* (2021) 'Epidemiology of Acute Myocarditis, Pericarditis in Hong Kong Adolescents Following Comirnaty Vaccination,' *Clinical Infectious Diseases*, 28 Nov.2021.

Chomsky, N. (1998) Profits Over People: Neoliberalism and the Global Order: Seven Stories Press.

Cull, N. J. *et al* (2003) Propaganda and Mass Persuasion: A Historical Encyclopaedia, 1500 to the Present: ABC-CLIO.

De keersmaecker, J. & Roets, A. (2017) 'Fake news': Incorrect, but hard to correct. The role of cognitive ability on the impact of false information on social impressions,' *Intelligence*: Vol. 65, Nov. 2017, Pp. 107-110.

Dionne, A. *et al* (2021) 'Association of Myocarditis With BNT162b2 Messenger RNA COVID-19 Vaccine in a Case Series of Children.' *JAMA Cardiology*, 10 Aug. 2021.

Duvat, V. (2019) 'A global assessment of atoll island planform changes over the past decades,' *WIREs Climate Change*, Volume10, Issue1 January/February 2019, e557.

Frenck, R. W. *et al* (2021) 'Safety, Immunogenicity, and Efficacy of the BNT162b2 Covid-19 Vaccine in Adolescents,' Supplementary Appendix, *New England Journal of Medicine* 2021; 385:239-250.

Ghislofi, S. *et al* (2020) 'Predicted COVID-19 fatality rates based on age, sex, comorbidities and health system capacity,' BMJ Global Health 2020

Greene, H. (1969) The Third Floor Front: A View of Broadcasting in the Sixties: The Bodley Head Ltd.

Greene, R. (2000) The 48 Laws of Power: Profile Books.

Gundry, S. (2021) 'Observational Findings of PULS Cardiac Test Findings for Inflammatory Markers in Patients Receiving mRNA Vaccines,' *Circulation*: November 16, 2021: Vol 144.

Hellwig, M. & Maia, A. (2021) 'A COVID-19 prophylaxis? Lower incidence associated with prophylactic administration of ivermectin,' *International Journal of Antimicrobial Agents:* 2021 Jan;57(1).~

Horowitz, L. *et al* (2021) 'Trends in COVID-19 Risk-Adjusted Mortality Rates,' *Journal of Hospital Medicine* (October 23, 2020).

Ioannidis, J. (2021) 'Infection fatality rate of COVID-19 inferred from seroprevalence data,' *Bulletin of the World Health Organization:* Jan 1; 99(1): 19–33F.

Ioannidis, J. (2021) 'Reconciling estimates of global spread and infection fatality rates of COVID-19: An overview of systematic evaluations,' *European Journal of Clinical Investigation*, May;51(5):e13554.

Kerr, L. *et al*. (2022) 'Ivermectin Prophylaxis Used for COVID 19: A Citywide, Prospective, Observational Study of 223,128 Subjects Using Propensity Score Matching,' *Cureus* 14(1).

Klokov, K. (2012) 'Changes in reindeer population numbers in Russia: an effect of the political context or of climate?' *Rangifer*, 32 (1), 2012.

Kory, P. *et al* (2021) 'Review of the Emerging Evidence Demonstrating the Efficacy of Ivermectin in the Prophylaxis and Treatment of COVID-19,' *American Journal of Therapeutics*, Nov-Dec 2021, 01;28(6).

Lasch, C. (1979) The Culture of Narcissism: American life in an age of diminishing expectations: W.W. Norton and Company.

Lawrence, J, *et al* (2021) 'The lesson of ivermectin: meta analyses based on summary data alone are inherently unreliable,' *Nature Medicine,* Vol. 27, November 2021: 1852 1857.

Levin, A. T. *et al*, (2020) 'Assessing the age specificity of infection fatality rates for COVID-19: systematic review, meta-analysis and public policy implications,' *European Journal of Epidemiology*, 2020 Dec;35 (12):1123-1138.

Le Vu, S. *et al* (2022) 'Age and sex-specific risks of myocarditis and pericarditis following Covid-19 messenger RNA vaccines. *Nature Communications* 13, 3633.

Lima-Morales, R. *et al* (2021) 'Effectiveness of a multidrug therapy consisting of Ivermectin, Azithromycin, Montelukast, and Acetylsalicylic acid to prevent hospitalization and death among ambulatory COVID-19 cases in Tlaxcala, Mexico,' *International Journal of Infectious Diseases*: 105 (2021) 598–605.

Lind, M. (2021) The News Class War: Saving Democracy from the Metropolitan Elite: Atlantic Books.

McEwen, B. & Sapolsky, R. (1995) 'Stress and cognitive function,' *Current Opinion in Neurobiology*, Vol. 5, Issue 2.

Majin, G. (2021) 'A catastrophic media failure? Russiagate, Trump and the illusion of truth: The dangers of innuendo and narrative repetition.' *Journalism*: 2021;22(10):2548-2565.

Mayer, M. *et al,* (2022) 'Safety and Efficacy of a MEURI Program for the Use of High Dose Ivermectin in COVID-19 Patients,' *Public Health*, Vol 10, Feb.

Meyerowitz-Katz, G. *et al* (2021) 'Is the cure really worse than the disease? The health impacts of lockdowns during COVID 19,' *BMJ Global Health* 2021;6.

Mills, T. (2016) The BBC: Myth of a Public Service: Verso.

Montford A. W. (2015) The Hockey Stick Illusion; Climategate and the Corruption of Science: Anglosphere Books.

Morgenstern, J. *et al* (2021) 'Ivermectin as a SARS-CoV-2 Pre Exposure Prophylaxis Method in Healthcare Workers: A Propensity Score-Matched Retrospective Cohort Study.' *Cureus*, 2021 Aug 26;13(8).

Neil, M. & Fenton, N. (2021) 'Bayesian Hypothesis Testing and Hierarchical Modelling of Ivermectin Effectiveness,' *American Journal of Therapeutics*, 28(5).

Rees W. G. *et al* (2008) 'Vulnerability of European reindeer husbandry to global change,' *Climatic Change*.

Schauer J. *et al* (2022) 'Persistent Cardiac MRI Findings in a Cohort of Adolescents with post COVID 19 mRNA vaccine myopericarditis,' *The Journal of Pediatrics*: 25 Mar. 2022.

Sedgwick, D. (2020) The Fake News Factory: Tales from BBC-land: Sandgrounder.

Stewart, C. (ed.) (1975) The Reith Diaries: Collins.

Talbot, D. (2016) The Devil's Chessboard: Allen Dulles, the CIA, and the Rise of America's Secret Government: William Collins.

Tanioka, H. *et al* (2021) 'Why COVID-19 is not so spread in Africa: How does Ivermectin affect it?' MedRxiv, 26 Mar. 2021.

Tsygankov, A. (2017) 'The dark double: The American media perception of Russia.' Politics 37(1): 19–35.

Tuvali, O. *et al* (2022) 'The Incidence of Myocarditis and Pericarditis in Post COVID-19 Unvaccinated Patients—A Large Population-Based Study.' *Journal of Clinical Medicine*: 2022, 11, 2219.

Uboni, A. *et al* (2016) 'Long-Term Trends and Role of Climate in the Population Dynamics of Eurasian Reindeer.' PLoS One. 2016 Jun 30;11.

Yagisawa, M. *et al* (2021) 'Global trends in clinical studies of ivermectin in COVID 19,' *The Japanese Journal of Antibiotics*, 74-1: Mar. 2021.

Notes

Introduction: BBC disinformation: Cui Bono?

[1] *The Culture of Narcissism*, p. 95.

[2] Omission is arguably the BBC's most potent disinformation weapon. Note, for example, its complete lack of coverage of Pfizer document dumps from January 2022 onwards. This information, which the FDA was forced to release after a court ruling, revealed that significant injuries (and deaths) had occurred in trials as a result of the company's Covid vaccine.

[3] 'Covid: Misleading vaccine claims target children and parents,' bbc.co.uk, 14 Dec. 2021. The same activist repeated this claim in yet another article titled 'Covid: Did boss cast doubt on his own vaccine?' in which she states: '…the virus itself comes with much greater risk than the vaccine of side-effects, including blood clotting, heart inflammation and death.'

[4] Tuvali *et al* (2022).

[5] Le Vu *et al* (2022).

[6] *Pick of the Year 2021*, BBC Radio 4, 1 Jan 2022.

[7] BBC News (UK) via Twitter, 5 Jun. 2022. While the person tasered had been black, unfortunately for the BBC the police officer involved had also been black, which no doubt explains why the story soon disappeared from the its news feed.

[8] As we shall see in the chapter which considers the Kyle Rittenhouse case, misleading the public can often be merely a case of substituting one word with another, a trick which only the most alert of consumers may notice.

[9] *The 48 Laws of Power*, p. xvii.

[10] The multitude of BBC stories which claimed Michael Cohen had accepted bribes from the Ukrainian president were shown at the High Court to be completely false; similarly, BBC

221

claims that Boris Johnson had colluded with the entrepreneur James Dyson were proven to be untrue: see the chapter titled: 'James Dyson is a prominent conservative supporter.'

Though it accuses just about any wrong-thinker of being a conspiracy theorist, the broadcaster is a prolific spreader of conspiracy in its own right. Russia-gate, Trump-Poroshenko, Dyson-Johnson, QAnon – BBC conspiracies invariably turn out to be false.

[11] Note the extent of BBC dedication to this narrative. Even as it tried every trick in the book to unseat Prime Minister Boris Johnson throughout 2020-22 – largely through incessant stories circulating around 'party-gate,' the broadcaster completely ignored a scandal that could have almost certainly sunk Johnson and his supposedly low-immigration Conservative government overnight: the (daily) Dover dinghy crossings.

[12] Though the master propagandist, as Lasch notes, strives to avoid overtly emotional appeals and associated risk of exposure, the BBC just can't help itself; for its propaganda to succeed requires an emotional, knee-jerk response, not clarity of thought. Its audience comprising largely the elderly and uninformed, the broadcaster calculates that it's a risk worth taking.

[13] While journalism does produce its share of scoops which expose the power structure and those who exploit it for gain e.g. MPs claiming expenses for duck ponds – it is window dressing. The moment journalism threatens to expose *the real power bases*, it will invariably find itself in deep trouble as Edward Snowden and Julian Assange discovered. Knowing which entities are off limits is part and parcel of mainstream media acculturation.

[14] *The BBC: The First Fifty Years*, p.100.

[15] *The BBC: Myth of a Public Service,* p.17.

[16] *The Reith Diaries*, p. 15.

[17] *Propaganda and Mass Persuasion: A Historical Encyclopaedia, 1500 to the Present*, p.37.

[18] One of the most persuasive techniques in terms of normalising the agenda of the 'elite' is celebrity endorsement. How many celebrities have you ever heard question the wisdom of the 'consensus?' Next time you get the chance, tune into the BBC's Frankie Boyle or the panel assembled on *Have I Got News for You* and listen as the 'comedians' attack and harangue any entity daring to make a stand against the global order.

[19] The broadcaster can sometimes punch up, *but only* if such targets are deemed problematical to global wealth and power i.e. Trump, Putin, Assad, Corbyn etc. It was only Jeremy Corbyn's anti-imperialist stance which made him problematical to global power; as far as other narratives were concerned the former Labour leader, like his US counterpart Bernie Sanders, was pretty much on message.

[20] Take lockdowns for example. The lockdowns of 2020-21 increased the wealth of the super-rich exponentially. As for the middle-class they were relatively unscathed. According to Stepchange Debt Charity, those earning less than £30k per annum meanwhile were likely to have fallen into debt during this period. The BBC not only lobbied on behalf of, but demanded the Johnson government put the UK into hard lockdown on a daily basis throughout this period.

[21] Politicians effectively acting as vaccine salesmen and women during 'coronavirus,' the boundary between the corporate and political has never been more blurred and is only set to continue converging.

[22] It is useful at this juncture to distinguish between permanent and temporary government. The British state and its components form a permanent bureaucracy of which the BBC is an integral part. It consists also of elements such as the 'faceless' civil service (i.e. Whitehall), the security agencies (MI5 etc.), City of London, Armed forces (i.e. MOD hierarchy), the judiciary, the Royal Family, the Labour-Tory party, House of Lords etc. Meanwhile, temporary government is the 'front of house' occupied by Ministers who come and go.

Although the BBC is often accused of being left or right-wing, and though BBC personnel in common with other middle-class 'socialists' typically support Labour, the broadcaster's loyalties actually lie with this permanent bureaucracy – the real seat of power in the UK, and which in turn is allied to US hegemonic power. Permanent (invisible) government represents the dominant minority while temporary (visible) government feigns to represent the interests of the majority.

[23] The last time the broadcaster took issue with a globalist-dictated narrative was arguably when 'rogue' BBC Today reporter Andrew Gilligan reported the WMD 45-minute claim made by the government of Tony Blair – a claim used by the US-(UK) to justify an illegal invasion of Iraq in order to requisition its valuable oil resources. Gilligan had reported the unease of a source Dr David Kelly, an internationally renowned weapons inspector. Kelly had been concerned with how intelligence had been mis-handled: Blair and his spin doctor Alistair Campbell had allegedly pressured British intelligence into exaggerating the threat posed by Iraq. These were revelations that rocked the Labour government – a scoop in every sense of the word.

The BBC had been right to expose these goings-on. Yet following a bitter and very public row the broadcaster apologised profusely to the government and its Chairman and Director General resigned. Ultimately it seems the BBC was not prepared to cross the UK permanent state and its US partners despite the fact it had been entirely correct to bring the issue to public attention. Since then – 2003 – the broadcaster has arguably become even more subservient to wealth and power, a case of once bitten twice shy?

[24] Meanwhile, a BBC news correspondent was flown back and forth to Ukraine a round trip of over 2.500 miles - in order to do a piece to camera in the middle of a supposed climate emergency…

[25] To understand how the system operates, consider the story of ex BBC activist Paul Mason. Exposed for his pro NATO, pro-war activities while posing as a man of the (anti-establishment) left,

in a series of leaked emails exposed by *The Grayzone,* Mason's close links to the British security state were revealed. Angered that independent media was exposing the nefarious war activities of the UK state, Mason asked his Foreign Office contact, Andy Pryce, what could be done to 'fight back.' Pryce advised him to ignore the revelations provided they received 'no traction outside of useful idiots sharing it with one another.'

What Pryce meant here is that the establishment only need worry if those in power are exposed to *independent* journalism. Otherwise, truth will soon hit a brick wall, have nowhere to travel – only back and forward between ordinary people whose opinions, after all, don't matter. Actors like Mason and Pryce ensure that the establishment is not exposed to truth, but to BBC narratives.

[26] During the coronavirus 'pandemic' BBC activists were among a small group of privileged individuals exempted from the same quarantine rigmarole imposed upon ordinary members of the public. Along with the rich and powerful, BBC personnel could thus fly as per normal throughout 2020-2022.

[27] Many Conservative voters marvel at how an organisation that is so profoundly anti-conservative should have thrived so much under Tory administrations. The Tories have been promising to address the issue of BBC anti-Tory bias since the 1980s when its anti-Thatcherism peaked. However, as exhibited by its coverage of climate change, Brexit, Trump, Ukraine etc. the value of BBC disinformation to the 'British' (permanent) state cannot be over-stated. Pity then the poor Tories; as a (political) proxy to wealth and power, the party is a solid ally of the BBC- pro-mass migration, neo-liberal, pro high levels of public spending, WEF-friendly, green zealotry, pro-lockdowns etc. On the other hand, grassroot supporters demand it deals with the same BBC whose worldview mirrors so well the party's own ideology. This affinity between broadcaster and the party of Cameron, Johnson *et al* explains why the Tories allow the BBC to harangue, attack

and shame its voter base: the modern Conservative party is not conservative in any meaningful sense of the word and so its supporters are fair game for BBC scorn and smears.

[28] As we write, the UK political establishment – Tory-Labour – is moving to make funding of the BBC compulsory for UK citizens via taxation thereby removing the right to opt-out – a policy fully commensurate with the uniparty's role as a fellow wealth and power proxy.

[29] 'The Typhoid Mary of Disinformation': Nicolle Wallace. Nobody Spreads it More Relentlessly.' Glenn Greenwald, Substack, 19 May 2022.

[30] How then do BBC activists who claim to operate with integrity and honesty square this circle? Easily. As Orwell illustrated in *1984* with the apocryphal Brotherhood, simply create imaginary demons for the activist to battle: QAnon, antivaxxers, the 'far right' etc. Then it's just a matter of convincing the BBC activist that he or she is therefore engaged in an epic *Star Wars* struggle between good and evil. Hence, telling lies, inverting reality, spreading disinformation becomes not only justifiable, but necessary – part of a far greater struggle. Lying can even become *a virtue*. Six-figure salaries and perks to match also help persuade individuals to act unconscionably.

'This is a paradise faced with extinction'

[1] This is a fairly typical BBC correction relating to an edition of Radio 4's *Today* programme broadcast Friday, 5 June 2020:

During the 8am news bulletin we reported that May this year was the hottest on record both globally and in the UK - according to Copernicus, the European Union's Earth Observation Programme. In fact, Copernicus found that global temperatures were 0.63 degrees warmer in May than the long-term average for the month…'

In other words, it had not been the 'hottest' May on record, but temperatures had been slightly higher than the long-term average for that month. The broadcaster regularly seizes upon such data and repurposes it in order to promote its alarmist messaging. Presenting incorrect information on its flagship news programme is a means by which the broadcaster can mislead several million listeners including, crucially, policy makers and politicians.

BBC reporting is saturated with superlatives like this e.g. 'Climate change: May was sunni*est* calendar month on record in UK,' (1 Jun. 2020) 'Met Office says 2010 'among hott*est* on record.' (26 Nov. 2010) etc.

2 But of course, correlation is not causation. Sceptics would point out that the current global warming period and age of increased CO_2 emissions, if not two completely unrelated phenomenon, are at best minimally interdependent.

3 'BBC Lies, Again, About Record Easter Warmth In The UK,' Climate Change Dispatch, 23 Apr. 2019.

4 Thus, when the broadcaster proclaims that the 'Met Office says 2010 'among hottest on record,' (26 Nov. 2010) what this means in terms of the wider historical significance is for the reader to decide.

5 'Sport 2050: Imagined sports news headlines in a warmer world,' bbc.co.uk/sport, 17 May 2021.

6 Though in common with its fellow travellers in the AGW lobby the crafty broadcaster is prone to frame the debate in terms of the catch-all phrase 'climate change' rather than the much more problematical concept of (man-made) global warming. After all, who can deny that the climate does indeed change?

7 'Call for anti-greenhouse action,' *The Canberra Times*, 26 Jan 1989.

8 In common with all quasi-religious movements where belief overrides fact, the climate change lobby, like Macbeth, is a group in blood stepp'd so far, returning were as tedious as go o'er. In other words, reversing their position given the

reputations at stake and staggering amounts of money involved, climate lobbyists have gone way beyond the point where they could reverse their extremist AGW position even if they wanted. Indeed, when cornerstones of the AGW theory are debunked the lobby hardly blinks. For example, not only has the '97% consensus' been debunked, but so too have hugely influential staples such as the fraudulent hockey stick curve. See: Montford (2015).

[9] 'Climate Change Is a $26 Trillion Growth Opportunity. 5 Business Models to Consider Today,' Inc.com.

[10] 'Follow the (Climate Change) Money,' Heritage.org, 18 Dec 2018.

[11] Ibid.

[12] For an introduction to the scope of vested interests driving the climate change agenda see the Climate Resistance YouTube video 'Intended consequences: energy price rises & inflation.'

[13] Despite or likely *because* of predicting in 2008 the disappearance of the ice caps would have occurred by 2013, climate warrior extraordinaire Al Gore has accumulated an estimated fortune of $330 million. Like many vociferous climate activists Gore's lifestyle belies his apocalyptic (and inaccurate) warnings. The former US vice president is the proud owner of a 6,500 square-foot seafront home in California – a rather risky if not foolhardy venture given the dire consequences of coastal erosion. Moreover, Gore's carbon footprint, like that of his fellow climate alarmists, is legend.

[14] Prof Richard Linzden: *Preface to Global Warming: A Case Study in Groupthink*, p. vii. Professor Lindzen was Alfred P. Sloan Professor of Meteorology at the Massachusetts Institute of Technology until his retirement in 2013. He is a member of the Academic Advisory Council of GWPF.

Professor Linzden knows what he is talking about. Climate 'science' is based on modelling which is itself based upon assumptions derived from political and (massive) financial imperatives. If one takes a turd and replicates it 1,000 times what one has is not more 'evidence' or a consensus but merely a lot more turds than when one began.

[15] 'Maldives Paradise soon to be lost,' bbc.co.uk, 28 July 2004.

[16] 'Threat to islands,' *The Canberra Times*, 26 Sep 1988.

[17] See Macrotrends.net.

[18] 'Maldives to open five new airports in 2019,' *Pacific Insider*, 20 May 2019.

[19] Ibid.

[20] See Duvat (2019).

[21] 'Hundreds of Pacific Islands are getting bigger despite global warming,' abc news, 7 Jan 2021.

[22] 'Minister Mausoom's estimation: 2 million tourists to arrive to Maldives next year,' Maldives News Network, 22 Sep 2021.

'The death toll is rising around the world'

[1] Rowlatt's sister allegedly is a member of extremist environmental groups Extinction Rebellion and Insulate Britain.

[2] The entire climate 'consensus' can be largely traced back to a paper by Cook *et al* (2013) which asserted that 97% of the world's 'climate scientists' agreed that climate change is 'real, man-made and dangerous.' The paper having been thoroughly debunked on numerous occasions, the BBC and its corporate-legacy allies quietly dropped the false 97% claim and pivoted instead to a new but equally disingenuous soundbite: 'the *vast majority* of climate scientists' now agree with the paper's nonsensical hypothesis. They do not; it would be more accurate to state that the vast majority of climate scientists *in receipt of funding* agree.

[3] The use of 'could' rather than 'will' strongly suggests that the science is in fact far from 'settled' and is indicative perhaps of numerous similar predictions that have failed to materialise from the disappearance of the Maldives to predictions of new ice ages. For a wider sample see: 'Wrong Again: 50 Years of

Failed Eco-apocalyptic Predictions,' Competitive Enterprise Institute, 18 Sept. 2019.

[4] 'See-saw to Wagon wheel: Safeguarding impartiality in the 21st century,' BBC Trust p.40.

[5] 'What a 100-degree day in Siberia really means,' *National Geographic,* 23 Jun. 2020.

[6] See: McEwen & Sapolsky (1995) pp. 205-16.

[7] 'Weather-related disasters increase over past 50 years, causing more damage but fewer deaths,' wmo.int, 31 Aug. 2021.

[8] A BBC Correction issued on 28 Mar. 2022, *18 months after the programme had aired* far from correcting the record doubled down: 'In retrospect it would have been better to have said 'the overall death toll is rising around the world and the forecast of extreme weather events is that worse is to come.'

[9] 'Climate-related mortality and hospital admissions, England and Wales: 2001 to 2020,' ONS, 17 Jan. 2022.

[10] 'Climate-related deaths fall in England and Wales – ONS,' bbc.co.uk, 17 Jan. 2022.

[11] *BBC Look North Yorkshire*, 7 Dec. 2020.

[12] At one point a business owner in the town of Hebden Bridge points to a plaque upon which historic flood levels are recorded. Unfortunately, the glimpse is so brief the viewer does not have chance to apprehend previous flood levels in the town, which appear to have been much higher than the present level.

[13] Britain has approximately 1,500 discrete river systems and about 200,000 km of waterways.

[14] Information is available via various sources including local libraries and newspaper archives. On the Internet, see: milltownmemories.org, eyeoncalderdale.com, 'The Calder Valley's History of Flooding' by Paul Homewood and Molly Sunderland's book, *It's Water Under the Bridge.*

[15] The 1946 flood affected many areas. For example, over 5,000 homes in Salford were flooded. The city's River Irwell has flooded many times in its history, the most well documented being the floods of 1866, 1946, 1954, 1980, and 2007.

[16] 'Yorkshire's flooding crisis laid bare with 20 years of storm damage, bursting rivers and houses swept away,' *The Yorkshire Examiner*, 22 Feb. 2022.

[17] 'The great coastal flood of 1099,' *The Times*, 11 Nov. 2019.

[18] 'Possibly the worst coastal flooding on record,' according to Horsburgh, K. & Horritt, M. 'The Bristol Channel Floods of 1607: reconstruction and analysis.' *Weather*, Oct. 2006, vol. 61, No. 10.

[19] This is just one of many severe floods discussed by Cicely M Botley in 'Historic Floods,' *Weather*, Mar. 1947. Pp. 66-68. Botley identifies the period 1086-1446 as the 'great period of tidal floods.' The 10th to 13th centuries is often referred to as the medieval warm period and indicates that flooding is related, as many non-BBC experts believe, primarily to solar activity.

'In steep decline because of climate change'

[1] The book's full title is: *The Grand Chessboard: American Primacy and its Geostrategic Imperatives*. Other chapters in the book include: 'The short road to global supremacy,' 'The First Global Power,' 'The American Global System,' etc.

[2] Tsygankov (2017).

[3] It might be. Or then again it may be that the Russian authorities do not especially trust the bastion of US-UK hegemonic power, the 'British' Broadcasting Corporation, to tell the truth.

[4] When the BBC says 'authoritarian' it is not including the kind of authority exerted by so-called western elites whose prejudices (and economic interests) control the public forum just as effectively – more so perhaps – than the truncheon wielding methods of former Communist states. On the contrary, provided it operates behind the scenes where it can

be ignored or underplayed this kind of intimidation seems just fine with the broadcaster.

Interestingly, when BBC right-thinkers like Emmanuel Macron revert to the truncheon (and tear gas) as witnessed during the *gilets jaunes* protests, the BBC stands silently by, fully approving of these police-state tactics. Does the broadcaster really disprove of hard tactics, or is it just a case of disapproval only when used by the other side as Orwell observed in his essay 'Notes on Nationalism?'

5 The world still awaits the broadcaster's investigations into any number of entities and relationships: The Clinton Foundation, Fusion GPs and the Democrat Party; the Biden's links with Ukraine etc. Such investigations will of course never happen.

6 Letter from Nigel Lawson via The Global Warming Policy Foundation, 30 Oct. 2017.

7 In fact, Kamchatka, location for Reeve's brush with reindeer herding, is named in Uboni's (2016) major study whereby the socio-economic conditions upon reindeer numbers is highlighted: 'the Arkhangelsk, Sakha, Chukotka, and *Kamchatka* populations experienced a period of stable dynamics during the Soviet Union time, a pronounced decline following the collapse of the Soviet Union (in 1991), and a slow recovery in the last decade.'

8 See: Klokov 2012.

9 The cartoonist was Stella Perrett formerly of *The Morning Star*.

10 While 'our' referendums are always paragons of virtue, 'theirs' are always corrupt – unless of course they deliver the 'correct' result e.g. the election of US-UK proxies such as Ukraine's Zelensky or Branco in 1964 (Brazil) etc.

11 Reeve appears to be alluding to Arkady Rotenberg, a judo sparring partner of Putin's and wealthy businessman. What, one wonders would Reeve have to say about the super wealthy connections of the Clintons, Obamas, Pelosis and Bidens of this world? Likely, not a lot.

[12] 'Moscow Renews Demolition Crusade Against Khrushchev's 1950s Apartment Blocks,' *The Moscow Times,* 9 Jun. 2014.

[13] 'Life inside a Kiev Khrushchyovka: Soviet architecture in Ukraine,' *Al Jazeera*, 25 Feb. 2019.

[14] 'Moscow's urban planning: rebuilding a part of the city,' We Build Value Digital Magazine, 20 Aug. 2018.

[15] As shall be seen later in the book, Putinsplaining is a common enough activity amongst BBC activists. Ironically, rather than Putin, Reeve's words actually sound more like they might have been said by BBC ally Klaus Schwab.

'The Brexit Murder?'

[1] BBC Radio 4, *Today*, 1st September 2016, Business Update, 8.40am.

[2] Even BBC reports acknowledged as much: 'A senior police officer says he is concerned at media reports that a murder was a 'hate crime' before a motive for the fatal attack has been established.' See: 'Harlow murder: Police concern at 'hate crime' label,' bbc.co.uk, 1 Sep 2016.

[3] At one point Fidgin remarks that upon journeying to the Stow precinct she was taken aback to observe a 'a tattered union flag flying out of a window.'

[4] See: 'The BBC's slur has caused my family misery,' *The Telegraph,* 19 Sept. 2017.

'Shot and killed two men during racial justice protests'

[1] According to News Sniffer, the sub-heading was deleted approximately 1.5 hours after being introduced into the third draft of the story.

[2] 'BBC defends censure of Naga Munchetty over Trump comments,' *The Guardian*, 27 Sep 2019.

[3] 'Homicide Trends in the United States, 1980-2008: Annual Rates for 2009 and 2010,' US Department of Justice.

[4] 'Lawlessness led to Rittenhouse trial,' *The Washington Times,*18 Nov. 2021.

[5] 'Kyle Rittenhouse: Calls for calm after US teen cleared of murder,' bbc.co.uk, 20 Nov. 2021.

[6] Ibid.

[7] The myth – 'a dangerous fiction' according to *Real Clear Politics* - that US police officers purposely kill black people is shamelessly used by left-wing politicians and media organisations intent on demonising law enforcement agencies as inherently racist. *Real Clear Politics* provides the context deliberately omitted by the BBC and friends e.g. black males are 6-7 times more likely to be involved in serious crime incidents than white males and that police killings of black males tend to occur in large, urban cities plagued by drug related crime.

'After accounting for these and other factors,' the analysis continues 'including averaged cultural differences in police departments, we found that black officers were at least as likely as their white peers to kill black suspects, but that black officers were more likely to kill unarmed blacks than were white officers.' See: 'Data Undercuts Myth of 'Racism' in Police Killings' *Real Clear Politics*, 21 Apr. 2021.

[8] One of the broadcaster's most enduring tricks when challenged over stories such as Johnson's is to state that it did in fact cover the case and that accusations to the contrary are therefore false even when that 'coverage' equates to a single, brief story safely tucked away on a regional BBC webpage. It's a ruse almost as common as the 'we get complaints from both sides' ploy.

[9] To what extent Johnson had been radicalised by the sort of (incessant) racially divisive content produced by the BBC and its fellow travellers in the corporate-legacy media was an avenue down which the broadcaster was reluctant to travel of course.

[10] After posting the racist comment, Jasmine Friedl, the Dropbox manager in question, promptly disappeared from social media and sites such as Linkedin.

[11] Examples abound; compare BBC coverage of the racially motivated murders of Kriss Donald and Stephen Lawrence;

also compare its coverage of the murders of the Conservative MP David Amess at the hands of a non-white perpetrator with that of Jo Cox (Labour) at the hands of a white male.

[12] Amongst a plethora of sweeping generalisations and falsehoods the programme claims that slavery 'started in the Caribbean' as a product of 'whiteness.' In fact, history is replete with examples of slave dynasties e.g. Egyptian, Babylonian, Ottoman, Abassid, Aztec, Incan, Mayan, Barbary, Persian etc. According to the Global Slavery Index, as of 2016 forty million people were enslaved worldwide – the vast majority in Africa, Asia and the Pacific region. As to why the broadcaster persistently attempts to exclusively link slavery with west European/Christian societies, the reader is free to speculate.

[13] The BBC has up its sleeve what it appears to think is a get out-jail card which it produces at such moments: *we were just following the rest of the media pack.* However, as a broadcaster with a unique system of funding (tax-payer funded via a compulsory television licence) in contrast to privately-funded media that do not operate under the jurisdiction of a royal charter, the broadcaster has an obligation to do precisely the opposite: *not blindly follow the crowd.* Or else, why grant it special privileges and dispensations?

[14] 'How we handle your complaint,' Overview: Step 2, bbc.co.uk.

'The [Pfizer] vaccine is 100% safe for children'

[1] In conversation with a caller named 'John' on his BBC Radio 2 show (11 Aug. 2021), after pointing out the dangers associated with Covid vaccines, presenter Jeremy Vine asked the caller if he happened to be virologist or an epidemiologist. As for Devi Sridhar, she is neither.

[2] Ghislofi et *al* (2020) estimate an IFR of 1 per 2.5 million in the 0-19 age group. Meanwhile, Levin *et al* (2020) estimate an IFR of 0.002% at age 10 and 0.01% at age 25.

[3] Frenck *et al* (2021).

[4] Meanwhile VAERS data reported 48 serious adverse reactions from a total of 1,497 doses given, a rate of 3%. It also reported the most common side effects in 12-15 year olds were Dizziness (28%) and Fainting (21%). Other side effects included loss of consciousness (9.5%) vomiting (8%) fall (5%). 'COVID-19 Vaccine Safety Updates: Vaccines and Related Biological Products Advisory Committee (VRBPAC), 10 June, 2021.

[5] Public Health England's findings of similar levels of viral load in the vaccinated and unvaccinated hinted as much i.e. that vaccination likely did not prevent transmission. See: 'Fully vaccinated people who catch Covid variants may pass virus on, study finds,' *The Telegraph*, 29 May 2021.

[6] In the accompanying article, Newsround makes the claim that, 'The Pfizer vaccine offers up to 95% protection against Covid-19...' It also states that, 'It's not unusual for vaccines to make people feel a bit unwell for a few hours after being jabbed...' 'Covid-19: Pfizer 'safe and effective' vaccine approved for 12- to 15-year-olds,' BBC Newsround, 4 Jun. 2021.

[7] 'Heart inflammation in young men higher than expected after Pfizer, Moderna vaccines -U.S. CDC,' Reuters, 10 Jun. 2021.

[8] 'Re: BBC Newsround – Pfizer Vaccine for 12 – 15 year olds.' Open Letter from the UK Medical Freedom Alliance to Professor Devi Sridhar – Chair of Global Public Health / University of Edinburgh, 14 Jun. 2021.

[9] Published in May 2021, the Fact Sheet was revised 3 Jan. 2022.

[10] Fact Sheet for Healthcare Providers Administering Vaccine: Emergency Use Authorization [EU] of the Pfizer-BioNTech Covid-19 Vaccine to Prevent Coronavirus Disease 2019 [Covid 19], p. 11.

[11] On page 12 of the fact sheet mentioned above, the FDA observes that: 'Adverse reactions in children 5 through 11

years included pain at the injection site, fatigue, headache, injection site redness, injection site swelling, muscle pain, chills, fever, joint pain, lymphadenopathy, nausea, malaise, decreased appetite, and rash. Meanwhile, adverse reactions in individuals 12 years of age and older included: Severe allergic reactions, including anaphylaxis, and other hypersensitivity reactions (e.g. rash, pruritus, urticaria, angioedema), diarrhoea, vomiting, pain in extremity (arm).

[12] Research by renowned cardiologist Steven Gundry (2021) found elevated PULS scores in recipients of Covid vaccines. The PULS test predicts risk of heart disease. Gundry concluded that: 'The mRNA vacs numerically increase all markers for denoting inflammation...of cardiac muscle, in a consecutive series of a single clinic patient population receiving mRNA vaccines without a control group.'

[13] Chua *et al* (2021).

[14] Op. Cit. 'Fact Sheet for Healthcare Providers Administering Vaccine,' p. 12.

[15] Sequelae is defined by Wikipedia as: a pathological condition resulting from a disease, injury, therapy, or other trauma. Derived from the Latin word, meaning 'sequel,' it is used in the medical field to mean a complication or condition following a prior illness or disease.

[16] Dionne *et al* (2021).

[17] VAERS ID:1071409.

[18] Worryingly, research conducted by Schauer *et al* (2022) at the Seattle Children's Hospital demonstrated 'persistence of abnormal findings' 3-6 months after hospitalisation via Cardiovascular magnetic resonance.

[19] 'Michigan boy dies in his sleep three days after getting vaccine,' *New York Post*, 5 July 2021.

[20] 'Tragisch: Herzkrankes Kind nach Corona-Impfung gestorben, ndr.de, 4 Nov. 2021.

[21] Priority question for written answer P-004862/2021 to the Commission, Rule 138, Francesca Donato (NI) 27 Oct. 2021.

The details of the three victims were as follows: On 9 Sept. a 16 yr-old female from Bastiglia died 16 hours after vaccination; on 13 Sept. a 14-year-old female from Bari died 48 hours after vaccination; on 1 Oct. a 13-year-old from Lecce died just hours after vaccination.

22 'Teen girl dies after second dose of COVID-19 vaccine in northern Vietnam,' Tuoi Tre News, 21 Jan. 2022.

23 'Mom details 12-year-old daughter's extreme reactions to COVID vaccine, says she's now in wheelchair,' Fox News, 2 July 2021.

24 Op. Cit. 'Fact Sheet for Healthcare Providers Administering Vaccine,' p. 14.

25 A total of 195 side effects in the 12-17 age group were reported by Ireland's Health Products Regulatory Authority (HPRA) following Covid vaccination: 'Three more cases of heart inflammation reported after Covid-19 vaccine,' Independent.ie, 6 Nov. 2021.

26 According to US VAERS data of 12,304 deaths reported in the 1 April 2022 release, 21% of them had occurred with 24 hours of receiving the Covid vaccination.

27 'The Misinformation Virus,' BBC Sounds, 17 Dec 2019.

28 For analysis of Sridhar's litany of Covid-19 misinformation see for example: 'Scottish Covid adviser's vaccine U-turn,' *The Spectator*, 25 May 2021. For an even more in depth analysis see: 'Devi Sridhar: Expert or Charlatan?' citizenjournos.com, 14 Nov. 2021.

29 See for example: 'COVID-19 child vaccination: safety and ethical concerns: An open letter from UK doctors to Dr June Raine, Chief Executive, MHRA.'

30 Ronny Cheung via Twitter, 2 Jan 2021.

31 RCPCH via Twitter, 2 Jan 2021.

32 The Evelina Hospital via Twitter, 8 Jan 2021.

33 'Confirmed: There Wasn't A 'Whole Ward of [Covid] Children' as Claimed by Laura Duffell of Kings College

Hospital,' citizenjournos.com, 10 Mar. 2021.

'Some racial slurs about Muslims can also be heard'

[1] 'Oxford Street: Images issued after men filmed spitting at Jews on bus,' bbc.co.uk, 2 Dec 2021. The article's title was also amended from: 'Oxford Street: Men filmed spitting at Jewish people on bus.'

[2] Confirmed in a tweet from BBC reporter Harry Farley: 'At about 3 seconds into the video you can just about hear someone on the bus saying 'dirty Muslims.' This was something actually picked up by my editors not me and they wanted to reflect that briefly in the piece.' Via Twitter, 13 Dec 2021.

[3] 'BBC's false equivalence tactic migrates to London reporting,' Camera-UK, 5 Dec 2021.

[4] Julia Lenarz via Twitter, 5 Dec 2021.

[5] 'The BBC has questions to answer on anti-Semitism,' *The Telegraph*, 6 Dec 2021.

[6] Letter to the BBC from the Jewish Board of British Jews, 7 Dec 2021.

[7] 'Police find 'no evidence' of anti-Muslim slur during Oxford Street hate incident,' *The Jewish Chronicle*, 13 Dec 2021.

[8] BBC pro-Palestinian and anti-Israel reporting is one of its most enduring biases, one that seeks to demonise the Israeli state while exonerating Palestinian acts of terror wherever possible.

[9] See page 4 of the report.

[10] Sixty-eight per-cent of respondents thought BBC coverage of Jewish affairs unfavourable, by far the highest level amongst mainstream British television channels: BBC: 68%, C4: 45%, ITV: 24%, Sky: 23% - See: Antisemitism Barometer 2020, Television Broadcasters: Coverage of Antisemitism, p.35.

[11] 'To restore public trust, the BBC must apologise,' *The Jewish Chronicle,* 30 Dec 2021.

[12] 'BBC's false equivalence tactic migrates to London reporting,' Camera-UK, 5 Dec 2021.

[13] Committee for Accuracy in Middle East Reporting and Analysis.

[14] Report by Professor Ghil'ad Zuckermann, 27 Dec 2021, p.12.

[15] 'Jewish BBC broadcaster resigns over antisemitism,' *The Jewish Chronicle*, 4 Jan 2022.

[16] 'BBC seeks swift response to bus anti-Semitism story complaints,' bbc.co.uk, 8 Jan 2022.

[17] Ibid.

[18] The full judgment can be read online via BBC Complaints website. To give a flavour of the level of tautology deployed here's how the ECU dismisses the objection that the broadcaster treated Jewish and Muslim insults differently, 'alleged' in the case of the former, de facto true in the latter:

We saw no evidence to suggest it [use of the word 'alleged'] *was intended to contrast with the treatment of the anti-Muslim slur claim – which was contextualised in the online item in a way the statements about the behaviour of those outside the bus were not, by the inclusion of a quote from one of the students on the bus, in which she denied hearing any such insults from her fellow passengers.*

The rest of the judgment continues in much the same manner.

[19] 'Oxford Street: Men filmed spitting at Jewish people on bus, BBC News Online (England) & BBC London News, BBC One (London), 2 December 2021,' bbc.co.uk, 26 Jan 2022.

[20] This part of the ECU judgement is even more of a triumph in tautology. The ECU is trying to persuade itself that the CST confirmed that 'dirty Muslims' had been said while not really confirming. At this juncture it is vital that the ECU provide evidence that the broadcaster sought views outside the 'seven' BBC staff who all agreed with one another – hence the contortions.

21 'Justice denied' as BBC defends its abominable reportage of antisemitic Oxford Street incident, prompting Ofcom to announce its own investigation,' Campaign Against Anti Semitism, 26 Jan 2022.

22 'The BBC must confront its long-held prejudices towards Jews,' *The Telegraph*, 30 Jan 2022.

'The material [on Trump] was of a sexual nature'

1 'BBC article showed anti-Trump bias,' *The Times*, 8 Aug 2020.

2 For more analysis on BBC promotion of the Trump-Russia conspiracy theory, see: *The Fake News Factory: Tales from BBC-land* pp. 232-256.

3 'More in U.S. Favor Diplomacy Over Sanctions for Russia,' Gallup, 20 Aug. 2018.

4 See: BBC Panorama: *The Kremlin Candidate?*

5 'Trump 'compromising' claims: How and why did we get here?' bbc.co.uk, 12 Jan. 2017.

6 '51% of Voters Think Russia Has 'Kompromat' on Trump,' Morning Consult.com, 12 Dec. 2018.

7 'There Remains No Evidence Of Trump-Russia Collusion,' Forbes, 23 May 2017.

8 'On the record: The U.S. administration's actions on Russia,' Brookings.edu, 31 Dec. 2019.

9 'Is Trump The Toughest Ever On Russia?' npr.org, 20 Jul. 2018.

10 The broadcaster's duplicity as well as its political bias is neatly illustrated by its coverage of the Nord Stream gas pipe saga. In late 2019 the Trump administration approved sanctions on any company working with Gazprom, Russia's state-owned gas company on the pipe line. In May 2021 the Biden administration waived these sanctions much to Russian relief. Predictably, the BBC did not accuse Mr Biden of being a Kremlin stooge nor of being Putin's 'best buddy' etc. as it had labelled Trump (and still does).

[11] Newsnight, 27 December 2018.

[12] 'After Weinstein, Trump sexual misconduct accusers demand action,' bbc.co.uk, 12 Dec. 2017.

[13] 'Trump camp puts forward witness to refute sex assault claim,' *The New York Post,* 14 Oct. 2016.

'Mr Trump suggested injecting patients with disinfectants might help treat coronavirus'

[1] 'Coronavirus: Trump's disinfectant and sunlight claims fact checked.' bbc.co.uk, 24 Apr. 2020.

[2] For example, in its 24 April 2020 edition Guardian.com ran an article titled: 'Please don't inject bleach': Trump's wild coronavirus claims prompt disbelief.' Even 12 months on certain factors of the US media were *still* making claims about bleach, e.g. 'It's been exactly one year since Trump suggested injecting bleach. We've never been the same,' Politico, 23 Apr. 2021.

[3] 'Coronavirus: US doctors warn 'don't take medical advice from Trump,' bbc.co.uk, 24 Apr. 2020.

[4] Ibid.

[5] 'Coronavirus: Trump's disinfectant and sunlight claims fact checked,' bbc.co.uk, 24 Apr. 2020.

[6] 'Coronavirus: Outcry after Trump suggests injecting disinfectant as treatment,' bbc.co.uk, 24 Apr. 2020.

[7] This is the transcript of this part of the president's speech:

So, supposing we hit the body with a tremendous, whether its ultraviolet or just very powerful light, and I think you said, that hasn't been checked but you're gonna test it. And then I said, supposing it brought the light inside the body, which you can either do either through the skin or some other way, and I think you said you're gonna test that too, sounds interesting.

8. A crucial point, but one that had to be ignored at all costs for the broadcaster to continue with its deceitful narrative.

9. 'Donald Trump told people to drink bleach to cure COVID 19,' Logically, 4 Mar. 2021.

10. 'On COVID-19, Donald Trump said that 'maybe if you drank bleach you may be okay,' Politifact, 9 Jul. 2020.

11. 'In Context: What Donald Trump said about disinfectant, sun and coronavirus,' Politifact, 24 Apr. 2020.

12. The broadcaster was just one of a number of entities within the corporate media axis circulating this same falsehood. For example, in its edition of 24 February, *The Independent* reported that: 'President Joe Biden has mocked his predecessor Donald Trump's infamous suggestion that injecting bleach could be considered as a treatment for coronavirus.'

'James Dyson is a prominent conservative supporter'

1. 'Boris Johnson told Sir James Dyson by text he would 'fix' tax issue,' bbc.co.uk, 21 April 2021.

2. The broadcaster never refers to individuals in the Remain camp as 'prominent supporters of the EU.' This is because, as it does when health-checking 'right-wing' or 'conservative' entities, the BBC uses its health-checks to encourage its believers they should judge the subject with scepticism; if anger can be stoked then so much the better: either way the BBC has attempted to discredit the subject in advance.

3. 'Billionaire Sir James Dyson moves residency back to the UK,' bbc.co.uk, 22 April 2021.

4. 'Sir James Dyson: the truth about my contact with Boris Johnson,' *The Telegraph*, 27 April 2021.

5. 'Sir James Dyson exclusive: BBC twisted the truth over my links to the Tories,' *The Telegraph*, 27 April 2021.

6. 'Dyson hits back: There was nothing wrong with my texts to Boris Johnson over ventilators and the BBC twisted

them to make it appear I was trying to 'extract favours,'
entrepreneur rages,' *Mail Online*, 28 April 2021.
[7] 'BBC apologises to Sir James Dyson,' Dyson.co.uk, 12 May
2021.
[8] 'The BBC's unfounded accusations deserve proper scrutiny
from Ofcom,' *The Telegraph*, 26 April 2021.

'1,162 died from coronavirus in a single day in the UK'

[1] 'My prediction of 100,000 cases per day was wrong, admits
Professor Neil Ferguson,' *The Telegraph*, 7 Aug. 2021.
[2] So determined seemed the government to increase the Covid
death toll, it may have sought to artificially increase numbers:
PCR testing and incentives aimed at encouraging inflated
diagnoses are just some of the methods which may have been
employed to achieve this objective. Whether or not this is
indeed the case will be up to an official enquiry to judge.
[3] Along with its fellow travellers in the corporate-legacy media
the BBC not only uncritically promoted this highly dubious
footage courtesy of the CCP and which sparked panic around
the world, but has still not assigned its army of
'disinformation' activists to 'fact-check' its veracity. Whilst
post-vaccination collapse/feinting is well documented,
Covid-19 infection appears not to result in immediate
death/blackout upon contact as depicted in the CCP footage.
[4] 'Covid made the world go mad – Here's what we know now
about the year of lockdown,' *The Telegraph*, 20 Feb. 2022.
The professor was referring to an especially deceitful tactic:
while the BBC promoted rare teenage deaths from Covid at
any opportunity, the same broadcaster all but ignored post
vaccination deaths in the same cohort, emphasising on those
rare occasions it did make an acknowledgement, that such
deaths were extremely rare etc.
[5] This story centred around a man who had 'died after a positive
Covid test…' In an interview with the *Shropshire Star a* friend
of Mr Matthews challenged the BBC story. Mr Matthews had
not in fact been a 'Covid denier' as per BBC reports, but had

been protesting about government lockdowns. See: 'Anti lockdown campaigner 'was not Covid denier' say friends,' *Shropshire Star,* 8 Feb. 2021.

Eager to exploit the death of a 'Covid denier' BBC Sounds produced a (10-part) podcast series in which a 'disinformation' reporter travels to Shrewsbury to investigate Mr Matthews' life and death. At the end of episode 4, the presenter, from the very same organisation now producing an extensive and one-sided programme featuring the dead man's family in order to push its fear-mongering agenda, actually says this: 'Next time we look at how the story spread in the media and how Gary's family were pulled into the orbit of people who wanted to use Gary's death to push their own agendas...'

When BBC employee Lisa Shaw died from the coronavirus vaccine having been assured (by, amongst others, her own employers) the vaccine was 'safe and effective' BBC Sounds did not produce a similar 10-part podcast series to unravel how, why and by whom she had been misled.

[6] 5 Live Drive: BBC Radio 5 Live, Monday 21 December 2020.

[7] 'State of fear: how ministers 'used covert tactics' to keep scared public at home,' *The Telegraph*, 3 Apr. 2021.

[8] See: Majin (2021).

[9] BBC Editorial Guidelines: Section 3: Accuracy – Introduction: Section 3.1.

[10] Newsnight: BBC Two, Wednesday 27 January 2021.

[11] 'Deaths involving COVID-19 in the care sector, England and Wales: deaths registered between week ending 20 March 2020 and week ending 2 April 20213,' ons.gov.uk.

[12] For the full story see: 'Shock as BBC admits Covid figures error,' *The Conservative Woman,* 16 Nov. 2021.

[13] *Today*, BBC Radio 4, Monday 13 December 2021.

[14] *Reporting Scotland*: BBC One Scotland, 14 January 2022.

[15] Readers should take a close look at the BBC's 'Reality Check' facility, which, just like the rest of its fellow

corporate-funded 'fact checkers,' invariably manages to declare as 'false' any position taken by the likes of Israel, Trump, Russia, Le Pen, Viktor Orban, Boris Johnson, Brexiteers, Conservatives, 'anti-vaxxers,' climate 'deniers' etc. - in fact any entity (apparently) opposed or critical of neo-liberal globalism and especially US-UK imperialist expansionism. Preposterous as such a ruse may appear to those of even meagre critical faculty, BBC adherents appear to indeed believe the judgements of BBC 'Reality Check.'

[16] 'BBC announces new documentary, Unvaccinated, with Professor Hannah Fry,' BBC Media Centre, 6 July 2022.

[17] Table 5 (page 65) of the UKHSA week 26 vaccine (1, 2 & 3 shots) reports a cumulative uptake of 70.2%.: Weekly national Influenza and COVID-19 surveillance report Week 27 report (up to week 26 data) 7 July 2022, UK Heath Security Agency.

'A pandemic of the unvaccinated'

[1] 'Pfizer, BioNTech, Moderna making $1,000 profit every second: analysis,' Medical Xpress, 16 Nov 2021.

[2] 'Thousands Of Swedes Are Inserting Microchips Under Their Skin,' npr, 22 Oct 2018.

[3] 'Covid 19 Vaccine Surveillance Report Week 1: 6 January 2022,' UK Health Security Agency, p.39.

[4] Ibid. p. 40.

[5] The rate of Covid vaccination in the UK population was generally acknowledged to be about 69% at the time; thus, the vaccinated were dying of Covid at a higher rate that the unvaccinated.

[6] 'Potential lessons from the Taiwan and New Zealand health responses to the COVID-19 pandemic,' The *Lancet Regional Health - Western Pacific Review:* Vol 4, 100044, November 01, 2020.

[7] Evidence is plentiful; for example, in their 50-country study Chaudhry *et al* (2020) concluded that, '[F]ull lockdowns and wide spread COVID-19 testing were not associated with

reductions in the number of critical cases or overall mortality.'

[8] VAERS COVID Vaccine Adverse Event Reports, openvaers.com.

[9] In order to further highlight the disparity between the wrong and the right-thinker the broadcaster will invariably ensure that its selected member of the former group will come across as inarticulate and ignorant. In order to achieve this end BBC producers invest considerable time pre-screening those it intends to platform for soundbites/interviews. While actively seeking out the gruff and incoherent to platform, similar care is taken to ensure articulate wrong-thinkers are prevented from making contributions.

[10] 'False Equivalence: The Problem with Unreasonable Comparisons,' Effectiviology.com.

[11] 'Icelanders argue over their ancestors,' *New Scientist*, 31 May 1996.

[12] 'Australia in the 1780s,' myplace.edu.au.

[13] Estimates vary. Researchers such as Horowitz (2021) estimate a standardised Covid mortality rate of 0.12 – 0.88 %. Meanwhile, Professor John Ioannidis (2021) has estimated the global IFR at 0.23 per cent overall and, for people under 70, 0.05 per cent. The point is of course that estimates are considerably lower than even the most conservative smallpox mortality estimates.

[14] On the issue of increasing uptake of vaccinia, the most common smallpox vaccine, Belognia & Nelway (2003) observe that, 'The federal government has indicated that voluntary vaccination of the general public may be approved after health care workers and first responders have been vaccinated. Increasing the number of vaccinated persons will inevitably lead to increases in morbidity and mortality due to vaccinia, and current evidence suggests net harm would result if smallpox vaccine were made available to the general public on a voluntary basis.'

[15] *Der Spiegel*, 19 Dec 2018. In an article entitled 'Germany's Leading Magazine Published Falsehoods about American Life,' *The Atlantic* observed that, '...the blame lies not only with Relotius or with a few careless checkers or even the publication's research methods, but with the mentality of its editors and readers.' *The Atlantic*, 3 Jan 2019.

[16] Poll available at: https://widget.civey.com/19008. The result of the poll was as follows: Agree – 49.1%, Somewhat Agree 13.1%, Neutral – 4.4.%, Somewhat Disagree – 7.7%, Disagree – 25.7%. Atkins appears to have got his maths wrong, too.

[17] 'Poll: Voters oppose new COVID-19 vaccine mandates to deal with omicron variant,' *Santa Barbara News Press,* 16 Dec 2021.

[18] Kliner M, Keenan A, Sinclair D, et al. Influenza vaccination for healthcare workers in the UK: appraisal of systematic reviews and policy options. BMJ Open 2016.

[19] 'COVID Cases Are Surging in the Five Most Vaccinated States,' *Newsweek*, 25 Nov 2021.

[20] 'COVID-19 Weekly Situation Report: State Overview,' Florida Health, 14 Jan 2022.

[21] 'Covid Scotland: Case rates lowest in unvaccinated as double jabbed elderly drive rise in hospital admissions,' *The Herald*, 13 Jan 2022.

[22] Covid 19 Cases in England by Vaccination Status 28th Feb – 27 March: UKSHA Vaccine Surveillance Report, Week 13, 2022.

'Wouldn't harm a fly: The Christian convert'

[1] 'Liverpool Cathedral to host city's annual Service of Remembrance,' Liverpool Cathedral.org, 14 Oct. 2021.

[2] As to who had intimated the bomber 'Wouldn't harm a fly' we are not informed. The phrase does not appear in the body paragraph and is thus left unattributed.

[3] 'Liverpool bomb: Suspect seemed a genuine Christian, says church worker,' bbc.co.uk, 16 Nov. 2021.

[4] 'Liverpool bomb: Judges had refused attacker permission to appeal to stay in UK,' bbc.co.uk, 16 Nov. 2021.

[5] Tribunal case: AA/06457/2015, 11 Jan 2017.

[6] 'Bishop who confirmed Emad al-Swealmeen says 'he chose a different path,' *The Guardian,* 16 Nob. 2021.

[7] 'Liverpool bomber had been planning attack since April,' bbc.co.uk, 17 Nov. 2021.

[8] bbc.co.uk, 17 Nov. 2021.

[9] Ibid.

[10] 'Concerns migrants are faking religious conversions at Liverpool Cathedral to help asylum claims,' *The Telegraph*, 16 Nov 2021.

[11] 'Liverpool bomber 'reverted to Islam' in months before attack,' *The Times*, 20 Nov. 2021.

[12] 'Poppy Day suicide bomber was at a mosque 'all day, every day' during Ramadan and in weeks leading up to botched bomb plot despite converting to Christianity in 2017 and used fake identity to claim asylum,' *The Daily Mail*, 18 Nov. 2021.

[13] 'We got lucky, say investigators who believe Liverpool bomb was set off by accident,' *The Telegraph*, 17 Nov. 2021.

[14] 'Liverpool bomb: What we know so far,' bbc.co.uk, 18 Nov. 2021.

[15] 'Liverpool bomber died from blast caused by device he made with 'murderous intent,' coroner rules,' ITV.com, 30 Dec. 2021.

[16] 'Liverpool bomber made device with murderous intent, coroner says,' bbc.co.uk, 30 Dec. 2021.

'Why people are using a horse drug'

[1] The Brooklyn Institute for Social Research according to its website is 'named after the Institute for Social Research in Frankfurt, Germany…' and is 'funded by public grants and private donations' – none of which are divulged. See: *Ros Atkins on… Joe Rogan and Spotify*, bbc.co.uk, 5 Feb, 2022.

[2] Rogan was not the only celebrity turning to Ivermectin. Eight days into his Covid-19 infection actor Louis Gossett Jr had been gravely ill. It was at this point he was directed to Dr Bruce L Boros of the non-profit Front Line Covid-10 Critical Care Alliance (FLCCC) who prescribed the octogenarian Ivermectin. According to Gossett Jr three days after starting treatment he had made a full recovery. In a Facebook post of 23 March 2021, the actor described Dr Boros as 'the angel that saved my life.' See: https://www.facebook.com/Dr Bruce-L-Boros-308111489273103

[3] Ivermectin is the generic name for Stromectol, developed in 1981 by Merck. Its patent expired in 1996.

[4] In November 2019 The FDA received a grant of $990,000 from the Bill and Melinda Gates Foundation.

[5] 'Y'all' is part of the vernacular of southern US states equating to 'everybody' in British English. Its use represented a clear dig at 'uneducated' Trump voters, just the types to ingest 'horse de-wormer.'

[6] During the corporate-legacy media onslaught which followed his Instagram post, a bewildered Rogan wondered why the likes of CNN and the BBC appeared not even slightly interested in the fact that he had shrugged off a nasty bout of Covid-19 in just a matter of a few days and what this could imply for treatment. Rather, the MSM attacked him for *recovering from illness…*

[7] 'How Ivermectin Saved Louis Gossett Jr. from Dying of COVID-19,' Rescue with Michael Capuzzo, 27 Sep. 2021.

[8] See: 'Gunshot Victims Left Waiting as Horse Dewormer Overdoses Overwhelm Oklahoma Hospitals, Doctor Says,' *Rolling Stone*, 3 Sep 2021. Even the image which accompanied the *Rolling Stone* article was clearly fake depicting as it did a long queue of people standing outside a building none of whom appeared to be bleeding from 'gunshot wounds' or any other type of wound. The (single) source for its article had been an emergency doctor affiliated to NHS Sequoyah, an Oklahoma hospital, which, following

the story, released a statement:

NHS Sequoyah has not treated any patients due to complications related to taking ivermectin. This includes not treating any patients for ivermectin overdose.

All patients who have visited our emergency room have received medical attention as appropriate. Our hospital has not had to turn away any patients seeking emergency care.

[9] The doctor in question was a certain Jason McElyea, the same doctor responsible for the false alarm gunshot story and whom the BBC platformed in an article published on 4 Sep. 2021 and whose opening paragraph begins:

A US doctor is urging people to stop taking the horse deworming drug Ivermectin to treat Covid-19.

Interestingly, when clicking through to the article the headline 'Don't take horse de-wormer for Covid, doctor pleads,' becomes 'Ivermectin: Oklahoma doctor warns against using drug for Covid treatment.'

[10] 'Horse-Bleep: How 4 Calls on Animal Ivermectin Launched a False FDA-Media Attack on a Life-Saving Human Medicine,' Mary Beth Pfeiffer and Linda Bonvie, Substack, 17 Oct. 2021.

[11] 'Demand Surges for Deworming Drug for Covid, Despite Scant Evidence It Works,' *The New York Times*, 30 Aug. 2021.

[12] 'CVS no longer filling ivermectin prescriptions,' *Vermont Daily Chronicle,* 15 Sep. 2021.

[13] As noted by the podcaster himself, CNN had deliberately changed the hue of Rogan's face on his original Instagram post to imply illness rather than health.

[14] The Joe Rogan Experience, #1718 Dr Sanjay Gupta, Oct. 2021.

A number of observations can be made about this figure not least the fact that under the auspices of the FDA, the entire US medical establishment was doing all it could to demonise Ivermectin as a treatment against Covid-19. A major part of that strategy was to deliberately conflate human and animal formulations e.g. labelling Joe Rogan's treatment as 'horse de-wormer.' The safety of the human form of Ivermectin well established, the 245% increase in poisonings could only have been caused by ingestion of the *animal variety*. And if that is the case, then a good proportion of blame lies on all those agencies conspiring to prevent the public from obtaining the human variety.

An article published on npr.org – a leading US establishment media website – entitled 'Poison Control Centers Are Fielding A Surge Of Ivermectin Overdose Calls' – illustrates the care required with mainstream 'facts' pertaining to Ivermectin. One paragraph reads:

The NPDS (National Poison Data System) says 1,143 ivermectin exposure cases were reported between Jan. 1 and Aug. 31. That marks an increase of 163% over the same period last year.

Note the use of the deliberately vague term 'exposure.' Note also the lack of discrimination re human or animal formulation of the drug. It also worth bearing in mind that a substantial number of calls logged by the Mississippi health authority had in fact been *enquiries* about Ivermectin.

The suggestion that Ivermectin was a dangerous 'horse de wormer' having been implanted in the public's mind, how many of that same public who had taken the human variety of the drug might now wonder about the wisdom of that decision? How much of the 245% had been 'exposures' to the perfectly safe human form of Ivermectin?

16 See: 'Covid-19: MedinCell Publishes an Extensive Ivermectin Safety Expert Analysis,' Bloomberg, 5 Mar. 2021.

[17] In a further dig at Dr Kory, Atkins goes on to say that: 'Kory ... described himself as the world's foremost expert on Ivermectin. It's fair to say that assessment isn't universal.'

[18] See 'About' page of the FLCCC website at: www.covid19criticalcare.com

[19] 'The FDA-approved drug ivermectin inhibits the replication of SARS-CoV-2 in vitro,' Caly *et al*, *Antiviral Research*, 2020 Jun; 178: 104787. This paper concluded that:

1. Ivermectin is an inhibitor of the COVID-19 causative virus (SARS CoV-2) in vitro.

2. A single treatment is able to effect 5000-fold reduction in virus at 48 h in cell culture.

[20] Hellwig, M. & Maia, A (2021).

[21] 'FLCCC Alliance Calls on National Health Authorities to Immediately Review Medical Evidence Showing the Efficacy of Ivermectin for the Prevention of COVID-19 and as an Early Outpatient Treatment,' News Wise.com, 4 Dec. 2020.

[22] Which is precisely what the 2-page opinion piece authored by student Jack Lawrence and cited by the BBC as having 'debunked' Ivermectin had done i.e. tried to hold Ivermectin trials to an entirely new standard.

[23] Concerns about the links between key government health advisers and their links to the pharmaceutical industry were expressed by the *British Medical Journal* in an article published on 6 December 2017 ('Tom Jefferson: The UK turns to Witty, Vallance, and Van Tam for leadership: revolving doors?') which observed that:

It is time that the government and the public took a close look at what is going on in the upper echelons of healthcare planning and delivery in this country and considered imposing a substantial time moratorium on hiring workers with close ties to industry.

[24] The Bill and Melinda Gates Foundation is the second largest donor to the World Health Organisation. GAVI, the vaccine organisation the Microsoft owner founded, is also a major WHO benefactor.

[25] In his analysis of Randomised Control Trials (RCTs), Hill concluded that Ivermectin demonstrated a 75% reduction in mortality viz moderate and severe Covid-19 infection. Under pressure he later revised his conclusions. In a subsequent interview, Dr Tess Lawrie asked Hill to explain his sudden U-turn. Hill said he had found himself in a 'very sensitive position.' He also intimated that a (Bill Gates-funded) company called Unitaid had exerted pressure on him. His new conclusion – that Ivermectin's efficacy was unproven and required more research – allowed the UK health authority to dismiss the drug and press ahead with its goal of mass vaccination.

It was later suggested that the new conclusion to Hill's paper had been amended by an academic at the University of Liverpool whose department, along with a company called Tandem Nano Ltd, signed a $40 million contract with Unitaid just days before the revised paper had been submitted for review.

For more information on Hill's inexplicable U-turn see: 'A Letter to Dr Andrew Hill,' by Dr Tess Lawrie produced by Oracle Films and in which Hill states his goal is to 'get Ivermectin approved' and he is doing everything he can to achieve that objective. In one segment of a recorded conversation between Hill and Lawrie, the former admits that if his own brother had Covid-19 he would want him to take Ivermectin. Hill also admits that unnamed Unitaid personnel had indeed altered the conclusion to his report – a course of action he had seemingly acquiesced to despite his knowledge of the drug's remarkable efficacy – presumably the 'sensitive position' alluded to.

[26] 'Pfizer and Moderna could score $32 billion in Covid-19 vaccine sales -- in 2021 alone,' cnn.com, 11 Dec. 2020.

[27] The latest Ivermectin studies and trials can be accessed online at https://c19ivermectin.com/

[28] According to those pushing for mass vaccinations such as the BBC, these trials with their inconvenient results are invariably dismissed as 'poor quality.' Interesting to note that virtually all the trials in question were not conducted by western European or American personnel or institutions, which may or may not help explain these recurring dismissals; a case of western ethnocentrism?

Furthermore, it's a phenomenon which may or may not be related to the strong pro-vaccine stance of major industrialised nations together with their national health authorities e.g. the pro-vaccine advocacy of the FDA which works in conjunction with equally enthusiastic pro-vaccine agencies including the Gates-funded GAVI and the WHO. In Europe, the EU is similarly robust in its support for mass vaccination and also works in conjunction with GAVI and the WHO. Lack of Ivermectin research in the US and Europe is reflected in these loyalties: rich and powerful entities have no interest whatsoever in funding the emergence of a potentially efficacious and cheap treatment for Covid-19 – a treatment that would deny £billions to those set to profit from mass vaccination

[29] Denied its request to suppress Pfizer's vaccine trial data for 75 years by a US district judge due to 'limited resources' the FDA was forced to disclose the data in early 2022. The appendix to Pfizer's document reports 1,291 side effects associated with its Covid vaccine. The 38-page report 'Cumulative Analysis of Post-authorization Adverse Event Reports' and marked CONFIDENTIAL can be accessed online.

'How false science created a Covid miracle drug'

[1] 'BBC appoints first specialist health disinformation reporter,' fipp.com, 27 Oct 2021. This is the same individual who

claimed that Myocarditis is more common after catching Covid than after the vaccine.

2 'Pfizer, Moderna will rake in a combined $93 billion next year on COVID-19 vaccine sales: report,' Fierce Pharma, 18 Oct. 2021.

3 'Trusted news initiative steps up global fight against disinformation and targets US presidential election,' European Broad-casting Union, 13 July 2020.

4 The so-called Trusted News Initiative has played a leading role on behalf of government and the pharmaceutical industry during the Covid-19 'pandemic.' Amongst its many achievements it has conspired to hide reporting of vaccine-induced deaths and injuries; attacked and smeared medical professionals not promoting mass vaccination; spearheaded disinformation campaigns against efficacious Covid treatment such as Ivermectin etc.

5 BBC Pension Scheme: Report and financial statements 2020 Pension, p.2.

6 The Bill and Melinda Gates Foundation.

7 'Bill Gates's stranglehold on the MSM: Part 1.' *The Conservative Woman*, 28 June 2021.

8 'Conservatives: Who funds them, and what's in it for them?' bbc.co.uk, 2 Oct. 2021.

9 'Bill Gates: The Best Investment I've Ever Made,' *The Wall Street Journal*, 16 Jan. 2019.

10 Bill Gates via Twitter: 19 Dec. 2019.

11 Already holding stock in Pfizer, in September 2019 the Bill and Melinda Gates Foundation invested $55 million in German vaccine manufacturer BioNTech which would likely reach $100 million. See: 'BioNTech Announces New Collaboration to Develop HIV and Tuberculosis Programs.'

12 Indeed, in March 2022 the son of a billionaire BioNTech investor splashed out $33 million on a mansion in an exclusive area of Sydney. Florian Struengmann, his father

and uncle had each received a $10.7 billion vaccine windfall thanks to sales of the Pfizer Covid vaccine.

[13] Chemical, Biological, Radiological and Nuclear materials.

[14] 'Emergency Use Authorization, US Food and Drug Administration, About Emergency Use Authorizations (EUAs).'

[15] Even more bizarrely, the entire 17-minute interview was also broadcast on BBC regional news programmes such as BBC North West. Taking Gates' $53 million donation as a starting point, this works out at about $3,133 500 per minute of prime air-time. Given the anticipated dividends from mass vaccination, it's a layout that might just represent fantastic value.

[16] Imagine if Donald Trump rather than Gates was the self-appointed vaccine czar of the world. Imagine how *that* BBC interview would have unfolded.

[17] Whether a conflict of interest exists between an individual with a substantial stake in vaccines, his $53 million donation to a BBC 'charity' and a plum spot on the same organisation's Breakfast Show allowing the same individual free reign to promote the products he is financially invested in, is a matter of course for Ofcom or *should be*. At the time of publication of this book, the BBC-friendly regulator has shown no interest in launching an investigation.

[18] Lawrence, J, *et al* (2021). The article was published online on 22 Sep. 2021.)

[19] 'Ivermectin: How false science created a Covid 'miracle' drug,' bbc.co.uk, 6 Oct. 2021.

[20] Titled, 'Debunking the BBC debunk of ivermectin,' as of August 2022 Dr Campbell's rebuttal has garnered almost 1.5 million views and has over 46k likes.

[21] The BBC 'disinformation' unit is charged with several tasks, prominent amongst which is the promotion of QAnon stories and labelling as 'false' any information which challenges the preferred narratives of the wealthy and powerful from Big

Pharma to the US military industrial complex right through to various state actors (e.g. CIA, FBI) including trans-national organisations such as the WHO, UN and EU.

[22] When last functioning (June 2021) the website routinely attacked conservatives and anything else it deemed 'right wing.' For example, after the Chinese-American journalist Andy Ngo had been viciously attacked in Portland on 29 June 2019 by Antifa thugs, in a post entitled 'So Antifa Isn't That Violent After All?' Grftr.news asserted that: 'Antifa has never been the 'big bad' the right would have people believe.' The same article goes onto claim that the January 6 'rioters' in Washington were: 'funded to the tune of hundreds and thousands of dollars through a combination of wealthy individuals $$ and small donors.'

[23] Note the use of the singular 'a fraud' here. Lawrence is referring to his supposed debunk of Elgazzar.

[24] 'Huge study supporting ivermectin as Covid treatment withdrawn over ethical concerns,' *The Guardian,* 15 July 2021.

[25] Bryant *et al* (2021).

[26] Indeed, well into 2022 and the Twitter-team are still mocking Elgazzar as well as circulating baseless conspiracy theories suggesting a major academic fraud had occurred e.g: 'I mean, even aside from the fraud Elgazzar and Niaee were always hugely suspect,' tweeted co-author Meyerowitz-Katz on 31 Mar. 2022, 'extremely poorly-done trials with obvious mistakes, but that was glossed over in studies published in peer-reviewed journals.'

Asked which journals had 'glossed over' the 'obvious mistakes' and for what possible reasons, Meyerowitz-Katz blocked the author of this book on Twitter. With Ivermectin costing but cents to mass produce and the likes of Pfizer and Moderna set to make billions from Covid vaccines, Meyerowitz-Katz's conspiracy theory makes little sense.

[27] Elgazzar Study: Letter to editor by Bryant *et al. American Journal of Therapeutics* 28, e573–e619 (2021). The

supposition was correct: the paper – 'Efficacy and Safety of Ivermectin for Treatment and prophylaxis of COVID-19 Pandemic,' was withdrawn by Research Square after receiving a complaint from...'Grrftr news' the apparently defunct student website and to where it actually refers researchers.

[28] Ibid.

[29] Neil & Fenton (2021).

[30] Professor John Ioannidis of Stanford University, one of the world's most cited academics, critiqued Meyerowitz-Katz's Covid IFR research methodology in the *European Journal of Clinical Investigation*. Prof Ioannidis and his colleagues were 'intrigued' by claims attributed to them by Meyerowitz-Katz who was attempting to discredit research that challenged his own alarmist Covid IFR estimates. In order to do this Professor Ioannidis highlighted how Meyerowitz-Katz had excluded studies demonstrating low IFR from his own study; thus, his flawed methodology resulted in 'inflated and, sometimes, overtly implausible results.'

[31] On an edition of BBC World Service (3 Jul. 2021) 'More or Less,' Meyerowitz-Katz falsely told host Tim Harford that Ivermectin was supported by 'a few scientists to border line conspiracy theorists.'

[32] Meyerowitz-Katz *et al*, (2021). Regarding this study Meyerowitz-Katz declared funding from New South Wales state government and Commonwealth of Australia. His co-authors declared funding from: MRC Centre for Global Infectious Disease Analysis, Imperial College COVID-19 Research Fund and Bill Melinda Gates Foundation. MRC is a research facility of Imperial College to whom the Gates Foundation has so far donated $303,875,383. Imperial College's MRC is also home to Professor Neal Ferguson whose catastrophically incorrect models were largely responsible for plunging the UK into lockdown. Thus, the pro-lockdown paper was effectively funded by the Gates Foundation. Lockdown was presumed by many

commentators to be a tool used to coerce individuals into submitting to vaccination.

[33] Evidence is extensive: '4 in 10 adults (40%) reported that the coronavirus was affecting their well-being this week,' according to the Office of National Statistics: 'Coronavirus and the social impacts on Great Britain': 14 August 2020,' ONS. See also for example, *Lockdown: Social Harm in the Covid-19 Era* by Briggs *et al*, Macmillan, 2021.

[34] Sheldrick describes himself in his blog as 'a medical doctor but not currently in clinical practice.' He goes on to reveal he receives extensive funding from the Australian government. His PhD research is funded by the AO Foundation headquartered in Davos. His activities appear to centre around 'debunking' any alternatives to Big Pharma drugs/medicine.

[35] Dr Keldrick did not respond to repeated requests regarding the location of his paper.

[36] See: kylesheldrick.blogspot.com.

[37] Author of the BBC 'debunk' Rachel Schraer did not reply to our emails (x 3) requesting clarification of the Sheldrick analysis quoted in her article. The main focus of the two-page opinion piece which forms the basis of her article, as noted, is the Elgazzar study. There is no mention in the op-ed of '26 studies.'

[38] A search of Google Scholar fails to return Sheldrick's 26 study investigation which, according to the BBC he co-authored with Dr James Heathers, Dr Gideon Meyerowitz-Katz and Dr Nick Brown. Dr Heathers was yet another member of this Twitter research team who did not reply to requests which sought to locate the study referred to by the BBC's 'specialist health disinformation reporter.' Only one result is returned on the entire Google scholar database which features this team: The 2 page *Nature* op-ed and its lead author Jack Lawrence...

'Groups such as QAnon have campaigned against the statue carved by Gill'

[1] The BBC article 'How Covid-19 myths are merging with the QAnon conspiracy theory,' explains the QAnon phenomenon thus:

QAnon's main strand of thought is that President Trump is leading a fight against child trafficking that will end in a day of reckoning with prominent politicians and journalists being arrested and executed.

Whether then President Trump was or was not leading such a fight seems somehow immaterial – the hope would be that *someone was/is*. Every available resource directed at fighting child trafficking and bringing the perpetrators (and enablers) to justice, who could possibly find such an idea objectionable?

[2] As an example of how the BBC and its allies seize upon everything QAnon despite the fact the psy-op is effectively dead and buried, consider this tweet from Will Sommer, a *Daily Beast* reporter and fanatical QAnon promoter, sent out 22 November 2021:

At least 100 QAnon supporters convinced JFK is coming back are still in Dallas. Today they stood on a bridge over Dealey Plaza for the anniversary of the assassination, but JFK and JFK Jr. never showed.

In a country of 330 million as many as '100' QAnon believers had hung around to witness the rebirth of JFK Jr, the movement's supposed saviour. That's how popular the psy-op is in reality.

[3] On 22 September 2020 a social media influencer called Nihal Arthanayake tweeted the following:

So Marianna Spring was at the save our children march in central London this weekend and a woman said to her 'beneath us babies are being kept for Prince Charles to eat.'

Spring re-tweeted this tweet adding: 'I spoke to Nihal on bbc5 live about how QAnon conspiracy theories could be impacting US voters - and are impacting the British public. Such as one lady who told me this about babies in tunnels.' Note the lack of context for this claim. Assuming this encounter did actually happen as described, did the woman in question introduce the topic of Prince Charles eating babies unprompted? Or did Spring, present at the rally purely to discredit it, ask leading questions?

During a podcast for Media Voices on 13 July 2020 titled 'The BBC's Specialist Disinformation Reporter Marianna Spring on proactively countering conspiracies,' Spring, who has used aliases on Facebook ('Marianna Claire' was one such identity until the cover was blown and a BBC reference was subsequently added to the profile.) had this to say about how she goes about her business of duping what she calls Facebook 'conspiracy theorists':

You don't have to lie but you also don't have to go on to the group and say, 'By the way, I'm a BBC journalist,' because actually the editorial justification for joining the group is greater than having to reveal who you are. You need to be in these spaces to monitor and analyse and investigate the content being shared. And if you told them you were a BBC journalist off the get go, you'd probably get kicked out.

Would an individual who assumes a false identity in order to spy on people have any qualms about engaging in such deceptive practices as entrapment? In the same podcast, Spring also makes the following claim:

The number of times I've sat in cabs during the pandemic, and cab drivers have said to me, 'Oh, my friend or my wife or my cousin has started contemplating conspiracies and they'd never normally do that, they're normally quite rational, but all of a sudden, they're interested in this stuff.

The choice of cab drivers is an interesting one not least because of its (inadvertent) acknowledgment of the broadcaster's notorious profligacy, which is of course funded by the tax-payer. Amongst the plethora of (predominantly] working-class) 'conspiracy theorists' who populate the activist's world, why should one particular sub-class – taxi drivers - be so grounded and so very...well, BBC? The Knowledge must have presumably expanded its remit way beyond the A-Z of London's streets into epidemiology...

While Spring and her fellow 'disinformation' activists spy on and attempt to discredit anti-paedophile groups, they have not, as far as can be ascertained, deployed the same subterfuge viz establishment protected and funded groups such as Antifa, BLM and Extinction Rebellion.

[4] Mike Wendling via Twitter, 24 Apr. 2021. The sense of moral outrage expressed in this tweet from an organisation that can quite credibly claim to be the world's biggest smear machine will no doubt put a smile on readers' faces.

[5] It is not immediately clear why 'conspiracy theorists' would contact the BBC via email or any other method. For reasons best known to itself, the emails, which would surely have made extremely interesting reading, are not reproduced in the article.

[6] The BBC calling out 'conspiracy theories' by creating one of its own is an irony seemingly lost on the broadcaster's 'anti-disinformation unit.'

[7] 'Can the art of a paedophile be celebrated?' bbc.co.uk, 5 Sep 2007.

[8] 'Call for paedophile's artwork to be removed from Dumbarton church,' *The Daily Record*, 11 July 2014.

[9] 'BBC told to remove work by pedophile sculptor Eric Gill,' news.com.au, 23 Apr 2013.

[10] Ibid.

[11] See the thread: 'Eric Gill and the BBC,' at mumsnet.com.

¹² The BBC 'disinformation' activist whose Twitter account is partly devoted to amplifying all things QAnon. For example, on 10 September 2020 Sardarizadeh tweeted the following about *Cuties* a Netflix film which featured pre-pubescent girls gyrating and posing provocatively for the camera – scenes which naturally caused widespread outrage amongst many people, especially concerned parents:

I haven't seen 'Cuties' on Netflix and therefore have no personal opinion for or against it. But let's be honest, the controversy surrounding the film is basically Christmas come early for the QAnon crowd, isn't it?

The tweet was subsequently deleted.

¹³ For a detailed expose of an arm of the BBC (i.e the ECU) even more deceitful than its colleagues in the news section, see, 'Liar, Liar, Pants on Fire: Anatomy of a BBC Complaint' in *The Fake News Factory*, pp. 276-300.

¹⁴ Even establishment-funded attack outfits in the mould of Hope not Hate could only muster the following muted expose re: Freedom For The Children:

FFTC was founded in the USA in June, and employs a 'big tent' approach, eschewing the esoterica of QAnon and broader theories about elite, Satanic paedophile cabals in its official branding. Instead, it has appropriated slogans from legitimate children's charities, such as 'Save the Children,' aiming for a broader appeal.

According to this assessment, FFTC displays no affinity to QAnon or Satanic paedophile theories; indeed, beyond the efforts of BBC 'disinformation' whereby they extrapolate and/or invent links, none actually exist.

¹⁵ Thai Paedophile Arrested For Child Pornography, CTN News, 13 Jun. 2022.

[16] Child sexual offences jump 57% in 5 years,' NSPPC, 8 Oct. 2020.

[17] In 2014 a former child protection officer revealed the existence of a 20-strong 'high-profile' UK paedophile ring which had operated in London for over six decades. See: 'UK: Paedophile ring had 20 high-profile members,' Gulf News, 9 Jul. 2014.

[18] Ofcom's Annual Report on the BBC 2020-21, pp. 82-88.

[19] Not only does Ofcom whitewash BBC disinformation, as can be seen in the following threat (Ofcom Broadcast on Demand Bulletin: 26 May 2020) during the coronavirus 'pandemic' it ensured government-WHO propaganda went unchallenged:

We remind all broadcasters of the significant potential harm that can be caused by material relating to the Coronavirus… We strongly advise you to take particular care when broadcasting…statements that seek to question or undermine the advice of public health bodies on the Coronavirus, or otherwise undermine people's trust in the advice of mainstream sources of information about the disease…Ofcom will consider any breach arising from harmful Coronavirus-related programming to be potentially serious and will consider taking appropriate regulatory action, which could include the imposition of a statutory sanction.

'The director of a large NHS trust has contacted the BBC'

[1] Thirty-two minutes after publication the article's title was changed to: 'NHS boss: 'I need gowns, can I call Burberry?' As to why a senior NHS figure would seek permission to order emergency supplies, the broadcaster doesn't say.

[2] 'NHS boss: 'I've hardly any gowns, can I call Burberry? bbc.co.uk, 17 Apr. 2020.

[3] If messages had been received via e-mail, then those sent by the respondent would have contained an official NHS e-mail suffix i.e. @nhs.net or @nhs.uk.

[4] When confirmation of key details would halt a narrative in its tracks, the BBC can become rather sloppy. For example, when

the broadcaster ill-advisedly revealed Lord McAlpine's name in relation to historic sexual abuse offences, *The Irish Times* reported that 'BBC failed to complete basic journalistic checks.' *The Irish Times*, 12 Nov 2012.

5   'BBC correction on Burberry coronavirus plea,' bbc.co.uk, 17 Apr 2020.

6   The only option would have been to suggest the broadcaster had itself been lied to – an even riskier ploy.

7   'BBC bias: Former Labour MP Kate Hoey orders BBC to apologise live on air,' The *Daily Express*, 19 Apr 2020.

8   For an example of how the ECU operates in practice, see 'Liar, Liar Pants on Fire: Anatomy of a BBC Complaint,' pp. 276-301, *The Fake News Factory: Tales from BBC-land.*

9   A key objective of a disinformation endeavour is to avoid any kind of public scrutiny where scrutiny can only lead to lies unravelling. Never explain or apologise – like royalty, maintain aloofness. Thus, it is essential to restrict any avenue whereby criticism could be aired and credibility undermined. And so, in 2022 Twitter is just about the only medium a BBC activist might encounter pushback. But even here critics can be dismissed as trolls or bots and blocked/muted.

10 At least this is a back-peddling ECU's rationale; the actual truth will likely never be known.

11 ECU lies are unravelling just as fast – faster than their colleagues in BBC news. The question of who actually contacted who aside, consider the scenario the arbitrator is painting here: a 'slick' BBC reporter is given the telephone number of a source who procures PPE by a third-party. What happens next? There are two possible scenarios: for reasons unknown the third-party falsely tells Browning the source works as an 'NHS trust boss' – an assertion the BBC reporter fails to check; or the third-party never mentions a job role and Browning never asks… though either scenario strains credulity to breaking point, it is necessary to believe in one or the other in order for the ECU to cover for its colleague's

farcical 'mistake' in assuming the source was an 'NHS trust boss.' (Chief Executive)

12 Nor is this behaviour an isolated incident. From the BBC corrections and clarification website:

We published a report on former President Farmajo which stated that he had paid a secret visit to Jerusalem in February 2020 and met with the then Israeli Prime Minister Benjamin Netanyahu.

This article did not meet the BBC's editorial standards and we have removed it from our website and social media accounts.

We produced the story based on a single source, and did not conduct our own investigations to establish whether the facts were correct. We did not contact former President Farmajo to give him a right of reply to the allegations in the article.

13 Durrand's profile at Oxford Academic Health Science Network's website reads: 'Paul joined Oxford AHSN in 2013. He has oversight of all its activities with a particular focus on governance, business planning, sustainability and partnerships with integrated care systems.'

14 Given that Durrands himself never claimed to be an NHS Trust 'Director,' then who did? If the ECU is to be believed, it can only have been the third-party who made the introductions. Thus, the third-party must have had virtually no knowledge of who Durrands was and what he actually did – yet it *still* suggested Browning make contact with him... Or maybe it knew exactly what Mr Durrands did. After all, it wasn't the third-party intent on creating lurid anti-government headlines.

15 The BBC reported very little about the actual telephone conversation. Presumably, the source had reached BBC switchboard after managing to locate the corporation's telephone number if not that of Burberry... What supposedly happened thereafter – to whom he was referred, whether he

managed to call Burberry etc. - the broadcaster very wisely never said…

16 The scenario of an unspoken job title hanging comedically in the air misleading all and sundry might sound like an Oscar Wilde plot, but it's the only option available to an ever more desperate ECU.

17 If for some reason the broadcaster could not have located Mr Durrands viz Linkedin, then it could always have contacted direct the 'large NHS Trust' he supposedly ran for confirmation.

18 Following ECU logic, Mr Durrands must have let slip that he 'oversaw' a *large* NHS Trust – a Trust which, tellingly, has never actually been named by the BBC… How then did the broadcaster come across the job title of 'NHS Director?' It can only have been via Durrands. But Durrands did not work for the NHS in any capacity let alone in a role that does not exist.

19 The mystery of 'Conservative' inaction is not so strange: the Tory-Labour uniparty is, like the BBC, a proxy of international corporate-political power. Broadcaster and political parties answer to precisely the same powers. BBC anti-Toryism is at best then a sideshow, a diversion. The Conservative Party knows and appreciates this and is more than happy to play the role of bad cop.

BBC attacks on conservatives are simply part of the same theatre: it is in fact immaterial to the corporation whether Labour or Tory govern – *provided one half of the uniparty does,* even if the broadcaster would prefer the former. BBC disdain for Johnson actually stems from his opportunistic support of Brexit. In this view, he betrayed both his and the BBC's class – the ruling class. Unforgiveable. Hence, the BBC vendetta against the prime minister was a grudge shared by those whom Brexit had so disjointed, that is the ultra-wealthy and powerful and their proxies.

'We can just refer her to our line again'

[1] 'Putin's False 'Nazi' Claims About Ukraine,' bbc.co.uk, 22 Mar. 2022. The programme's blurb reads thus: 'Ros Atkins looks at the untruths that Russia is spreading about Nazis in Ukraine.' However it was BBC Panorama that reported it had witnessed 'serious racism' in Ukraine on the dawn of the Euro 2012 football tournament; it was BBC Newsnight that had visited Kiev in 2014 warning about the 'rise of the far right' and interviewing a young volunteer soldier who told the broadcaster he wanted his country to be a 'bit like Hitler' etc. Had the devious broadcaster engaged in a spot of extrapolation? Was their respondent truly representative of wider Ukraine society?

What then was the truth regarding the BBC flip-flop apparent by 2022? Given the broadcaster's propensity of painting (mainly European) nationalists as far-right racists and Nazis, its portrayal of Ukrainian nationalism between 2014-2021 replete with the usual unsubtle dog-whistles was only to be expected. But was it true? For its part, Ukraine militia such as the Azov battalion described itself as patriots, not far right nationalists as per BBC reporting. Thus, if Ros Atkins is correct and Putin's assessment was indeed 'false,' then by linking certain elements in Ukraine to far-right and extremism the BBC must have indeed been misleading its audience throughout 2014-2021.

[2] In David Talbot's book *The Devil's Chessboard* the author relates an incident whereby former CIA boss Allen Dulles once faced unexpected public scrutiny. The incident occurred in the aftermath of The Warren Commission – the investigation into the Kennedy assassination accused of whitewash and onto which Dulles had somehow managed to inveigle himself. Talbot's theory is that the embittered Dulles had orchestrated the assassination and had subsequently joined the commission in order to secure a cover-up. Not long after the report was published to hoots of derision, Dulles went on a lecture tour in winter 1965. In one event held at ULCA the veteran spymaster was confronted by a student who had read and dissected the entire report – all 26 volumes. Talbot relates how the room fell

silent. With the US mainstream media firmly in his pocket – *The New York Times, Washington Post, Time* etc. - this was possibly the first time in his life the immensely powerful and well-connected Dulles had ever been publicly challenged. And it was showing. To the student's assertion that *The Nation* had interviewed eye-witnesses to the assassination, the CIA boss resorted to the trusted tactics of smearing and mockery – "The Nation? Ha, ha, ha." However, nobody in the theatre was laughing. Talbot goes onto relate that suddenly Dulles found himself isolated; the smear had not worked and the spymaster began to unravel – presumably because he had never been required to justify his actions in public before. The student, remarks Talbot, "was the only person who ever gave Allen Dulles a taste of what it would have been like for him to be put on the witness stand." (See *The Devil's Chessboard*, p 591 592.)

[3] Notice for example how RT is labelled as 'Russian state media' while the BBC is never similarly labelled as 'British state media.'

[4] Observe the understatement in this 'correction':

We said a government cleaner who worked in Downing Street and had been surrounded by people breaking the rules had contracted Covid and died.

In fact, he worked at the Ministry of Justice.

His family was reported to have been told by medical staff that he had died from coronavirus but the post-mortem recorded hypertensive heart disease as the official cause of death.

We are sorry for the mistake.
26/05/20

But this was not just any old 'mistake.' It was in fact part of the broadcaster's campaign to oust Boris Johnson out of Downing Street. The implication was that an innocent party had contracted coronavirus in *Downing Street* as a result of the infamous socialising that had gone on there. Thus, in breaking the rules Johnson and his team bore at least some responsibility for the death. However, as noted the BBC's original story had been wholly misleading – a calculated and serious act of deception one sneaked onto the corrections website with minimal fanfare.

5 'More Than a White Lie,' *Psychology Today*, 9 Jun. 2016.

6 BBC Complaints reference: CAS-5475670-4V5T7D.

7 'BBC hit by new Martin Bashir shame: Outrage at derisory efforts to find Babes In The Wood victim's bloodied clothes after disgraced reporter took them from her mother – then lost them,' M*ail Online*, 18 Sep. 2021.

8 Ibid.

9 'BBC 'extremely sorry' over loss of murdered schoolgirl's clothes,' bbc.co.uk, 19 Sep. 2021.

10 E-mail sent by BBC Press Office, 25 May 2021.

11 Whether BBC indifference had anything to do with the humble backgrounds of the family and victims is for the reader to decide. Had the victims also been middle-class would that have made the families worthy of respect in BBC eyes?

12 Jody Doherty-Cohen via Twitter, 25 May 2021.

13 See for example: 'BBC's deceit over Diana interview worsened my parents' relationship – William,' bbc.co.uk, 21 May 2021.

14 In 2016 Martin Bashir was re-hired by the BBC as Religious Affairs Correspondent. In 2018, the role was upgraded to Religion Editor. He left the BBC in May 2021, the week before publication of the Dyson report.

'[Donald Trump] long-time fan-boy of Putin'

1 'Russia's Natural Resources Valued at 60% of GDP,' *The Moscow Times*, 14 Mar. 2019.

2 *The Third Floor Front,* p. 32.

3 A leaked phone conversation between Victoria Nuland, the lead US diplomat during the Ukraine crisis, confirmed direct

US involvement in the coup.

4 The broadcaster was caught red-handed misleading its audience when showing viewers of its 25 Feb 2022 breakfast broadcast dramatic footage of what it claimed was Russia's 'invasion' of Ukraine. The footage was in fact of a military rehearsal which had occurred in May 2020. See: 'BBC Breakfast uses old footage of Russian parade rehearsal to show invasion of Ukraine.' Fullfact.org, 25 Feb. 2022.

5 This wasn't the first time the article's author Nick Bryant had produced such work. As recently as August 2020 the broadcaster's Executive Complaints Unit upheld a complaint regarding a similarly seething, ad-hominem attack on another archetypal BBC wrong-thinker then US president Donald Trump and which had also clearly broken impartiality guidelines. 'The finding' reported the EUC, 'was discussed with those responsible for the article and reported to the Board of BBC News.' Judged by the scathing, cynical tone of the current article, Bryant and his editors had typically not learnt any lessons.

As observed in the consistent misreporting of the 'four white' officers involved in the George Floyd case, although the broadcaster swears its activists have been informed of the 'error' in question with the implication that it will not be repeated, the same transgressions just keep on occurring over and over again ...for the full complaint see: 'Coronavirus: What this crisis reveals about US - and its president, bbc.co.uk,' 6 Aug. 2020.

6 For a fuller list detailing the astonishing record of US activity in the affairs of sovereign countries see Wikipedia: 'United States involvement in regime change.'

7 'Why Is America the World's Police?' The Boston Review, 19 Oct 2020.

8 In its analysis HRW state that the Syrian government was 'almost certainly responsible' for what it terms 'likely' chemical weapon attacks in Ghouta. It reached these conclusions via Skype chats with 10 'witnesses' and 3

doctors.

It also 'reviewed' video footage. And if the sheer weight of such high-quality non-partisan investigative work fails to convince, it was also assisted by the CIA & Atlantic Council funded 'Bellingcat' an organisation that produces anti-Russian and anti-Syrian propaganda. See: 'Attacks on Ghouta: Analysis of Alleged Use of Chemical Weapons in Syria,' HRW, 10 Sept. 2013.

[9] See: *The Chemical Attacks on East Ghouta to Justify Military Right to Protect Intervention in Syria*, ISTEAMS, 11 Sept. 2013.

[10] 'Facebook Says Russian Accounts Bought $100,000 in Ads During the 2016 Election,' *Time*, 6 Sept. 2017.

[11] For more of the same see the Wikipedia page: 'Russian interference in the 2016 United States elections.'

[12] Indeed, Trump's 2015 announcement that he would be contesting the Republican nomination was met by huge swathes of amazement as well as mockery by the mainstream media. The announcement literally shocked America.

[13] 'U.S. pension fund CalSTRS has investments in Russia, monitors risks to portfolio. Reuters, 25 Feb. 2022.

[14] 'Four US lawmakers or their spouses personally invested in Russian companies: documents, *Business Insider*, 1 Mar. 2022.

[15] 'Who Is Felix Sater, and Why Is Donald Trump So Afraid of Him?' *The Nation*, 8 Sept. 2017.

[16] 'There Remains No Evidence Of Trump-Russia Collusion,' Forbes, 23 May 2017.

You will own nothing and be happy

[1] The statement was 'fact-checked' by various wealth and power proxies including Reuters who produced arguably one its most absurd truth-benders to date: 'Fact check: The World Economic Forum does not have a stated goal to have people own nothing by 2030,' Reuters, 25 Feb 2021. The scramble to run cover for

273

Schwab's notoriously incautious organisation by the likes of Reuters and co was hardly unexpected.

[2] For a good overview of public unease see: 'You will own nothing, and you will be happy': Warnings of 'Orwellian' Great Reset,' SkyNews.com.au.

[3] World Economic Forum via Medium.com, 12 Nov. 2016.

[4] World Economic Forum via Twitter, 22 Mar. 2022. The blowback from this latest WEF proclamation duly triggered the entire establishment 'fact-checking' network, according to whom the WEF had not actually sent the tweet – despite the fact it had been sent via the organisation's official Twitter account. To non-partisan actors what had happened was clear enough: having been mocked and derided after posting the tweet, the WEF had simply deleted it. Google and Facebook funded Full-Fact were one of several wealth and power proxies charged with the onerous task of running cover for this latest WEF faux pas. Its admittedly very funny attempt can be accessed here: 'WEF didn't say that property ownership would become 'unsustainable,' Full-Fact, 1 Apr. 2022.

[5] 'How the code of secrecy among Davos attendees works, *Quartz*, 22 Jan 2014.

[6] When requested via a Freedom of Information (RFI20211544) request to reveal how many members of its staff are currently affiliated with the WEF, the broadcaster refused to answer.

[7] Over the years Schwab has also articulated his vision of a trans-human future, a melding together of man and machine. 'At first we will implant them in our clothes,' replied Schwab in an interview with Swiss channel RTS in January 2016 on the subject of microchips, 'And then we could imagine that we will implant them in our brains, or in our skin. And in the end maybe there will be a direct communication between our brain and the digital world. What we see is a kind of fusion of the physical, digital and biological world.'

[8] 'UK and World Economic Forum to lead regulation

revolution to foster industries of the future,' gov.uk, 23 Jan 2019.

[9] This dangerous and wholly irrational initiative had been laid out in a glossy WEF publication *The Net Zero Challenge* and distributed to members. According to the WEF its net zero challenge was 'voluntary…' The concept of net zero is usually attributed to a group of climate activists who met at the Scottish estate of one of its central figures – a (green) investment fund manager...This small group included individuals linked to the UN and World Bank. Using their contacts, the plot dreamed up by this group over coffee made its way into the mainstream where, despite the misgivings of many regarding long term impacts especially on the poorest in society, it has remained and where the UK became the first nation to sign up to net zero in 2019.

[10] For an excellent analysis of The Great Reset see the YouTube video: 'You will OWN NOTHING, and you will be HAPPY: Douglas Kruger debunks Great Reset.'

[11] Ironically, the average BBC activist will often – inadvertently - set out claims which approximate to truth while simultaneously implying 'conspiracy.' Take the following sentence for example:

Believers spin dark tales about an authoritarian socialist world government run by powerful capitalists and politicians - a secret cabal that is broadcasting its plan around the world.

Since 2020, under the aegis of Covid, governments in places as disparate as Austria and Australia have been brutally beating up citizens protesting the erosion of their rights. Some governments have introduced mandatory 'vaccinations,' others implementing coercive measures to increase uptake – authoritarianism last witnessed in liberal democracies in the 1930s. Is the world run by 'powerful capitalists and politicians?' Are powerful meta-democratic organisations such as Bilderberg and WEF secretive? As for 'broadcasting its plans around the world' start by checking out all those 'flashy' WEF videos.

[12] In a WEF publication titled *Emerging Pathways towards a Post-COVID-19 Reset and Recovery* listed are what the think tank terms its 'Members of the Community of Economists' – a who's of who of international finance comprising representatives from, amongst others: Deutsche Bank, IMF, HSBC, Bank of America, Deloitte, Barclays, Microsoft, Unilever, Allianz etc.

[13] According to global risk analysis firm Criminal Justice International Associates, 'socialist' Venezuelan president Hugo Chavez was worth between $1 billion and $2 billion at his death. Similarly, Romanian communist dictator Nicolae Ceausescu kept $470 million in a Swiss bank account. Meanwhile, as of 2013 it had been estimated that North Korea's communist dictator Kim Jong Un had assets of at least $5 billion spread around 200 foreign bank accounts.

[14] While the BBC struggles to envisage the world described by Schwab plenty of others are able to offer educated guesses. For example, in its assessment of 'stakeholder capitalism' a key WEF concept, Resilience.org note with concern the prominence of Big Corporations and Big Tech in this model together with the shrinking role of government. See: 'Conspiracy theories aside, there is something fishy about the Great Reset,' Resilience.org, 24 Aug. 2021. Although the BBC seemingly failed to locate it, there exists a growing body of critical enquiry into Schwab's vision.

[15] Interview at 'Summit on the Global Agenda 2015.'

[16] 'Build Back Better: our plan for growth,' www.gov.uk.

BOOKS BY THE SAME AUTHOR

BBC: Brainwashing Britain? How and Why the BBC Controls Your Mind

In this ground-breaking study and Amazon best-seller, the author analyses the methods as well as the reasons why the BBC habitually attacks the truth and those who dare tell it.

Using Orwell's nightmarish dystopia as articulated in *1984* as its guide, the BBC is placed within a specific socio-cultural context. The corporation, argues the book, is the very embodiment of Orwell's nightmarish Ministry of Truth, a cult of dogged and ideologically extreme 'right-thinkers.'

Essential reading for those seeking to understand an especially dishonest milieu where reality is defined not by our perceptions and experiences, but by the proclamations of those who work for the Inner Party aka The British Broadcasting Corporation, this book may radically alter the reader's opinion of 'Auntie.'

The Fake News Factory: Tales from BBC-land

From chlorine-washed chicken through Russia-gate, grooming scandals and even taking in Sir Cliff Richard, in this follow-up to the acclaimed *BBC: Brainwashing Britain* extended case studies of BBC malfeasance are put under the microscope.

The UK state broadcaster pumps out an impressive stream of globalist propaganda. Unable to modify its playbook by a single degree however, the corporation faces an existential crisis. More hated than loved, the BBC unravels in front of our eyes.

Using myriad examples of unethical BBC practice, *The Fake News Factory* takes the reader on a disturbing journey into the very heart of dishonesty.

Pironi: The Champion That Never Was

Short-listed for the RAC sports book of the year, the remarkable story of French motor racing enigma Didier Pironi takes the reader on a rollercoaster ride from the depths of despair to the heights of triumph.

The dashing Parisian had it all: looks, panache, money and talent. But on a grim August morning in 1982 his gilded world came crashing down around him in the mangled cockpit of his Ferrari.

The book charts a tragedy of Shakespearean proportions as the misunderstood Frenchman battled to regain his life and the F1 world championship so cruelly denied him on that fateful morning - a battle that would ultimately end in defeat.

The Power and The Glory: Senna, Prost and F1's Golden Era

Set amid the glamour, bravado and testosterone of 1980s Formula One, *The Power and The Glory* relates the story of a rivalry unsurpassed in motor-racing history.

By the mid-80s Alain Prost had firmly established himself as leader of the F1 pack. Winning Grands Prix almost at will, the French ace radiated invincibility. But then came the emergence of Ayrton Senna, sparking a decade-long battle for supremacy which peaked during their tenure as Mclaren-Honda team-mates.

An intimate portrait of two unique competitors, *The Power and The Glory* is a supercharged story of acrimony and sheer ambition.

"A cracking good read" (Foyle's Bookshop)

Imagining A Murder: The Cartland Case Revisited
(As "Stockton Heath")

In the early hours of Monday, 19th March 1973, the mutilated body of British businessman and academic John Basil Cartland was discovered on waste ground near the town of Pélissanne in the south of France. Why would anyone wish to murder Mr Cartland and in such brutal fashion?

Described as a 'Brighton headmaster' over the coming days and weeks a picture of an exceptionally complex individual would emerge. Cartland was a man with a past - a very colourful past.

Suspicion eventually fell upon his son Jeremy who had been travelling with his father through France on the night of the murder. Had a son killed his father? The story made headlines around the world throughout and beyond 1973.

Vengeance, lies and political machinations, 'Imagining a Murder' relates a gripping story of human frailty and betrayal.

"Everything a true crime book ought to be" (Bookwormex)

Printed in Great Britain
by Amazon

16123463R00159